AUTHOR'S GUIDE TO JOURNALS
in Psychology, Psychiatry & Social Work

AUTHOR'S GUIDE TO JOURNALS

in psychology, psychiatry & social work

Edited by

Allan Markle, Ph.D.
and
Roger C. Rinn, Ph.D.

THE HAWORTH PRESS, NEW YORK

To
our mentors,
Morgan Worthy and Mitchel C. Morrow,

who made this book possible
by teaching us to respect and value research

CONTENTS

CONTENTS

ACKNOWLEDGMENTS

We would like to express our appreciation to the editors and publishers of the journals included in this book. Without their cooperation and assistance in providing the information contained herein, this project would not have been possible.

Our very special thanks are due to Sherry Belsha who spent long hours carefully typing the manuscript. We are also appreciative of Anna Sasnette, who, along with Ms. Belsha, assisted us in the preparation and mailing of questionnaires to the various journals.

We are most grateful to our families for their patience and understanding throughout the development of this book.

Finally, we wish to express our sincere thanks and appreciation to Bill Cohen of The Haworth Press for his skillful guidance and numerous helpful suggestions and for his encouragement and generous support.

AM
RCR

INTRODUCTION

If necessity is the mother of invention, then the development of this book was inevitable. Researchers, practitioners, administrators, students, and other scholars in psychology, psychiatry, and social work have strong professional and personal needs to publish their papers and reports. Unfortunately, there has been no truly helpful resource to assist them in answering that commonest of questions: "Where shall I publish my paper?"

Any professional is naturally well acquainted with the most important journals in his or her own field. At the same time, however, anyone who has gone through the publishing gauntlet soon learns that the process of article submission can be a harrowing and time-consuming affair. This volume has been designed to include sufficient information about the major journals in psychology, psychiatry, and social work to take a great deal of guesswork out of article submission, and to help professionals locate journals where acceptance is most probable, quick, and most attuned to the author's specific needs.

Information Included

For each journal included, there is a table of information of importance to contributors. This information was obtained primarily through a questionnaire sent directly to the journal editors themselves. Occasionally an editor did not respond to the questionnaire, and the data were obtained either from the publisher or the journal itself. Where pertinent information could not be obtained, this is entered as "not given" in the text. A complete description of each informational category is presented in Table 1.

Selection of Journals

The number of journals directly in, or related to, the fields of psychology, psychiatry, and social work would add up to many thousands. A selection strategy was decided upon that would reduce to a minimum any subjective assessments as to whether a particular journal title would be included or excluded. This selection strategy is presented in Table 2. Naturally, some journals may be appearing on the market after publication of this book, and could not be included.

TABLE 1
Information Included for Each Journal

JOURNAL TITLE: The correct, current title of the journal.

MANUSCRIPT ADDRESS: The correct address for submitting manuscripts.

MAJOR CONTENT AREAS: The broad topics which are of prime interest to the journal, as indicated by the journal's present editor.

ARTICLES USUALLY ACCEPTED: The types of articles (research, review, theoretical, etc.) which the present editor indicates he or she will usually accept for publication. This section also includes any unusual restrictions and requirements of authorship (e.g., society members only, psychologists only, etc.).

TOPICS PREFERRED: A list of topics which the present editor indicates he or she currently prefers to publish.

INAPPROPRIATE MANUSCRIPTS: Types of manuscripts identified by the editor as frequently received but "wish I hadn't." Inappropriate submissions usually deal with content, but other reasons may be explained in this entry.

INDEXED/ABSTRACTED IN: A comprehensive listing of where the journal is indexed or abstracted.

SUBSCRIPTION ADDRESS: Correct address for ordering subscriptions.

SUBSCRIPTION COST: Cost of individual and institutional subscriptions. Where these are identical, only one price is given. It should be noted that some journals also have special rates for students, association members, etc. Since complete information on special financial arrangements could not be included for each journal, it would be advisable before ordering to check recent issues or write to the subscription address for complete information on frequency, special supplements, availability of an annual index, etc.

PUBLICATION LAG TIME: The editor's estimate of the usual interval between the time an article is accepted for publication and the actual time it is published.

EARLY PUBLICATION OPTION: Whether the journal will publish an article sooner than its normal lag time. There is normally an early publication charge for this service, and the advantages gained fluctuate considerably from year to year. The editor should be contacted if additional and current information on this option is desired.

REVIEW PERIOD: The editor's estimate of the average time interval between the time a manuscript is received and the time the author is notified whether it has been accepted or rejected. It must be noted that these are averages, and any given paper may require more or less review time.

ACCEPTANCE RATE: The editor's estimate of the approximate percentage of manuscripts accepted for publication.

STYLE SHEET: Whether the editor will send a copy of the journal's complete style requirements to prospective authors. The notation "with SSAE" means that a stamped, self-addressed envelope must accompany the request.

STYLE REQUIREMENTS: The style requirements followed by the journal. A list of the abbreviations used for this entry may be found in Table 4.

CIRCULATION: The size of the journal's circulation.

REPRINT POLICY: The policy of the journal regarding the purchase of reprints. If the journal provides a quantity of free reprints, the number provided is indicated. Additional ones may usually be purchased for an extra fee. The notation "purchase required" indicates that authors must purchase reprints if an article is accepted for publication. "Optional purchase" means that no free reprints are given, but that they may be purchased after publication.

TABLE 2
Journal Selection Strategy

JOURNALS INCLUDED IN THE AUTHOR'S GUIDE
1. Journals covered by *Psychological Abstracts.*
2. Journals covered by *Abstracts for Social Workers.*
3. Journals covered by Section 32 (Psychiatry) of *Excerpta Medica.*
4. Journals covered by *Current Contents: Social and Behavioral Sciences* and also listed under the sections of psychology, psychiatry, and social work in the annual "Source Publications" listing of *Current Contents.*
5. Journals listed under the sections of psychology, psychiatry, and social work in the 1976 Edition of *Ulrich's International Guide to Periodicals* (R.R. Bowker Company).

JOURNALS EXCLUDED FROM THE AUTHOR'S GUIDE
1. Non-English language journals.
2. Newsletters.
3. Hardbound serial publications and annual review publications that accept only solicited articles.
4. Irregular serial publications issued by local government agencies, foundations, and other institutions and associations.
5. Journals which, according to questionnaires returned, only rarely accept articles written by psychologists, psychiatrists, or social workers.
6. Minor state and local periodicals.

Indexing and Abstracting Information

A special effort was made to carefully list where each journal is indexed or abstracted. While this information is normally of interest only to library professionals, it was our opinion that authors should pay additional attention to where a journal is indexed or abstracted before they make their final submission choice for the manuscript. For example, an article on correctional psychology should be sent to an appropriate journal with the thought in mind that the journal chosen is covered by a standard indexing or abstracting service in the criminal justice field. The purpose is to ensure that the results of one's research are readily available to other researchers via the specialized reference tools which may be consulted at some future time.

Information on indexing and abstracting was collected by 1) requesting the information from the journal editors themselves; 2) checking through the major abstracting and indexing services in psychology, psychiatry, and social work; 3) checking the 1976 edition of *Ulrich's International Periodicals Directory* (R.R. Bowker Company); 4) checking *Chicorel's Guide to Indexing and Abstracting Services.* Naturally, indexing services add new titles all the time, but an effort was made to make this section as accurate as possible up to the point of press time.

It is unfortunate that important research does not always find its way into print only because it was submitted to inappropriate journals. It is our hope that this book will be of assistance to you in the publication of your scholarly works.

Allan Markle, Ph.D.
Roger C. Rinn, Ph.D.

ABBREVIATIONS USED

Abstracting and Indexing Services

ARGPL	Abridged Readers Guide to Periodical Literature	CICF	Current Issues in Commerce and Finance
AA	Abstracts in Anthropology	CLA	Current Literature on Aging
ACP	Abstracts in Criminology and Penology	CPI	Christian Periodical Index
AES	Abstracts in English Studies	DSHA	Deafness, Speech and Hearing Abstracts
AHM	Abstracts of Hospital Management	DNP	Digest of Neurology and Psychiatry
AHMS	Abstracts of Hospital Management Studies	EBSCO	Ebsco Subscription Services
APC	Abstracts of Popular Culture	EE	Economia de la Empresa
ASW	Abstracts for Social Workers	EA	Economic Abstracts
ADPA	Accounting and Data Processing Abstracts	EAA	Education Administration Abstracts
		EI	Education Index
ABCPS	Advance Bibliography of Contents, Political Science and Government	ERA	Employment Relations Abstracts
		EPB	Environmental Periodicals Bibliography
AHL	American History and Life	EY	Europa Yearbook
AL	American Librarian	ECA	Exceptional Child Abstracts
AI	Anthropological Index	ECEA	Exceptional Child Education Abstracts
AATA	Art and Archeology Technical Abstracts	EM	Excerpta Medica
AEI	Australian Education Index	GR	Genetic Research
APAIS	Australian Public Affairs Information Service	GAA	Graphic Arts Abstracts
		GPE	Guide to Periodicals in Education
BI	Bibliographic Index	GSSRPL	Guide to Social Science and Religion in Periodical Literature
BA	Biological Abstracts	HA	Historical Abstracts
BIS	Biosciences Information Service	HLI	Hospital Literature Index
BRD	Book Review Digest	HB	Human Behavior
BRI	Book Review Index	I	Iitgelezen
BAA	British Archeological Abstracts	ICS	Index Clinicus Sandoz
BEI	British Education Index	IEP	Index to Educational Publications
BHI	British Humanities Index	ILP	Index to Legal Periodicals
BS	Bulletin Signaletique	IM	Index Medicus
BPI	Business Periodicals Index	IPAPL	Index to Periodical Articles Pertaining to Law, 1970
CEI	Canadian Education Index	IPARL	Index to Periodical Articles Related to Law
CECD	Catalogo dell'Emeroteca del Centro di Documentazione	IRPL	Index to Religious Periodical Literature
CPLI	Catholic Periodical and Literature Index	IEA	Indian Education Abstracts
CNRS	Centre National de Recherche Scientifique	IPsA	Indian Psychological Abstracts
		ISA	Information Science Abstracts
CA	Chemical Abstracts	INSPEC	INSPEC Science Abstracts
CDA	Child Development Abstracts	IL	Institute of Living
CGCI	Chronicle Guidance Career Index	IBSS	International Bibliogaphy of Social Science
CSPA	College Student Personnel Abstracts		
CDL	Crime and Delinquency Literature	IIMI	International Index to Multi-Media Information
CJPI	Criminal Justice Periodicals Index	ILD	International Labor Documentation
CINL	Cumulative Index to Nursing Literature	Inte	Interation
CB	Current Biography	INI	International Nursing Index
CCCP	Current Contents, Clinical Practice	IPA	International Pharmaceutical Abstracts
CCSBS	Current Contents, Social and Behavioral Sciences	IPSA	International Political Science Abstracts
CIJE	Current Index to Journals in Education		

ISIR	International Statistical Institute Review
JEL	Journal of Economic Literature
JHE	Journal of Home Economics
K	Kompass
LLBA	Language and Language Behavior Abstracts
LISA	Library and Information Science Abstracts
MA	Management Abstracts
MI	Management Index
MDA	Marketing and Distribution Abstracts
MCR	Medical Care Review
MSRS	Medical Socioeconomic Research Studies
MHBRI	Mental Health Book Review Index
MHD	Mental Health Digest
MRA	Mental Retardation Abstracts
MLA	Modern Language Association
MMRI	Multi-Media Reviews Index
MI	Music Index
NSA	Nuclear Science Abstracts
NA	Nursing Abstracts
NSI	Nursing Studies Index
NAR	Nutrition Abstracts and Reviews
OL	Ophthalmic Literature
PRAJ	Peace Research Abstract Journal
PL	Personnel Literature
PMA	Personnel Management Abstracts
PTA	Personnel and Training Abstracts
PI	Philosophers Index
PHRA	Poverty and Human Resources Abstracts
PA	Psychological Abstracts
PRG	Psychological Readers Guide
PpA	Psychopharmacology Abstracts
PAISB	Public Affairs Information Service Bulletin
RGPL	Readers Guide to Periodical Literature
REAPP	Reference Encyclopedia of American Psychology and Psychiatry
RL	Rehabilitation Literature
RTA	Religious and Theological Abstracts
RHEA	Research into Higher Education Abstracts
RICS	RICS Abstracts and Reviews
SCI	Science Citation Index
SLTCPP	Selected List of Tables of Contents in Psychiatric Periodicals
SES	Social and Educational Sciences
SSCI	Social Sciences Citation Index
SSHI	Social Sciences and Humanities Index
SA	Sociological Abstracts
TC	Tables of Contents
TSI	Theater and Speech Index
T	Topicator
TMA	Top Management Abstracts
U	Uitgelezen
URS	Universal Reference Systems
VI	Vision Index
WRA	Work Related Abstracts
WSA	Woman Studies Abstracts
WLSP	World List of Scientific Periodicals
WMP	World Medical Periodicals
WTA	World Textile Abstracts
WAH	Writings on American History
YPMH	Yearbook of Psychology and Mental Health

ABBREVIATIONS USED

Style Manuals

AAA	American Anthropological Association
AAAS	American Association for the Advancement of Science
AIBS	American Institute of Biological Sciences
AIP	American Institute of Physics
APA	American Psychological Association
ASA	American Sociological Association
BPS	British Psychological Society
CBE	Council of Biological Editors (formerly SMBJ)
Chicago	A Manual of Style, University of Chicago Press
GPO	U. S. Government Printing Office
Ind Med	Index Medicus
IPS	Indian Psychiatric Society
JAMA	American Medical Association
LSA	Linguistic Society of America
Sage	Sage Publications
SMBJ	Style Manual for Biological Editors (now CBE)

STYLE MANUAL PUBLISHERS

If writers cannot locate certain style manuals in their libraries or through university bookstores, inquire at these publishers' addresses.

AAA	American Anthropological Association Publications Department 1703 New Hampshire Avenue, N. W. Washington DC 20009
AAAS	American Association for the Advancement of Science 1776 Massachusetts Avenue, N. W. Washington DC 20036
AIBS	American Institute of Biological Sciences 1401 Wilson Boulevard Arlington VA 22209
AIP	American Institute of Physics 335 East 45th Street New York NY 10017
APA	American Psychological Association Publications Department *Publication Manual of the APA, 2nd Ed., 1974* 1200 Seventeenth Street, N. W. Washington DC 20036
CBE	Council of Biological Editors Committee on Form and Style *CBE Style Manual* 3900 Wisconsin Avenue, N. W. Washington DC 20016
Chicago	University of Chicago Press *A Manual of Style* 5801 Ellis Avenue Chicago IL 60637
GPO	U. S. Government Printing Office Washington DC 20402
Ind Med	*Index Medicus* U. S. Government Printing Office Washington DC 20402
JAMA	American Medical Association *Journal of the AMA Style Book and Editorial Manual* 535 North Dearborn Street Chicago IL 60610
LSA	Linguistic Society of America 1611 North Kent Street Arlington VA 22209
Sage	Swallow Press, Inc. *Sage Publications Style Manual* 1139 South Wabash Avenue Chicago IL 60605

JOURNAL TITLE: Academic Therapy

MANUSCRIPT ADDRESS: Editor, Academic Therapy Publications
1539 Fourth Street
San Rafael, CA 94901

MAJOR CONTENT AREAS: Clinical, educational, learning, perception

ARTICLES USUALLY ACCEPTED: Theoretical, research, and program descriptions;
Letter of inquiry should be submitted first

TOPICS PREFERRED: Diagnosis & remediation of learning dysfunct-
ions in intellectually capable individuals.

INAPPROPRIATE MANUSCRIPTS: Those dealing with the mentally retarded;
highly involved statistical research studies.

INDEXED/ABSTRACTED IN: PA, BS, CCSBS, CIJE, DSHA, EI, ECEA, LLBA,
RL

SUBSCRIPTION ADDRESS: 1539 Fourth Street
San Rafael, CA 94901

SUBSCRIPTION COST:	$7		
PUBLICATION LAG TIME:	1 year	STYLE SHEET:	Yes
EARLY PUBLICATION OPTION:	Yes (limited)	STYLE REQUIREMENTS:	Chicago
REVIEW PERIOD:	6 weeks	CIRCULATION:	9,000
ACCEPTANCE RATE:	25%	REPRINT POLICY:	50 free

JOURNAL TITLE: Academy of Management Journal

MANUSCRIPT ADDRESS: Dr. L. L. Cummings, Editor, Graduate School
of Business, University of Wisconsin,
1155 Observatory Drive, Madison, WI 53706

MAJOR CONTENT AREAS: Management

ARTICLES USUALLY ACCEPTED: Research only

TOPICS PREFERRED: None

INAPPROPRIATE MANUSCRIPTS: None

INDEXED/ABSTRACTED IN: PA, ADPA, BPI, CCSBS, EE, ERA, IBSS, ILD,
JHE, MDA, PTA, TMA

SUBSCRIPTION ADDRESS: Dr. Roderick A. Forsgren, College of Business
Administration, University of Maine
Orono, ME 04473

SUBSCRIPTION COST:	$20		
PUBLICATION LAG TIME:	18 months	STYLE SHEET:	Yes
EARLY PUBLICATION OPTION:	No	STYLE REQUIREMENTS:	Own style
REVIEW PERIOD:	6-12 weeks	CIRCULATION:	4,700
ACCEPTANCE RATE:	10%	REPRINT POLICY:	Optional purchase

1

JOURNAL TITLE: Acta Neurochirurgica

MANUSCRIPT ADDRESS: Dr. P.R.R. Clarke, Middlesbrough Gen. Hosp.
Ayresome Green Lane
Middlesbrough, Cleveland TS5 5AZ, U.K.

MAJOR CONTENT AREAS: Neurosurgery

ARTICLES USUALLY ACCEPTED: Research, clinical

TOPICS PREFERRED: Those useful to research and clinical
work in neurosurgery, surgical technique

INAPPROPRIATE MANUSCRIPTS: None

INDEXED/ABSTRACTED IN: Not given

SUBSCRIPTION ADDRESS: Springer-Verlag New York, Inc.
175 Fifth Avenue
New York, NY 10010

SUBSCRIPTION COST: $71.90
PUBLICATION LAG TIME: 3-4 months
EARLY PUBLICATION OPTION: No
REVIEW PERIOD: Not given
ACCEPTANCE RATE: Not given

STYLE SHEET: Yes
STYLE REQUIREMENTS: Own style
CIRCULATION: Not given
REPRINT POLICY: 100 free

JOURNAL TITLE: Acta Psychologica

MANUSCRIPT ADDRESS: P.A. Vroon, Psychological Institute
Rynsburgerweg 16g
Leiden, The Netherlands

MAJOR CONTENT AREAS: Experimental, general, learning, perception
physiological, mathematical models

ARTICLES USUALLY ACCEPTED: Research, review, theoretical

TOPICS PREFERRED: Psychonomically oriented articles

INAPPROPRIATE MANUSCRIPTS: Comparative, personality, psychometric, social
and biological psychology

INDEXED/ABSTRACTED IN: PA, CCSBS, RHEA

SUBSCRIPTION ADDRESS: North-Holland Publishing Co., P. O. Box 211
Amsterdam, The Netherlands

SUBSCRIPTION COST: $21
PUBLICATION LAG TIME: 9 months
EARLY PUBLICATION OPTION: Yes
REVIEW PERIOD: 2 months
ACCEPTANCE RATE: 58%

STYLE SHEET: Yes
STYLE REQUIREMENTS: North-Holland
CIRCULATION: 900
REPRINT POLICY: 25 free

JOURNAL TITLE: Addictive Behaviors

MANUSCRIPT ADDRESS: Dr. Peter M. Miller, Editor, Dept of Psychiatry
University of Mississippi Medical Center
Jackson, MS 39216

MAJOR CONTENT AREAS: Addictive behaviors

ARTICLES USUALLY ACCEPTED: Clinical research, case studies (with data),
review, theoretical

TOPICS PREFERRED: Alcoholism, drug abuse, obesity, smoking

INAPPROPRIATE MANUSCRIPTS: Program descriptions and case studies with
no data

INDEXED/ABSTRACTED IN: None as yet (new journal)

SUBSCRIPTION ADDRESS: Pergamon Press, Inc.
Maxwell House, Fairview Park
Elmsford, NY 10523

SUBSCRIPTION COST: $22.50 individual, $45 institutional

PUBLICATION LAG TIME: 6-8 months   STYLE SHEET: Yes

EARLY PUBLICATION OPTION: Yes   STYLE REQUIREMENTS: APA

REVIEW PERIOD: 8-10 weeks   CIRCULATION: Not yet known

ACCEPTANCE RATE: 60%   REPRINT POLICY: 25 free

JOURNAL TITLE: Addictive Diseases: An International Journal

MANUSCRIPT ADDRESS: P. O. Box 249087
University of Miami
Coral Gables, FL 33124

MAJOR CONTENT AREAS: Addictive diseases

ARTICLES USUALLY ACCEPTED: Research, review, theoretical, book review;
articles are normally invited, but unsolicited
papers will be reviewed

TOPICS PREFERRED: Each issue focuses on a specific topic

INAPPROPRIATE MANUSCRIPTS: None

INDEXED/ABSTRACTED IN: CCSBS

SUBSCRIPTION ADDRESS: Spectrum Publications
86-19 Sancho Street
Holliswood, NY 11423

SUBSCRIPTION COST: $15 individual, $28 institutional

PUBLICATION LAG TIME: 8-10 months   STYLE SHEET: No

EARLY PUBLICATION OPTION: Yes   STYLE REQUIREMENTS: APA

REVIEW PERIOD: 1-2 months   CIRCULATION: 2,500

ACCEPTANCE RATE: Most articles   REPRINT POLICY: 20 free
solicited

3

JOURNAL TITLE: Administration in Mental Health

MANUSCRIPT ADDRESS: P. O. Box 2088
Rockville, MD 20852

MAJOR CONTENT AREAS: Community psychology, mental health
administration

ARTICLES USUALLY ACCEPTED: Research, review, theoretical

TOPICS PREFERRED: Administration in mental health

INAPPROPRIATE MANUSCRIPTS: None

INDEXED/ABSTRACTED IN: IM, ASW, CCSBS

SUBSCRIPTION ADDRESS: P. O. Box 2088
Rockville, MD 20852

SUBSCRIPTION COST:	$12 individual, $17 institutional		
PUBLICATION LAG TIME:	3 months	STYLE SHEET:	Yes
EARLY PUBLICATION OPTION:	No	STYLE REQUIREMENTS:	Own style
REVIEW PERIOD:	3 months	CIRCULATION:	2,000
ACCEPTANCE RATE:	10%	REPRINT POLICY:	Optional purchase

JOURNAL TITLE: Administration in Social Work

MANUSCRIPT ADDRESS: Dr. Simon Slavin
School of Social Administration, Temple Univ.
Ritter Annex, Philadelphia, PA 19122

MAJOR CONTENT AREAS: Applied behavior analysis, administration,
organizational psychology, social issues

ARTICLES USUALLY ACCEPTED: Research, review, theoretical, case studies

TOPICS PREFERRED: Administration of social services, executive
performance, accountability

INAPPROPRIATE MANUSCRIPTS: None

INDEXED/ABSTRACTED IN: Not yet available

SUBSCRIPTION ADDRESS: The Haworth Press
174 Fifth Avenue
New York, NY 10010

SUBSCRIPTION COST:	$20 individual, $32 institutional		
PUBLICATION LAG TIME:	5-12 months	STYLE SHEET:	Yes
EARLY PUBLICATION OPTION:	Yes	STYLE REQUIREMENTS:	Chicago
REVIEW PERIOD:	2 months	CIRCULATION:	Not yet known
ACCEPTANCE RATE:	Not yet known	REPRINT POLICY:	50 free

JOURNAL TITLE: Administrative Science Quarterly

MANUSCRIPT ADDRESS: Malott Hall
Cornell University
Ithaca, NY 14853

MAJOR CONTENT AREAS: Community, industrial/organizational, social,
methodology, management

ARTICLES USUALLY ACCEPTED: Theoretical, research, book review

TOPICS PREFERRED: Varied

INAPPROPRIATE MANUSCRIPTS: Those lacking empirical data, case studies,
those unrelated to administrative science

INDEXED/ABSTRACTED IN: PA, ASW, SA, AHMS, BS, BPI, CCSBS, CIJE, EE,
EA, EAA, ERA, HA, IPAPL, IPARL, ILD, IBSS,
IPSA, MA, MR, PMA, PAISB, RHEA

SUBSCRIPTION ADDRESS: Subscriptions, ASQ
Malott Hall, Cornell University
Ithaca, NY 14853

SUBSCRIPTION COST: $14
PUBLICATION LAG TIME: 4-6 months   STYLE SHEET: Yes
EARLY PUBLICATION OPTION: No   STYLE REQUIREMENTS: Own style
REVIEW PERIOD: 3-6 months   CIRCULATION: 5,200
ACCEPTANCE RATE: 40%   REPRINT POLICY: 50 free

JOURNAL TITLE: Adolescence

MANUSCRIPT ADDRESS: Libra Publishers, Inc. P. O. Box 165
391 Willets Rd.
Roslyn Heights, L.I., NY 11577

MAJOR CONTENT AREAS: Almost all areas as related to adolescence

ARTICLES USUALLY ACCEPTED: Research, review, theoretical, book review
from psychologists, psychiatrists,
physiologists, sociologists, and educators

TOPICS PREFERRED: None

INAPPROPRIATE MANUSCRIPTS: None

INDEXED/ABSTRACTED IN: PA, SA, AA, ACP, BS, CSPA, CCSBS, CIJE,
DSHA, EI, ECEA, IBSS, LLBA, RHEA, WSA

SUBSCRIPTION ADDRESS: Libra Publishers, Inc.
P. O. Box 165, 391 Willets Road
Roslyn Heights, L.I., NY 11577

SUBSCRIPTION COST: $10
PUBLICATION LAG TIME: Up to 2 years   STYLE SHEET: Yes
EARLY PUBLICATION OPTION: No   STYLE REQUIREMENTS: APA
REVIEW PERIOD: 2-3 weeks   CIRCULATION: 3,000
ACCEPTANCE RATE: 30%   REPRINT POLICY: Optional
purchase

JOURNAL TITLE: Aggressive Behavior

MANUSCRIPT ADDRESS: Dr. K. E. Moyer, Editor-in-Chief
Psychology Dept., Carnegie-Mellon University
Pittsburgh, PA 15213

MAJOR CONTENT AREAS: All areas as related to aggression

ARTICLES USUALLY ACCEPTED: Research, review, theoretical, book review
(book reviews by invitation only)

TOPICS PREFERRED: Aggressive behavior only

INAPPROPRIATE MANUSCRIPTS: None

INDEXED/ABSTRACTED IN: CCSBS

SUBSCRIPTION ADDRESS: Alan R. Liss, Inc.
150 Fifth Avenue
New York, NY 10011

SUBSCRIPTION COST: $30
PUBLICATION LAG TIME: 6 months   STYLE SHEET: Yes
EARLY PUBLICATION OPTION: No   STYLE REQUIREMENTS: APA
REVIEW PERIOD: 1-3 months   CIRCULATION: Not given
ACCEPTANCE RATE: 35-40%   REPRINT POLICY: Optional
purchase

JOURNAL TITLE: Aging

MANUSCRIPT ADDRESS: Dept. of HEW; Administration on Aging
400 Sixth Street, S.W.
Washington, DC 20201

MAJOR CONTENT AREAS: Gerontology

ARTICLES USUALLY ACCEPTED: Research

TOPICS PREFERRED: Any in the area of gerontology

INAPPROPRIATE MANUSCRIPTS: None

INDEXED/ABSTRACTED IN: ASW, AHMS, RGPL, U

SUBSCRIPTION ADDRESS: Superintendent of Documents
Government Printing Office
Washington, DC 20402

SUBSCRIPTION COST: $5.05
PUBLICATION LAG TIME: 7 weeks   STYLE SHEET: Yes
EARLY PUBLICATION OPTION: Yes   STYLE REQUIREMENTS: Not given
REVIEW PERIOD: 1 month   CIRCULATION: 12,000
ACCEPTANCE RATE: Not given   REPRINT POLICY: One free

JOURNAL TITLE: American Behavioral Scientist

MANUSCRIPT ADDRESS: Sage Publications, Inc.
275 South Beverly Drive
Beverly Hills, CA 90212

MAJOR CONTENT AREAS: All areas that would be of interest to the
general public

ARTICLES USUALLY ACCEPTED: All types; a special theme with a guest editor
each issue; most manuscripts are solicited
by the guest editor

TOPICS PREFERRED: General, social

INAPPROPRIATE MANUSCRIPTS: None

INDEXED/ABSTRACTED IN: PA, ABCPS, AA, BS, CDL, CCSBS, CIJE, EAA,
IPAPL, ISA, IBSS, IPSA, JHE, PRAJ, SSHI,
WSA

SUBSCRIPTION ADDRESS: Sage Publications, Inc.
275 South Beverly Drive
Beverly Hills, CA 90212

SUBSCRIPTION COST: $12 individual, $24 institutional
PUBLICATION LAG TIME: Not given   STYLE SHEET: Yes
EARLY PUBLICATION OPTION: Not given   STYLE REQUIREMENTS: Sage
REVIEW PERIOD: Not given   CIRCULATION: Not given
ACCEPTANCE RATE: Not given   REPRINT POLICY: 24 free

JOURNAL TITLE: American Educational Research Journal

MANUSCRIPT ADDRESS: Dr. Maryellen McSweeney, 464 Erickson Hall
Michigan State University,
East Lansing, MI 48823

MAJOR CONTENT AREAS: Educational, experimental, learning, perception, psychometrics, statistics/methodology

ARTICLES USUALLY ACCEPTED: Original reports of empirical or theoretical
research relating to education

TOPICS PREFERRED: None

INAPPROPRIATE MANUSCRIPTS: None

INDEXED/ABSTRACTED IN: PA, BS, CGCI, CSPA, CCSBS, CIJE, EI, EAA,
ECEA, EY, LLBA, RHEA, SPD

SUBSCRIPTION ADDRESS: AERA 1126 16th. St., N.W.
Washington, DC 20036

SUBSCRIPTION COST: $12 individual, $14 institutional
PUBLICATION LAG TIME: 3-6 months   STYLE SHEET: No
EARLY PUBLICATION OPTION: No   STYLE REQUIREMENTS: APA
REVIEW PERIOD: 2-4 months   CIRCULATION: 14,000
ACCEPTANCE RATE: Not yet available REPRINT POLICY: 50 free

JOURNAL TITLE: American Journal of Art Therapy

MANUSCRIPT ADDRESS: P. O. Box 4918
Washington, DC 20008

MAJOR CONTENT AREAS: Clinical, educational, experimental, mental
retardation, & others as related to art therapy

ARTICLES USUALLY ACCEPTED: Research, review, theoretical, book review

TOPICS PREFERRED: None

INAPPROPRIATE MANUSCRIPTS: None

INDEXED/ABSTRACTED IN: PA, IM, CCSBS, ECEA

SUBSCRIPTION ADDRESS: P. O. Box 4918
Washington, DC 20008

SUBSCRIPTION COST: $10

PUBLICATION LAG TIME: Not given	STYLE SHEET:	Yes
EARLY PUBLICATION OPTION: No	STYLE REQUIREMENTS:	Own style
REVIEW PERIOD: Not given	CIRCULATION:	850
ACCEPTANCE RATE: Not given	REPRINT POLICY:	6 free copies of issue

JOURNAL TITLE: The American Journal of Clinical Hypnosis

MANUSCRIPT ADDRESS: Sheldon B. Cohen, M.D., Editor
401 Peachtree St., N.E., Suite 804
Atlanta, GA 30308

MAJOR CONTENT AREAS: Hypnosis, psychotherapy, personality

ARTICLES USUALLY ACCEPTED: Research, theoretical, case studies

TOPICS PREFERRED: None

INAPPROPRIATE MANUSCRIPTS: None

INDEXED/ABSTRACTED IN: PA, BI, CCCP, CCSBS, WSA

SUBSCRIPTION ADDRESS: The American Society of Clinical Hypnosis
2400 East Devon Ave., Suite 218
Des Plaines, IL 60018

SUBSCRIPTION COST: $12

PUBLICATION LAG TIME: 3-9 months	STYLE SHEET:	Not given
EARLY PUBLICATION OPTION: Not given	STYLE REQUIREMENTS:	Not given
REVIEW PERIOD: Not given	CIRCULATION:	1,200
ACCEPTANCE RATE: Not given	REPRINT POLICY:	Not given

JOURNAL TITLE: American Journal of Community Psychology

MANUSCRIPT ADDRESS: Charles D. Spielberger, Univ. of South Florida
Department of Psychology
Tampa, FL   33620

MAJOR CONTENT AREAS: Community, applied social, community mental health

ARTICLES USUALLY ACCEPTED: Research, theoretical, review

TOPICS PREFERRED: Empirical research on community psychology

INAPPROPRIATE MANUSCRIPTS: Clinical psychology, abnormal psychology, descriptions of clinical services

INDEXED/ABSTRACTED IN: PA, CCSBS

SUBSCRIPTION ADDRESS: Plenum Publishing Corp.
227 West 17th Street
New York, NY   10011

SUBSCRIPTION COST: $16 individual, $32 institutional

PUBLICATION LAG TIME:	10-14 months	STYLE SHEET:	Yes
EARLY PUBLICATION OPTION:	No	STYLE REQUIREMENTS:	APA
REVIEW PERIOD:	2-4 months	CIRCULATION:	800
ACCEPTANCE RATE:	35-40%	REPRINT POLICY:	Optional purchase

JOURNAL TITLE: American Journal of Diseases of Children

MANUSCRIPT ADDRESS: Gilbert B. Forbes, M.D., Chief Editor
601 Elmwood Avenue
Rochester, NY   14642

MAJOR CONTENT AREAS: Clinical, developmental, educational, learning, methodology

ARTICLES USUALLY ACCEPTED: Research, review, theoretical, book review

TOPICS PREFERRED: None

INAPPROPRIATE MANUSCRIPTS: None

INDEXED/ABSTRACTED IN: PA, IM, ASW, BS, CCCP, DSHA, ECEA, JHE, LLBA, WSA, WAH

SUBSCRIPTION ADDRESS: American Medical Association
535 North Dearborn St.
Chicago, IL   60610

SUBSCRIPTION COST: $18

PUBLICATION LAG TIME:	6 months	STYLE SHEET:	Yes
EARLY PUBLICATION OPTION:	Yes	STYLE REQUIREMENTS:	AMA
REVIEW PERIOD:	Not given	CIRCULATION:	25,000
ACCEPTANCE RATE:	30%	REPRINT POLICY:	Optional purchase

JOURNAL TITLE: American Journal of Mental Deficiency

MANUSCRIPT ADDRESS: Dr. H. C. Haywood, Editor
Box 503, Peabody College
Nashville, TN 37203

MAJOR CONTENT AREAS: Mental retardation

ARTICLES USUALLY ACCEPTED: Original research, theoretical articles, and systematic reviews

TOPICS PREFERRED: Articles from the various disciplines concerned with mental retardation

INAPPROPRIATE MANUSCRIPTS: Program descriptions, personal accounts, anecdotal case studies, & research applications

INDEXED/ABSTRACTED IN: PA, BS, CCSBS, CIJE, DSHA, EI, ECEA, LLBA

SUBSCRIPTION ADDRESS: American Association on Mental Deficiency
5201 Connecticut Ave., N.W.
Washington, DC 20015

SUBSCRIPTION COST: $20 individual, $40 institutional

PUBLICATION LAG TIME:	6 months	STYLE SHEET:	Yes
EARLY PUBLICATION OPTION:	No	STYLE REQUIREMENTS:	Modified APA
REVIEW PERIOD:	4 months	CIRCULATION:	13,527
ACCEPTANCE RATE:	25%	REPRINT POLICY:	Optional purchase

JOURNAL TITLE: American Journal of Nursing

MANUSCRIPT ADDRESS: 10 Columbus Circle
New York, NY 10019

MAJOR CONTENT AREAS: All areas as related to nursing

ARTICLES USUALLY ACCEPTED: Research, review, theoretical, book review, humor, personal interest, how-to-do-it

TOPICS PREFERRED: Nursing and health care

INAPPROPRIATE MANUSCRIPTS: None

INDEXED/ABSTRACTED IN: PA, IM, ASW, AHMS, CA, CCCP, CCSBS, HLI, INI, JHE, LLBA, MMRI, PAISB, WSA, WAH

SUBSCRIPTION ADDRESS: 10 Columbus Circle
New York, NY 10019

SUBSCRIPTION COST: $10

PUBLICATION LAG TIME:	6-18 months	STYLE SHEET:	Yes
EARLY PUBLICATION OPTION:	No	STYLE REQUIREMENTS:	Chicago
REVIEW PERIOD:	3-4 months	CIRCULATION:	305,000
ACCEPTANCE RATE:	10%	REPRINT POLICY:	100 free

JOURNAL TITLE: American Journal of Occupational Therapy

MANUSCRIPT ADDRESS: 616 Tanner Marsh Road
Guilford, CT   06437

MAJOR CONTENT AREAS: Occupational therapy in psychiatry, work issues

ARTICLES USUALLY ACCEPTED: Research, review, theoretical, case studies

TOPICS PREFERRED: None

INAPPROPRIATE MANUSCRIPTS: Those on psychoanalysis

INDEXED/ABSTRACTED IN: PA, IM, AHMS, CCSBS, CIJE, ECEA

SUBSCRIPTION ADDRESS: 6000 Executive Boulevard
Rockville, MD   20852

SUBSCRIPTION COST: $15 individual, $18 institutional
PUBLICATION LAG TIME: 4-12 months   STYLE SHEET: Yes
EARLY PUBLICATION OPTION: Not given   STYLE REQUIREMENTS: APA
REVIEW PERIOD: 2-3 months   CIRCULATION: 18,000
ACCEPTANCE RATE: 60%   REPRINT POLICY: Purchase
required

JOURNAL TITLE: American Journal of Orthopsychiatry

MANUSCRIPT ADDRESS: 1775 Broadway
New York, NY   10019

MAJOR CONTENT AREAS: Almost all areas of psychiatry

ARTICLES USUALLY ACCEPTED: Clinical, theoretical, research, review;
no unsolicited book reviews

TOPICS PREFERRED: Multidisciplinary approaches to mental health,
prevention and treatment of mental illness

INAPPROPRIATE MANUSCRIPTS: None

INDEXED/ABSTRACTED IN: PA, ASW, BI, CSPA, CCCP, CIJE, DSHA, EI,
ECEA, IPAPL, IPARL, IBSS, JHE, LLBA, PRAJ,
WSA

SUBSCRIPTION ADDRESS: 49 Sheridan Ave.
Albany, NY   12210

SUBSCRIPTION COST: $16
PUBLICATION LAG TIME: 3-4 months   STYLE SHEET: Yes
EARLY PUBLICATION OPTION: No   STYLE REQUIREMENTS: Own style
REVIEW PERIOD: 3-4 months   CIRCULATION: 9,500
ACCEPTANCE RATE: 15%   REPRINT POLICY: 1 free copy
of issue

JOURNAL TITLE: American Journal of Psychiatry

MANUSCRIPT ADDRESS: 1700 Eighteenth St.
Washington, DC 20009

MAJOR CONTENT AREAS: Psychiatry, all clinical areas

ARTICLES USUALLY ACCEPTED: Research, review, theoretical, book review

TOPICS PREFERRED: Psychotherapy, social issues of interest to
psychiatrists, psychiatric education

INAPPROPRIATE MANUSCRIPTS: Single case reports, program descriptions

INDEXED/ABSTRACTED IN: PA, IM, EM, ASW, AHMS, BI, BA, CA, CSPA,
CCCP, CCSBS, DSHA, HLI, IPAPL, IPARL, IBSS,
INI, JHE, LLBA, NAR, PHRA, WSA, WAH

SUBSCRIPTION ADDRESS: 1700 Eighteenth Street
Washington, DC 20009

SUBSCRIPTION COST: $18	
PUBLICATION LAG TIME: 8-12 months	STYLE SHEET: Yes
EARLY PUBLICATION OPTION: Yes	STYLE REQUIREMENTS: Own style
REVIEW PERIOD: 4-6 months	CIRCULATION: 28,000
ACCEPTANCE RATE: 25%	REPRINT POLICY: Optional purchase

JOURNAL TITLE: American Journal of Psychoanalysis

MANUSCRIPT ADDRESS: Helen A. DeRosis, M.D.
329 East 62nd Street
New York, NY 10021

MAJOR CONTENT AREAS: Psychoanalysis

ARTICLES USUALLY ACCEPTED: Research, theoretical, book review,
personal opinion

TOPICS PREFERRED: Diverse theoretical points of view within
the area of psychoanalysis

INAPPROPRIATE MANUSCRIPTS: None

INDEXED/ABSTRACTED IN: PA, ASW, BI, BS, CCSBS

SUBSCRIPTION ADDRESS: Association for the Advancement of Psychoanalysis
329 East 62nd Street
New York, NY 10021

SUBSCRIPTION COST: $12 individual, $22 institutional	
PUBLICATION LAG TIME: Not given	STYLE SHEET: No
EARLY PUBLICATION OPTION: Not given	STYLE REQUIREMENTS: Own style
REVIEW PERIOD: Not given	CIRCULATION: 1,500
ACCEPTANCE RATE: Not given	REPRINT POLICY: Optional purchase

JOURNAL TITLE: American Journal of Psychology

MANUSCRIPT ADDRESS: 425 Psychology Building
University of Illinois
Champaign, IL 61820

MAJOR CONTENT AREAS: Clinical, developmental, all experimental
areas, industrial/organizational, social

ARTICLES USUALLY ACCEPTED: Research, book review, theoretical, review

TOPICS PREFERRED: General experimental psychology

INAPPROPRIATE MANUSCRIPTS: Original "fiction"

INDEXED/ABSTRACTED IN: PA, IM, BA, BS, CA, CCSBS, CIJE, DSHA,
JHE, LLBA, RHEA

SUBSCRIPTION ADDRESS: Marilyn Morey
University of Illinois Press
Champaign, IL 61820

SUBSCRIPTION COST:	$15		
PUBLICATION LAG TIME:	6 months	STYLE SHEET:	No
EARLY PUBLICATION OPTION:	No	STYLE REQUIREMENTS:	APA
REVIEW PERIOD:	3-6 months	CIRCULATION:	3,500
ACCEPTANCE RATE:	33%	REPRINT POLICY:	Optional purchase

JOURNAL TITLE: American Journal of Psychotherapy

MANUSCRIPT ADDRESS: 114 East 78th Street
New York, NY 10021

MAJOR CONTENT AREAS: All clinical areas

ARTICLES USUALLY ACCEPTED: Research

TOPICS PREFERRED: Psychotherapy

INAPPROPRIATE MANUSCRIPTS: None

INDEXED/ABSTRACTED IN: PA, IM, ASW, BI, CCSBS, LLBA

SUBSCRIPTION ADDRESS: Mrs. E. Hyde, Business Manager
119-21 Metropolitan Avenue
Jamaica, NY 11415

SUBSCRIPTION COST:	$16		
PUBLICATION LAG TIME:	9-12 months	STYLE SHEET:	No
EARLY PUBLICATION OPTION:	Yes	STYLE REQUIREMENTS:	Ind. Med.
REVIEW PERIOD:	3 months	CIRCULATION:	4,500
ACCEPTANCE RATE:	25%	REPRINT POLICY:	Optional purchase

JOURNAL TITLE: American Journal of Public Health

MANUSCRIPT ADDRESS: American Public Health Association
1015 18th Street, N.W.
Washington, DC 20036

MAJOR CONTENT AREAS: All aspects of public health

ARTICLES USUALLY ACCEPTED: Research, demonstration, evaluation

TOPICS PREFERRED: Original articles covering the current
aspects of public health

INAPPROPRIATE MANUSCRIPTS: Those too clinical or anecdotal; speeches

INDEXED/ABSTRACTED IN: IM, EM, ASW, BA, BS, CECD, CA, CCCP, DSHA,
EPB, HLI, IPAPL, NSA, PHRA, PAISB, WSA

SUBSCRIPTION ADDRESS: American Public Health Association
1015 18th Street, N.W.
Washington, DC 20036

SUBSCRIPTION COST: $30
PUBLICATION LAG TIME: 6-8 months   STYLE SHEET: Yes
EARLY PUBLICATION OPTION: Yes   STYLE REQUIREMENTS: Ind. Med.
REVIEW PERIOD: 3 months   CIRCULATION: 30,000
ACCEPTANCE RATE: 15-20%   REPRINT POLICY: Optional
                                                      purchase

JOURNAL TITLE: American Journal of Sociology

MANUSCRIPT ADDRESS: 1130 East 59th Street
Chicago, IL 60637

MAJOR CONTENT AREAS: Sociology

ARTICLES USUALLY ACCEPTED: Research, review, theoretical; book reviews
are solicited

TOPICS PREFERRED: Those of substantial significance for sociology
or the sociology-psychology interface

INAPPROPRIATE MANUSCRIPTS: Those of interest only to psychologists

INDEXED/ABSTRACTED IN: ASW, SA, ABCPS, AA, AI, BRD, BRI, BS, CSPA, CCSBS
CIJE, EAA, ERA, GSSRP, HA, IPAPL, IPARL, IBSS, IL
IPSA, JHE, LLBA, PRAJ, RHEA, SSHI, WSA, WAH

SUBSCRIPTION ADDRESS: University of Chicago Press, Journals Division
5801 Ellis Avenue
Chicago, IL 60637

SUBSCRIPTION COST: $15 individual, $20 institutional
PUBLICATION LAG TIME: 8 months   STYLE SHEET: Yes
EARLY PUBLICATION OPTION: No   STYLE REQUIREMENTS: Own style
REVIEW PERIOD: 2-3 months   CIRCULATION: 11,500
ACCEPTANCE RATE: 7%   REPRINT POLICY: Optional
                                                      purchase

JOURNAL TITLE: American Psychologist

MANUSCRIPT ADDRESS: Charles A. Keisler, Editor
APA, 1200 17th Street, N.W.
Washington, DC 20036

MAJOR CONTENT AREAS: All areas if they are current issues in psychology

ARTICLES USUALLY ACCEPTED: Research, theoretical, practical, review

TOPICS PREFERRED: None

INAPPROPRIATE MANUSCRIPTS: None

INDEXED/ABSTRACTED IN: PA, ASW, BI, CSPA, CCSBS, DSHA, EE, ERA, ECEA, IPAPL, IPARL, ISA, IBSS, JHE, LLBA, PRAJ

SUBSCRIPTION ADDRESS: APA Subscription Office
1200 17th Street, N.W.
Washington, DC 20036

SUBSCRIPTION COST: $15

PUBLICATION LAG TIME:	5 months	STYLE SHEET:	No
EARLY PUBLICATION OPTION:	No	STYLE REQUIREMENTS:	APA
REVIEW PERIOD:	Variable	CIRCULATION:	45,000
ACCEPTANCE RATE:	10%	REPRINT POLICY:	20 free

JOURNAL TITLE: American Quarterly

MANUSCRIPT ADDRESS: Box 1, Logan Hall CN
University of Pennsylvania
Philadelphia, PA 19174

MAJOR CONTENT AREAS: History & systems, American culture

ARTICLES USUALLY ACCEPTED: Research, historical, book review

TOPICS PREFERRED: Interdisciplinary articles analyzing American society, past and present

INAPPROPRIATE MANUSCRIPTS: Topics that are too narrow or pertain only to one discipline

INDEXED/ABSTRACTED IN: ASW, AES, ALA, HA, IPAPL, IRPL, MLA, SSHI, SSCI, WSA, WAH

SUBSCRIPTION ADDRESS: American Studies Association
4025 Chestnut Street
Philadelphia; PA 19174

SUBSCRIPTION COST: $15

PUBLICATION LAG TIME:	6 months	STYLE SHEET:	Yes
EARLY PUBLICATION OPTION:	No	STYLE REQUIREMENTS:	MLA
REVIEW PERIOD:	3 months	CIRCULATION:	5,500
ACCEPTANCE RATE:	5%	REPRINT POLICY:	25 free

JOURNAL TITLE:	American Scientist
MANUSCRIPT ADDRESS:	345 Whitney Avenue New Haven, CT 06511
MAJOR CONTENT AREAS:	Experimental, learning, perception, personality, physiological, social
ARTICLES USUALLY ACCEPTED:	Research, review
TOPICS PREFERRED:	Any topic with a solid body of evidence and perhaps some integrative theory
INAPPROPRIATE MANUSCRIPTS:	Editorials, polemics, case studies
INDEXED/ABSTRACTED IN:	PA, IM, AES, AA, BA, BAA, CA, CCSBS, INSPEC, ISA, JHE, LLBA, NSA, PRAJ, SCI, WSA, WAH
SUBSCRIPTION ADDRESS:	345 Whitney Avenue New Haven, CT 06511

SUBSCRIPTION COST:	$12		
PUBLICATION LAG TIME:	one issue	STYLE SHEET:	Yes
EARLY PUBLICATION OPTION:	No	STYLE REQUIREMENTS:	APA
REVIEW PERIOD:	1-2 months	CIRCULATION:	125,000
ACCEPTANCE RATE:	40-50%	REPRINT POLICY:	100 free

JOURNAL TITLE:	American Sociological Review
MANUSCRIPT ADDRESS:	Dept. of Sociology Stanford University Stanford, CA 94305
MAJOR CONTENT AREAS:	Sociology
ARTICLES USUALLY ACCEPTED:	Research, theoretical
TOPICS PREFERRED:	Sociology
INAPPROPRIATE MANUSCRIPTS:	None
INDEXED/ABSTRACTED IN:	PA, ASW, SA, ABCPS, AA, AHM, APAIS, BRI, BS, CSP, CB, CCSBS, EE, EAA, ERA, ECEA, GSSRPL, HA, IPAPL, IBSS, ILD, IPSA, JHE, LLBA, PRAJ, RHEA, SSHI, WS
SUBSCRIPTION ADDRESS:	Executive Office, American Sociological Assoc. 1722 N Street, N.W. Washington, DC 20036

SUBSCRIPTION COST:	$15 individual, $30 institutional		
PUBLICATION LAG TIME:	6 months	STYLE SHEET:	Yes
EARLY PUBLICATION OPTION:	No	STYLE REQUIREMENTS:	APA
REVIEW PERIOD:	3 months	CIRCULATION:	18,000
ACCEPTANCE RATE:	10%	REPRINT POLICY:	Optional purchase

JOURNAL TITLE: Animal Behaviour

MANUSCRIPT ADDRESS: Jack P. Hailman, Dept. of Zoology
Birge Hall, Univ. of Wisconsin
Madison, WI 53706

MAJOR CONTENT AREAS: Comparative, physiological, ethology

ARTICLES USUALLY ACCEPTED: Research, theoretical; non-members must
pay a nominal editorial fee

TOPICS PREFERRED: Animal behavior

INAPPROPRIATE MANUSCRIPTS: Laboratory animal learning studies

INDEXED/ABSTRACTED IN: PA, BI

SUBSCRIPTION ADDRESS: Dr. C. Richard Terman, Dept. of Biology
College of William and Mary
Williamsburg, VA 23185

SUBSCRIPTION COST: $17.50 individual, $60 institutional	
PUBLICATION LAG TIME: 6-9 months	STYLE SHEET: Yes
EARLY PUBLICATION OPTION: No	STYLE REQUIREMENTS: CBE
REVIEW PERIOD: 3 months	CIRCULATION: Not given
ACCEPTANCE RATE: 30%	REPRINT POLICY: Optional purchase

JOURNAL TITLE: Animal Learning and Behavior

MANUSCRIPT ADDRESS: Dr. M. D'Amato
Rutgers University
New Brunswick, NJ 08903

MAJOR CONTENT AREAS: Comparative, developmental, experimental,
learning

ARTICLES USUALLY ACCEPTED: Research, theoretical, review

TOPICS PREFERRED: Animal learning, behavior development,
psychophysics, motivation, conditioning

INAPPROPRIATE MANUSCRIPTS: Very few, if any

INDEXED/ABSTRACTED IN: PA, PRG

SUBSCRIPTION ADDRESS: Publications Office, The Psychonomic Society
1108 West 34th Street
Austin, TX 78705

SUBSCRIPTION COST: $7.50 individual, $15 institutional	
PUBLICATION LAG TIME: 5-6 months	STYLE SHEET: Yes
EARLY PUBLICATION OPTION: No	STYLE REQUIREMENTS: APA, AIP
REVIEW PERIOD: 3-6 weeks	CIRCULATION: 1,700
ACCEPTANCE RATE: 30%	REPRINT POLICY: Purchase required

JOURNAL TITLE: Applied Psychological Measurement

MANUSCRIPT ADDRESS: David T. Weiss, Editor
N660 Elliott Hall, University of Minnesota
Minneapolis, MN 55455

MAJOR CONTENT AREAS: Applications of psychometrics to most areas of psychology.

ARTICLES USUALLY ACCEPTED: Research on the application of measurement techniques, review, book review, summaries of measurement-related computer programs

TOPICS PREFERRED: Empirical research on the application of techniques of psychological measurement

INAPPROPRIATE MANUSCRIPTS: Articles which are not data based (except for reviews)

INDEXED/ABSTRACTED IN: Not yet available

SUBSCRIPTION ADDRESS: Larry Schneider, West Publishing Co.
50 W. Kellogg Blvd.
St. Paul, MN 55102

SUBSCRIPTION COST: $20 individual, $30 institutional

PUBLICATION LAG TIME: 9-12 months   STYLE SHEET: Yes

EARLY PUBLICATION OPTION: No   STYLE REQUIREMENTS: APA

REVIEW PERIOD: 2-3 months   CIRCULATION: Not yet known

ACCEPTANCE RATE: 30-35%   REPRINT POLICY: Undecided

JOURNAL TITLE: Archives of General Psychiatry

MANUSCRIPT ADDRESS: Daniel X. Freedman, M.D., Editor
Dept. of Psychiatry, Univ. of Chicago
950 E. 59th St., Chicago, IL 60637

MAJOR CONTENT AREAS: All areas of psychiatry

ARTICLES USUALLY ACCEPTED: Research, review, book review

TOPICS PREFERRED: None

INAPPROPRIATE MANUSCRIPTS: None

INDEXED/ABSTRACTED IN: PA, IM, ASW, CSPA, CCCP, CCSBS, IPAPL, LLBA, WAH

SUBSCRIPTION ADDRESS: Subscription Manager
535 North Dearborn St.
Chicago, IL 60610

SUBSCRIPTION COST: $18

PUBLICATION LAG TIME: 2-12 months   STYLE SHEET: Yes

EARLY PUBLICATION OPTION: Yes   STYLE REQUIREMENTS: Own style

REVIEW PERIOD: 2-4 months   CIRCULATION: 20,880

ACCEPTANCE RATE: 35%   REPRINT POLICY: 200 free

JOURNAL TITLE: Archives of Psychiatry and Neurological Sciences

MANUSCRIPT ADDRESS: Depends upon area of research; contact New York office for list of addresses

MAJOR CONTENT AREAS: Psychiatry, psychotherapy, neurology, psychopharmacology

ARTICLES USUALLY ACCEPTED: Research

TOPICS PREFERRED: Psychotherapy, social and community psychiatry, evaluation of mental health services

INAPPROPRIATE MANUSCRIPTS: None

INDEXED/ABSTRACTED IN: CCCP

SUBSCRIPTION ADDRESS: Springer-Verlag New York, Inc.
175 Fifth Avenue
New York, NY 10010

SUBSCRIPTION COST: Not given
PUBLICATION LAG TIME: 3-4 months   STYLE SHEET: Yes
EARLY PUBLICATION OPTION: No   STYLE REQUIREMENTS: Own style
REVIEW PERIOD: Not given   CIRCULATION: Not given
ACCEPTANCE RATE: Not given   REPRINT POLICY: 50 free

JOURNAL TITLE: Archives of Sexual Behavior

MANUSCRIPT ADDRESS: Dept. of Psychiatry and Behavioral Sciences, Health Sciences Center, State University of New York, Stony Brook, NY 11794

MAJOR CONTENT AREAS: Most areas as related to sexual behavior

ARTICLES USUALLY ACCEPTED: Research, review

TOPICS PREFERRED: Sex research, primarily human, but may include non-human primates

INAPPROPRIATE MANUSCRIPTS: None

INDEXED/ABSTRACTED IN: PA, IM, EM, BA, CCSBS, WSA

SUBSCRIPTION ADDRESS: Plenum Publishing Corp.
227 W. 17th St.
New York, NY 10011

SUBSCRIPTION COST: $19 individual, $54 institutional
PUBLICATION LAG TIME: 10-13 months   STYLE SHEET: No
EARLY PUBLICATION OPTION: Yes   STYLE REQUIREMENTS: SMBJ
REVIEW PERIOD: 2 months   CIRCULATION: 1,000
ACCEPTANCE RATE: 33%   REPRINT POLICY: Optional purchase

JOURNAL TITLE: Art Psychotherapy

MANUSCRIPT ADDRESS: Pergamon Press
Headington Hill Hall
Oxford OX3 OBW, England

MAJOR CONTENT AREAS: Clinical, psychotherapy, art therapy

ARTICLES USUALLY ACCEPTED: Research, review, theoretical

TOPICS PREFERRED: Art; creativity and therapy

INAPPROPRIATE MANUSCRIPTS: Case studies

INDEXED/ABSTRACTED IN: CCSBS

SUBSCRIPTION ADDRESS: Pergamon Press
Headington Hill Hall
Oxford OX3 OBW, England

SUBSCRIPTION COST: $40
PUBLICATION LAG TIME: 6 months   STYLE SHEET: Yes
EARLY PUBLICATION OPTION: No   STYLE REQUIREMENTS: APA
REVIEW PERIOD: 2-3 months   CIRCULATION: Not given
ACCEPTANCE RATE: 60-70%   REPRINT POLICY: Purchase
required

JOURNAL TITLE: Audiovisual Instruction

MANUSCRIPT ADDRESS: AECT
1201 16th Street, N.W.
Washington, DC 20036

MAJOR CONTENT AREAS: Educational

ARTICLES USUALLY ACCEPTED: Practical articles about uses, management,
and programs of educational technology; list-
ing of themes included in author guidelines

TOPICS PREFERRED: Media in classrooms, technology in education
and training

INAPPROPRIATE MANUSCRIPTS: None

INDEXED/ABSTRACTED IN: PA, CIJE, EI, ECA, ECEA, ISA, INSPEC, IIMMI,
LLBA, MI, MMRI, RHEA

SUBSCRIPTION ADDRESS: AECT
1201 16th Street, N.W.
Washington, DC 20036

SUBSCRIPTION COST: $18
PUBLICATION LAG TIME: 10 weeks   STYLE SHEET: Yes
EARLY PUBLICATION OPTION: No   STYLE REQUIREMENTS: APA, Chicago
REVIEW PERIOD: 6-8 weeks   CIRCULATION: 20,000
ACCEPTANCE RATE: 30%   REPRINT POLICY: 2 free

JOURNAL TITLE: Australian Journal of Psychology

MANUSCRIPT ADDRESS: Department of Psychology
University of Sydney
Sydney, 2006, Australia

MAJOR CONTENT AREAS: Almost all non-clinical areas

ARTICLES USUALLY ACCEPTED: Research, review, theoretical, book review

TOPICS PREFERRED: All experimental areas plus industrial/
organizational, social and personality

INAPPROPRIATE MANUSCRIPTS: Applied or professional

INDEXED/ABSTRACTED IN: PA, AEI, BI, CSPA, CCSBS, CIJE, LLBA, RHEA

SUBSCRIPTION ADDRESS: National Science Centre
191 Royal Parade
Parkville, Victoria 3052, Australia

SUBSCRIPTION COST:	$A8.50		
PUBLICATION LAG TIME:	3 months	STYLE SHEET:	Yes
EARLY PUBLICATION OPTION:	Yes	STYLE REQUIREMENTS:	APA
REVIEW PERIOD:	3 months	CIRCULATION:	3,000
ACCEPTANCE RATE:	36%	REPRINT POLICY:	25 free

JOURNAL TITLE: Australian and New Zealand Journal of
Psychiatry

MANUSCRIPT ADDRESS: Maudsley House
107 Rathdowne Street
Carlton, Victoria 3053, Australia

MAJOR CONTENT AREAS: All areas of psychiatry

ARTICLES USUALLY ACCEPTED: Research, theoretical, clinical, review; book
reviews on request

TOPICS PREFERRED: Psychiatry, psychotherapy, psychoanalysis and
associated fields of work and research

INAPPROPRIATE MANUSCRIPTS: None

INDEXED/ABSTRACTED IN: IM, EM, APAIS, CCCP, CCSBS, IL, MHD, YPMH

SUBSCRIPTION ADDRESS: Maudsley House
107 Rathdowne Street
Carlton, Victoria 3053, Australia

SUBSCRIPTION COST:	1976, AUS $15, 1977 AUS $20		
PUBLICATION LAG TIME:	3-6 months	STYLE SHEET:	Yes
EARLY PUBLICATION OPTION:	No	STYLE REQUIREMENTS:	Own style
REVIEW PERIOD:	3 months	CIRCULATION:	1,300
ACCEPTANCE RATE:	33%	REPRINT POLICY:	1 free copy of issue

JOURNAL TITLE: Australian Psychologist

MANUSCRIPT ADDRESS: Editor, Australian Psychologist
Dept. of Psychology, University of Queensland
St. Lucia, Queensland 4067, Australia

MAJOR CONTENT AREAS: General

ARTICLES USUALLY ACCEPTED: Research, review, theoretical, book review
(of general interest to Society membership)

TOPICS PREFERRED: Professional issues - occupational, counselling,
test standardization, role of psychologist

INAPPROPRIATE MANUSCRIPTS: None

INDEXED/ABSTRACTED IN: PA, AEI, CCSBS, PRG

SUBSCRIPTION ADDRESS: Australian Psychological Society
National Science Centre, 191 Royal Parade
Parkville, Victoria 3052, Australia

SUBSCRIPTION COST: $9

PUBLICATION LAG TIME: 3 months   STYLE SHEET: No

EARLY PUBLICATION OPTION: No   STYLE REQUIREMENTS: APA

REVIEW PERIOD: 2-6 months   CIRCULATION: 2,200

ACCEPTANCE RATE: Not given   REPRINT POLICY: 25 free

JOURNAL TITLE: Australian Social Work

MANUSCRIPT ADDRESS: Mary McLelland, Editor
Box 59, North Richmond
Victoria 3121, Australia

MAJOR CONTENT AREAS: Social work

ARTICLES USUALLY ACCEPTED: Not given

TOPICS PREFERRED: Not given, tabloid format

INAPPROPRIATE MANUSCRIPTS: Not given

INDEXED/ABSTRACTED IN: APAIS

SUBSCRIPTION ADDRESS: Australian Association of Social Workers
Box 59, North Richmond
Victoria 3121, Australia

SUBSCRIPTION COST: $3Australian

PUBLICATION LAG TIME: Not given   STYLE SHEET: Not given

EARLY PUBLICATION OPTION: Not given   STYLE REQUIREMENTS: Not given

REVIEW PERIOD: Not given   CIRCULATION: 2,250

ACCEPTANCE RATE: Not given   REPRINT POLICY: Not given

JOURNAL TITLE: AV Communication Review

MANUSCRIPT ADDRESS: R. Heinich
AV Center, Indiana University
Bloomington, IN 47401

MAJOR CONTENT AREAS: Educational, learning, instructional systems

ARTICLES USUALLY ACCEPTED: Research, review, theoretical

TOPICS PREFERRED: Psychological principles of learning and instruction involving the use of media

INAPPROPRIATE MANUSCRIPTS: Non-research, descriptive articles

INDEXED/ABSTRACTED IN: PA, CCSBS, CIJE, EI, ISA, IBSS, LLBA, T

SUBSCRIPTION ADDRESS: 1201 16th Street, N.W.
Washington, DC 20036

SUBSCRIPTION COST: $18 months
PUBLICATION LAG TIME: 6 months
EARLY PUBLICATION OPTION: Yes
REVIEW PERIOD: 9 weeks
ACCEPTANCE RATE: 8-12%

STYLE SHEET: Yes
STYLE REQUIREMENTS: APA
CIRCULATION: 7,000
REPRINT POLICY: 3 free copies of issue

JOURNAL TITLE: Behavior Genetics

MANUSCRIPT ADDRESS: S. G. Vandenberg
Dept. of Psychology, University of Colorado
Boulder, CO 80302

MAJOR CONTENT AREAS: Behavior genetics

ARTICLES USUALLY ACCEPTED: Research, review, theoretical

TOPICS PREFERRED: Behavior genetics

INAPPROPRIATE MANUSCRIPTS: Single case descriptions

INDEXED/ABSTRACTED IN: PA, IM, AA, CCSBS, GR

SUBSCRIPTION ADDRESS: Plenum Publishing Corp.
227 West 17th Street
New York, NY 10011

SUBSCRIPTION COST: $16 individual, $19.50 institutional
PUBLICATION LAG TIME: 9-10 months   STYLE SHEET: Yes
EARLY PUBLICATION OPTION: No   STYLE REQUIREMENTS: SMPJ
REVIEW PERIOD: 3 months   CIRCULATION: 657
ACCEPTANCE RATE: 65%   REPRINT POLICY: 25 free

JOURNAL TITLE: Behavior Modification

MANUSCRIPT ADDRESS: Michael Hersen, Editor-in-Chief, Western
Psychiatric Inst. & Clinic, U. of Pitt. School of
Med., 3811 O'Hara St., Pittsburgh, PA 15261

MAJOR CONTENT AREAS: Behavior therapy, applied behavior analysis

ARTICLES USUALLY ACCEPTED: Research, review, theoretical, case studies

TOPICS PREFERRED: Detailed reports of behavior analysis and
modification

INAPPROPRIATE MANUSCRIPTS: Not yet known

INDEXED/ABSTRACTED IN: Will appear in PA, CCSBS, PHRA, PRG, PAISB,
SSCI

SUBSCRIPTION ADDRESS: Sage Publications, Inc.
275 South Beverly Drive
Beverly Hills, CA 90212

SUBSCRIPTION COST: $15 individual, $30 institutional
PUBLICATION LAG TIME: 6-9 months (expected)STYLE SHEET: Yes
EARLY PUBLICATION OPTION: No   STYLE REQUIREMENTS: APA
REVIEW PERIOD: 1 month (expected) CIRCULATION: Not yet known
ACCEPTANCE RATE: Not yet known   REPRINT POLICY: 25 free

JOURNAL TITLE: Behavior Research Methods and Instrumentation

MANUSCRIPT ADDRESS: Dr. Joseph B. Sidowski
Department of Psychology, Univ. of South Fla.
Tampa, FL 33620

MAJOR CONTENT AREAS: Computer technology, instrumentation,
neuropsychology, psychochemistry

ARTICLES USUALLY ACCEPTED: Review, applied techniques and instruments,
computer program abstracts, research (pure
and applied)

TOPICS PREFERRED: Instrumentation techniques, computer
technology

INAPPROPRIATE MANUSCRIPTS: None

INDEXED/ABSTRACTED IN: PA, CCSBS, DSHA, ISA, LLBA, PRG

SUBSCRIPTION ADDRESS: Psychonomic Society, Inc.
1108 West 34th Street
Austin, TX 78705

SUBSCRIPTION COST: $10 individual, $20 institutional
PUBLICATION LAG TIME: 8 weeks   STYLE SHEET: Yes
EARLY PUBLICATION OPTION: No   STYLE REQUIREMENTS: APA, AIP
REVIEW PERIOD: 1-4 weeks   CIRCULATION: 1,000
ACCEPTANCE RATE: 48-50%   REPRINT POLICY: Purchase
required

JOURNAL TITLE: Behavior Research and Therapy

MANUSCRIPT ADDRESS: Prof. H. J. Eysenck, Institute of Psychiatry
De Crespigny Park
London SE5, England

MAJOR CONTENT AREAS: Behavior therapy

ARTICLES USUALLY ACCEPTED: Research, theoretical, case studies

TOPICS PREFERRED: Experimental clinical research in behavior
therapy

INAPPROPRIATE MANUSCRIPTS: None

INDEXED/ABSTRACTED IN: PA, CCSBS, DSHA

SUBSCRIPTION ADDRESS: Pergamon Press
Headington Hill Hall
Oxford, England

SUBSCRIPTION COST: $25 individual, $50 institutional
PUBLICATION LAG TIME: 9 months   STYLE SHEET: Yes
EARLY PUBLICATION OPTION: No   STYLE REQUIREMENTS: Old APA
REVIEW PERIOD: 3 months   CIRCULATION: 3,000
ACCEPTANCE RATE: 15%   REPRINT POLICY: 25 free

JOURNAL TITLE: Behavior Science Research

MANUSCRIPT ADDRESS: Box 2015 YS
New Haven, CT 06520

MAJOR CONTENT AREAS: Cross-cultural

ARTICLES USUALLY ACCEPTED: Research, theoretical, annotated
bibliographies

TOPICS PREFERRED: Cross-cultural research

INAPPROPRIATE MANUSCRIPTS: Ethnographics of a travelogue nature

INDEXED/ABSTRACTED IN: AA, CCSBS

SUBSCRIPTION ADDRESS: Box 2015 YS
New Haven, CT 06520

SUBSCRIPTION COST: $5 individual, $10 institutional
PUBLICATION LAG TIME: 6-12 months   STYLE SHEET: Yes
EARLY PUBLICATION OPTION: No   STYLE REQUIREMENTS: Chicago
REVIEW PERIOD: 3 months   CIRCULATION: 1,100
ACCEPTANCE RATE: 50%   REPRINT POLICY: 100 free

JOURNAL TITLE: Behavior Therapy

MANUSCRIPT ADDRESS: Cyril M. Franks, GSAPP, Psych. Bldg. Rm. 105
Busch Campus, Rutgers University
New Brunswick, NJ 08903
MAJOR CONTENT AREAS: Behavior therapy

ARTICLES USUALLY ACCEPTED: Research, review, theoretical, book review,
case studies

TOPICS PREFERRED: None

INAPPROPRIATE MANUSCRIPTS: Animal studies, anecdotal reports

INDEXED/ABSTRACTED IN: PA, BI, CCSBS, CIJE, DSHA, ECEA, PRG

SUBSCRIPTION ADDRESS: Academic Press, Inc.
111 Fifth Avenue
New York, NY 10003
SUBSCRIPTION COST: $22 individual, $36 institutional
PUBLICATION LAG TIME: 1 year   STYLE SHEET: Yes
EARLY PUBLICATION OPTION: No   STYLE REQUIREMENTS: APA
REVIEW PERIOD: 6 weeks   CIRCULATION: 4,000
ACCEPTANCE RATE: 10%   REPRINT POLICY: 50 free

JOURNAL TITLE: Behavioral Biology

MANUSCRIPT ADDRESS: Dept. of Psychobiology, School of Biological
Science, University of California
Irvine, CA   92717

MAJOR CONTENT AREAS: Comparative, physiological

ARTICLES USUALLY ACCEPTED: Research, review, theoretical

TOPICS PREFERRED: Biological bases of behavior

INAPPROPRIATE MANUSCRIPTS: None

INDEXED/ABSTRACTED IN: PA, DSHA

SUBSCRIPTION ADDRESS: Academic Press, Inc.
111 Fifth Avenue
New York, NY   10003

SUBSCRIPTION COST:	$115.50		
PUBLICATION LAG TIME:	6 months	STYLE SHEET:	Not given
EARLY PUBLICATION OPTION:	No	STYLE REQUIREMENTS:	Own style
REVIEW PERIOD:	6 weeks	CIRCULATION:	Not given
ACCEPTANCE RATE:	40-50%	REPRINT POLICY:	Optional purchase

JOURNAL TITLE: Behavioral Disorders

MANUSCRIPT ADDRESS: Dr. Albert H. Fink, Editor
2805 East Tenth Street
Bloomington, IN   47401

MAJOR CONTENT AREAS: All areas with educational implications
for behavioral disorders

ARTICLES USUALLY ACCEPTED: Research, theoretical, review, book review

TOPICS PREFERRED: Educationally relevant interventions for
behaviorally disordered

INAPPROPRIATE MANUSCRIPTS: Case analyses of problem children

INDEXED/ABSTRACTED IN: None as yet (new journal) but several
are pending

SUBSCRIPTION ADDRESS: Dr. Albert H. Fink, Editor
2805 East Tenth Street
Bloomington, IN   47401

SUBSCRIPTION COST:	$12.50		
PUBLICATION LAG TIME:	9-12 months	STYLE SHEET:	Yes
EARLY PUBLICATION OPTION:	Not given	STYLE REQUIREMENTS:	APA
REVIEW PERIOD:	3-4 months	CIRCULATION:	4,000
ACCEPTANCE RATE:	Not yet known	REPRINT POLICY:	Optional purchase

JOURNAL TITLE: Behavioral Ecology and Sociobiology

MANUSCRIPT ADDRESS: Dr. Hubert Markl, Fachbereich Biologie
Universitat Kanstranz
Postfach 7733, D-7750 Konstanz

MAJOR CONTENT AREAS: Comparative, experimental, physiological, social biology

ARTICLES USUALLY ACCEPTED: Research, occasional theoretical

TOPICS PREFERRED: Experimental analysis of animal behavior, ecological adaptations of behavior, sociobiology

INAPPROPRIATE MANUSCRIPTS: Purely descriptive or highly speculative material

INDEXED/ABSTRACTED IN: CCSBS, SCI

SUBSCRIPTION ADDRESS: Springer-Verlag New York, Inc.
175 Fifth Avenue
New York, NY 10010

SUBSCRIPTION COST: $71.40

PUBLICATION LAG TIME: 3-4 months

EARLY PUBLICATION OPTION: No

REVIEW PERIOD: 2-3 months

ACCEPTANCE RATE: Not given

STYLE SHEET: Yes

STYLE REQUIREMENTS: Springer

CIRCULATION: 1,000

REPRINT POLICY: 50 free

JOURNAL TITLE: Behavioral Engineering

MANUSCRIPT ADDRESS: P. O. Box 1473
Grand Island, NE 68801

MAJOR CONTENT AREAS: Behavior therapy, engineering, experimental, physiological, instrumentation

ARTICLES USUALLY ACCEPTED: Research, review, theoretical, book review

TOPICS PREFERRED: Safety/ethical/legal/technical issues related to instrumentation

INAPPROPRIATE MANUSCRIPTS: Case studies, safety topics dealth with inadequately

INDEXED/ABSTRACTED IN: PA

SUBSCRIPTION ADDRESS: P.O. Box 1473
Grand Island, NE 68801

SUBSCRIPTION COST: Undecided

PUBLICATION LAG TIME: 3-6 months

EARLY PUBLICATION OPTION: No

REVIEW PERIOD: 2 months

ACCEPTANCE RATE: 60%

STYLE SHEET: Yes

STYLE REQUIREMENTS: APA

CIRCULATION: 1,650

REPRINT POLICY: 25 free

JOURNAL TITLE: Behavioral Neuropsychiatry

MANUSCRIPT ADDRESS: 61 East 86th Street
New York, NY 10028

MAJOR CONTENT AREAS: Clinical, experimental, learning, mental
retardation, physiological, personality
ARTICLES USUALLY ACCEPTED: Research, review, theoretical

TOPICS PREFERRED: Psychiatry, neurology, neurological surgery,
and allied behavioral sciences
INAPPROPRIATE MANUSCRIPTS: None

INDEXED/ABSTRACTED IN: PA, IM, BS

SUBSCRIPTION ADDRESS: 61 East 86th Street
New York, NY 10028

SUBSCRIPTION COST:	$48.50		
PUBLICATION LAG TIME:	2-4 months	STYLE SHEET:	Yes
EARLY PUBLICATION OPTION:	Yes	STYLE REQUIREMENTS:	Ind. Med.
REVIEW PERIOD:	4 weeks	CIRCULATION:	23,000
ACCEPTANCE RATE:	12%	REPRINT POLICY:	Optional purchase

JOURNAL TITLE: Behavioral Science

MANUSCRIPT ADDRESS: P. O. Box 1055
Louisville, KY 40201

MAJOR CONTENT AREAS: Comparative, experimental, learning, general
systems
ARTICLES USUALLY ACCEPTED: Research, theoretical, book reviews, systems
simulation

TOPICS PREFERRED: General systems research, especially analysis
of isomorphisms across systems
INAPPROPRIATE MANUSCRIPTS: Computer programs & abstracts, philosophical/
discussion papers, nursing, elementary educ.
INDEXED/ABSTRACTED IN: PA, ASW, ABCPS, AA, AI, BI, BA, BS, CCSBS,
EAS, ECEA, IBSS, IPSA, JHE, LLBA, PRAJ, WSA

SUBSCRIPTION ADDRESS: P. O. Box 1055
Louisville, KY 40201

SUBSCRIPTION COST:	$18 individual, $30 institutional		
PUBLICATION LAG TIME:	2-4 months	STYLE SHEET:	Yes
EARLY PUBLICATION OPTION:	Yes	STYLE REQUIREMENTS:	Own style
REVIEW PERIOD:	6 months	CIRCULATION:	4,000
ACCEPTANCE RATE:	15%	REPRINT POLICY:	1-4 free

JOURNAL TITLE: Behaviorism: A Forum for Critical Discussion

MANUSCRIPT ADDRESS: Dr. Willard F. Day, Editor
Dept. of Psychology, University of Nevada
Reno, NV 89507

MAJOR CONTENT AREAS: Behaviorism

ARTICLES USUALLY ACCEPTED: Those dealing with behaviorism at a conceptual
or philosophical level

TOPICS PREFERRED: Conceptual issues related to behaviorism

INAPPROPRIATE MANUSCRIPTS: Empirical research studies, except for highly
new and innovative ones

INDEXED/ABSTRACTED IN: PI

SUBSCRIPTION ADDRESS: Dr. Willard F. Day, Editor
Dept. of Psychology, University of Nevada
Reno, NV 89507

SUBSCRIPTION COST: $10 individual, $15 institutional

PUBLICATION LAG TIME: 4 months   STYLE SHEET: Yes
EARLY PUBLICATION OPTION: No   STYLE REQUIREMENTS: APA
REVIEW PERIOD: 4 months   CIRCULATION: 1,000
ACCEPTANCE RATE: 35%   REPRINT POLICY: Optional
                                                      purchase

JOURNAL TITLE: Biochemical Pharmacology

MANUSCRIPT ADDRESS: Yale University School of Medicine
333 Cedar Street
New Haven, CT 06510

MAJOR CONTENT AREAS: Pharmacology

ARTICLES USUALLY ACCEPTED: Research

TOPICS PREFERRED: None

INAPPROPRIATE MANUSCRIPTS: None

INDEXED/ABSTRACTED IN: PA, IM, CA

SUBSCRIPTION ADDRESS: Pergamon Press
Headington Hill Hall
Oxford OX3 OBW, England

SUBSCRIPTION COST: $40 individual, $200 institutional

PUBLICATION LAG TIME: 7 months   STYLE SHEET: No
EARLY PUBLICATION OPTION: No   STYLE REQUIREMENTS: Not given
REVIEW PERIOD: 6-10 weeks   CIRCULATION: Not given
ACCEPTANCE RATE: 60%   REPRINT POLICY: 100 free

JOURNAL TITLE: Biofeedback and Self Regulation

MANUSCRIPT ADDRESS: Dr. Johann Stoyva, Dept. of Psychiatry
Box C258, Univ. of Colorado Medical Center
4200 E. 9th Ave., Denver, CO 80220

MAJOR CONTENT AREAS: Behavior therapy, clinical, physiological

ARTICLES USUALLY ACCEPTED: Research, review, theoretical

TOPICS PREFERRED: Biofeedback and voluntary control of
physiological functions

INAPPROPRIATE MANUSCRIPTS: None as yet (new journal)

INDEXED/ABSTRACTED IN: Not yet available

SUBSCRIPTION ADDRESS: Plenum Publishing Corp.
227 West 17th Street
New York, NY 10011

SUBSCRIPTION COST: $15 individual, $36 institutional
PUBLICATION LAG TIME: 4-5 months   STYLE SHEET: Yes
EARLY PUBLICATION OPTION: No   STYLE REQUIREMENTS: APA
REVIEW PERIOD: 4 months   CIRCULATION: Not yet known
ACCEPTANCE RATE: 35%   REPRINT POLICY: Optional
                                                                        purchase

JOURNAL TITLE: Biological Psychiatry

MANUSCRIPT ADDRESS: J. Wortis, Editor, Dept. of Psychiatry
Health Sciences Center, State Univ. of New York
Stony Brook, NY 11794

MAJOR CONTENT AREAS: Behavior therapy, clinical, physiological,
general psychiatry

ARTICLES USUALLY ACCEPTED: Research, review, theoretical

TOPICS PREFERRED: Experimental psychiatry

INAPPROPRIATE MANUSCRIPTS: Animal research

INDEXED/ABSTRACTED IN: PA, IM, EM, CCSBS

SUBSCRIPTION ADDRESS: Plenum Publishing Corp.
227 West 17th Street
New York, NY 10011

SUBSCRIPTION COST: $19 individual, $65.00 institutional
PUBLICATION LAG TIME: 6 months   STYLE SHEET: Yes
EARLY PUBLICATION OPTION: Not given   STYLE REQUIREMENTS: AIBS
REVIEW PERIOD: 2 months   CIRCULATION: 1,200
ACCEPTANCE RATE: 60%   REPRINT POLICY: Optional
                                                                        purchase

JOURNAL TITLE: Biological Psychology

MANUSCRIPT ADDRESS: Dr. M. H. Lader
Institute of Psychiatry
Decrespigny Park, London   SE5, U.K.

MAJOR CONTENT AREAS: Physiological, methodology, biochemical

ARTICLES USUALLY ACCEPTED: Research, review, brief communications,
methods, case reports

TOPICS PREFERRED: Psychophysiology: GSR, EEG, AER, & CNV

INAPPROPRIATE MANUSCRIPTS: None

INDEXED/ABSTRACTED IN: PA, CCSBS

SUBSCRIPTION ADDRESS: North-Holland Publishing Co.
P. O. Box 211
Amsterdam, The Netherlands

SUBSCRIPTION COST: $30
PUBLICATION LAG TIME: 6 months   STYLE SHEET: Yes
EARLY PUBLICATION OPTION: No   STYLE REQUIREMENTS: APA
REVIEW PERIOD: 2 months   CIRCULATION: 600
ACCEPTANCE RATE: 60%   REPRINT POLICY: 25 free

JOURNAL TITLE: Brain, Behavior and Evolution

MANUSCRIPT ADDRESS: Dr. Walter Riss
Dept. of Anatomy, SUNY Downstate Medical Center
Brooklyn, NY   11203

MAJOR CONTENT AREAS: Comparative, physiological

ARTICLES USUALLY ACCEPTED: Research, review, theoretical

TOPICS PREFERRED: None

INAPPROPRIATE MANUSCRIPTS: None

INDEXED/ABSTRACTED IN: PA, IM

SUBSCRIPTION ADDRESS: S. Karger, AG
Basel, Switzerland

SUBSCRIPTION COST: $29 individual, $72 institutional
PUBLICATION LAG TIME: 6 months   STYLE SHEET: Yes
EARLY PUBLICATION OPTION: No   STYLE REQUIREMENTS: Not given
REVIEW PERIOD: 1 month   CIRCULATION: 1,000
ACCEPTANCE RATE: 40%   REPRINT POLICY: Optional
purchase

JOURNAL TITLE: Brain and Language

MANUSCRIPT ADDRESS: Professor Harry A. Whitaker
Dept. of Psychology, University of Rochester
Rochester, NY 14627

MAJOR CONTENT AREAS: Experimental, physiological, mental retardation,
neuropsychology, neurolinguistics

ARTICLES USUALLY ACCEPTED: Research, review, theoretical, book review

TOPICS PREFERRED: Any aspect of human language related to the
brain or brain function

INAPPROPRIATE MANUSCRIPTS: None

INDEXED/ABSTRACTED IN: CCSBS, LLBA

SUBSCRIPTION ADDRESS: Academic Press, Inc.
111 Fifth Avenue
New York, NY 10003

SUBSCRIPTION COST: $19.50 individual, $38.50 institutional

PUBLICATION LAG TIME: 9 months   STYLE SHEET: Yes

EARLY PUBLICATION OPTION: No   STYLE REQUIREMENTS: Own style

REVIEW PERIOD: 2-3 months   CIRCULATION: 1,500

ACCEPTANCE RATE: 60-65%   REPRINT POLICY: 50 free

JOURNAL TITLE: British Journal of Disorders of
Communication

MANUSCRIPT ADDRESS: Mrs. B. Byers Brown, Dept. of Audiology
University of Manchester
Manchester M 13 QPL, England

MAJOR CONTENT AREAS: Speech pathology and therapy, behavior therapy,
counseling, mental retardation

ARTICLES USUALLY ACCEPTED: Research, case studies; preference given
to articles by speech therapists

TOPICS PREFERRED: Clinically oriented papers on speech pathology
and other communication disorders

INAPPROPRIATE MANUSCRIPTS: Minute and insignificant statistical
correlations

INDEXED/ABSTRACTED IN: PA, BEI, BS, CCSBS, DSHA, ECEA, LLBA

SUBSCRIPTION ADDRESS: College of Speech Therapists
4Y St. John's Wood High Street
London NW8 7NJ, England

SUBSCRIPTION COST: $11.20

PUBLICATION LAG TIME: 1 year   STYLE SHEET: Yes

EARLY PUBLICATION OPTION: No   STYLE REQUIREMENTS: Not given

REVIEW PERIOD: 1 month   CIRCULATION: 4,500

ACCEPTANCE RATE: Not given   REPRINT POLICY: Optional
purchase

JOURNAL TITLE: The British Journal of Educational
Psychology

MANUSCRIPT ADDRESS: Department of Educational Research
Cartmel College
Bailrigg, Lancaster LA1 4YL, England

MAJOR CONTENT AREAS: Counseling, developmental, educational,
mental retardation, psychometrics

ARTICLES USUALLY ACCEPTED: Research, review, theoretical

TOPICS PREFERRED: Any related to educational research
with psychological relevance

INAPPROPRIATE MANUSCRIPTS: Studies without theoretical rationale or
research hypotheses

INDEXED/ABSTRACTED IN: PA, BEI, CSPA, CCSBS, CIJE, DSHA, EI, JHE,
LLBA, RHEA, WSA

SUBSCRIPTION ADDRESS: Scottish Academic Press, Ltd.
33 Montgomery Street
Edinburgh, Scotland

SUBSCRIPTION COST: $20

PUBLICATION LAG TIME: 6-9 months   STYLE SHEET: No

EARLY PUBLICATION OPTION: No   STYLE REQUIREMENTS: BPA

REVIEW PERIOD: 2-3 months   CIRCULATION: 3,500

ACCEPTANCE RATE: 25%   REPRINT POLICY: 50 free

JOURNAL TITLE: The British Journal of Mathematical and
Statistical Psychology

MANUSCRIPT ADDRESS: Dept. of Psychology
The University of Lancaster
Lancaster LA1 4YF, England

MAJOR CONTENT AREAS: Experimental, learning, perception, social,
methodology

ARTICLES USUALLY ACCEPTED: All types which have some formal (often
symbolic) expression of theory related to
data

TOPICS PREFERRED: Formal expressions of theory and methods of
data analysis in any area of psychology

INAPPROPRIATE MANUSCRIPTS: Minor developments of statistical theory
not related to substantive problems in psychology

INDEXED/ABSTRACTED IN: PA, BI, BEI, BS, CCSBS, ISIR, LLBA, RHEA,
SSCI

SUBSCRIPTION ADDRESS: The British Psychological Society
18-19 Albemarle Street
London W1X 4DN, England

SUBSCRIPTION COST: $34

PUBLICATION LAG TIME: 6-12 months   STYLE SHEET: No

EARLY PUBLICATION OPTION: No   STYLE REQUIREMENTS: BPS

REVIEW PERIOD: 1-3 months   CIRCULATION: 850

ACCEPTANCE RATE: 40%   REPRINT POLICY: 50 free

JOURNAL TITLE: The British Journal of Psychiatry

MANUSCRIPT ADDRESS: Dr. Edward Hare, Editor
17 Belgrave Square
London SW1X 8PG, England

MAJOR CONTENT AREAS: All areas of psychiatry

ARTICLES USUALLY ACCEPTED: Research

TOPICS PREFERRED: Clinical psychiatry; biochemical, genetic, & psychological aspects of psychiatry

INAPPROPRIATE MANUSCRIPTS: None

INDEXED/ABSTRACTED IN: PA, BI, CCCP, CCSBS, HA, IPAPL, LLBA, SSCI, WSA

SUBSCRIPTION ADDRESS: Headley Brothers, Ltd.
Invicta Press
Ashford, Kent, England

SUBSCRIPTION COST:	$100		
PUBLICATION LAG TIME:	8-12 months	STYLE SHEET:	Yes
EARLY PUBLICATION OPTION:	Yes	STYLE REQUIREMENTS:	Own style
REVIEW PERIOD:	4-6 weeks	CIRCULATION:	9,000
ACCEPTANCE RATE:	40%	REPRINT POLICY:	Optional purchase

JOURNAL TITLE: British Journal of Medical Psychology

MANUSCRIPT ADDRESS: Prof. Arthur A. Crisp, Psychiatric Research Unit, Atkinson Morley's Hospital, Copse Hill London SW20 ONE, England

MAJOR CONTENT AREAS: Clinical, psychotherapy

ARTICLES USUALLY ACCEPTED: Research, book review, theoretical

TOPICS PREFERRED: None

INAPPROPRIATE MANUSCRIPTS: None

INDEXED/ABSTRACTED IN: PA, IM, BI, BEI, BHI, CCCP, CCSBS, LLBA, RHEA

SUBSCRIPTION ADDRESS: Cambridge University Press
32 E. 57th Street
New York, NY 10022

SUBSCRIPTION COST:	$36 individual, $48 institutional		
PUBLICATION LAG TIME:	18 months	STYLE SHEET:	Yes
EARLY PUBLICATION OPTION:	No	STYLE REQUIREMENTS:	BPA
REVIEW PERIOD:	6 weeks	CIRCULATION:	2,400
ACCEPTANCE RATE:	30%	REPRINT POLICY:	50 free

JOURNAL TITLE: British Journal of Mental Subnormality

MANUSCRIPT ADDRESS: Dr. H. C. Gunzburg, Editor
Monyhull Hospital, Monyhull Hall Road
Birmingham B30 3QB, England

MAJOR CONTENT AREAS: All areas as related to mental retardation

ARTICLES USUALLY ACCEPTED: Research, review

TOPICS PREFERRED: Anything related to mental retardation

INAPPROPRIATE MANUSCRIPTS: None

INDEXED/ABSTRACTED IN: PA, BS, CCSBS, ECEA, SSCI

SUBSCRIPTION ADDRESS: Subscription Department
Monyhull Hospital, Monyhull Hall Road
Birmingham B30 3QB, England

SUBSCRIPTION COST: $6.50
PUBLICATION LAG TIME: 6-12 months   STYLE SHEET: Yes
EARLY PUBLICATION OPTION: No   STYLE REQUIREMENTS: APA
REVIEW PERIOD: 3-6 months   CIRCULATION: 1,500
ACCEPTANCE RATE: 50%   REPRINT POLICY: 10 free

JOURNAL TITLE: British Journal of Psychology

MANUSCRIPT ADDRESS: Prof. A.D.B. Clarke, Dept. of Psychology
The University
Hull HU6 7RX, England

MAJOR CONTENT AREAS: General, experimental, statistics/methodology

ARTICLES USUALLY ACCEPTED: Research, book review

TOPICS PREFERRED: None

INAPPROPRIATE MANUSCRIPTS: None

INDEXED/ABSTRACTED IN: PA, IM, BI, BA, BEI, BHI, CCSBS, CIJE,
DSHA, ISA, JHE, LLBA, RHEA, SSCI

SUBSCRIPTION ADDRESS: Cambridge University Press
32 E. 57th Street
New York, NY 10022

SUBSCRIPTION COST: $48 individual, $60 institutional
PUBLICATION LAG TIME: Not given   STYLE SHEET: Yes
EARLY PUBLICATION OPTION: Not given   STYLE REQUIREMENTS: BPA
REVIEW PERIOD: Not given   CIRCULATION: 3,200
ACCEPTANCE RATE: Not given   REPRINT POLICY: 50 free

JOURNAL TITLE: British Journal of Social and Clinical Psychology

MANUSCRIPT ADDRESS: Social Psychology articles:
Univ. of Edinburgh, 60 The pleasance,
Edinburgh EH8 9TJ, Scotland

MAJOR CONTENT AREAS: Behavior therapy, clinical, personality, social

ARTICLES USUALLY ACCEPTED: Research, review, theoretical; send clinical articles to: H.R. Beech, Withington Hosp., Manchester M20 8LR, Eng.

TOPICS PREFERRED: Clinical; developmental and educational papers of social import, personality, social

INAPPROPRIATE MANUSCRIPTS: Topics are not a problem - poor papers are

INDEXED/ABSTRACTED IN: PA, BI, BEI, BS, CCSBS, DSHA, IBSS, LLBA, PRG, RHEA, SSCI, WSA

SUBSCRIPTION ADDRESS: Cambridge University Press
32 East 57th Street
New York, NY   10022

SUBSCRIPTION COST: $57

PUBLICATION LAG TIME: 15 months	STYLE SHEET:	Yes
EARLY PUBLICATION OPTION: No	STYLE REQUIREMENTS:	BPS
REVIEW PERIOD: 6 weeks	CIRCULATION:	2,750
ACCEPTANCE RATE: 20%	REPRINT POLICY:	50 free

JOURNAL TITLE: The British Journal of Social Work

MANUSCRIPT ADDRESS: Professor P. Parsloe, Univ. of Aberdeen
Dept. of Social Work, King's College
Old Aberdeen AB9 2UB, Scotland

MAJOR CONTENT AREAS: Social work

ARTICLES USUALLY ACCEPTED: Research, review, theoretical, practice-oriented

TOPICS PREFERRED: Discussions of social work practice

INAPPROPRIATE MANUSCRIPTS: Ph.D. theses of no relevance to social work

INDEXED/ABSTRACTED IN: PA, ASW, BHI, CCSBS, I, SSCI

SUBSCRIPTION ADDRESS: British Association of Social Workers
Publications Dept., 16 Kent Street
Birmingham B5 6RD, England

SUBSCRIPTION COST: $30

PUBLICATION LAG TIME: Highly variable	STYLE SHEET:	Yes
EARLY PUBLICATION OPTION: No	STYLE REQUIREMENTS:	Own style
REVIEW PERIOD: 4-6 weeks	CIRCULATION:	3,000
ACCEPTANCE RATE: 25%	REPRINT POLICY:	25 free

JOURNAL TITLE: Bulletin of the Menninger Clinic

MANUSCRIPT ADDRESS: Managing Editor,
The Menninger Foundation, Box 829
Topeka, KS 66601

MAJOR CONTENT AREAS: Behavior therapy, clinical, community
psychoanalysis, psychotherapy, history

ARTICLES USUALLY ACCEPTED: Original articles in clinical areas, book
reviews

TOPICS PREFERRED: Psychiatry, neurology, psychology,
psychoanalysis, child psychiatry

INAPPROPRIATE MANUSCRIPTS: Statistical studies with few results

INDEXED/ABSTRACTED IN: PA, EM, ASW, ACP, BA, BS, CNRS, CCSBS, DSHA,
IPAPL, IBSS, LLBA, PRAJ

SUBSCRIPTION ADDRESS: Circulation Manager,
The Menninger Foundation, Box 829
Topeka, KS 66601

SUBSCRIPTION COST: $15
PUBLICATION LAG TIME: 9-12 months
EARLY PUBLICATION OPTION: No
REVIEW PERIOD: 6 weeks
ACCEPTANCE RATE: 25%

STYLE SHEET: Yes
STYLE REQUIREMENTS: Chicago
CIRCULATION: 3,500
REPRINT POLICY: Optional purchase

JOURNAL TITLE: Bulletin of the Psychonomic Society

MANUSCRIPT ADDRESS: 1108 West 34th Street
Austin, TX 78705

MAJOR CONTENT AREAS: Experimental

ARTICLES USUALLY ACCEPTED: Research; must be authored by or sponsored
by members of the Psychonomic Society

TOPICS PREFERRED: None

INAPPROPRIATE MANUSCRIPTS: None

INDEXED/ABSTRACTED IN: PA, CCSBS, DSHA, LLBA

SUBSCRIPTION ADDRESS: 1108 West 34th Street
Austin, TX 78705

SUBSCRIPTION COST: $20 individual, $40 institutional
PUBLICATION LAG TIME: 3-6 months
EARLY PUBLICATION OPTION: No
REVIEW PERIOD: 1 week
ACCEPTANCE RATE: 95%

STYLE SHEET: Yes
STYLE REQUIREMENTS: APA
CIRCULATION: 1,300
REPRINT POLICY: Optional purchase

JOURNAL TITLE: Canada's Mental Health

MANUSCRIPT ADDRESS: Health and Welfare Canada
6th floor, Jeanne Mance Building
Ottawa, Ontario, Canada K1A 1B4

MAJOR CONTENT AREAS: Almost all areas as related to mental health

ARTICLES USUALLY ACCEPTED: Research, review, theoretical, book review

TOPICS PREFERRED: All phases of mental health

INAPPROPRIATE MANUSCRIPTS: Those more suited to medical journals

INDEXED/ABSTRACTED IN: PA, ASW, AHMS, CEI, CCSBS, CIJE, ECEA, HLI,
PHRA, PAISB

SUBSCRIPTION ADDRESS: Health and Welfare Canada
6th floor, Jeanne Mance Building
Ottawa, Ontario, Canada K1A 1B4

SUBSCRIPTION COST:	$3		
PUBLICATION LAG TIME:	3-6 months	STYLE SHEET:	Yes
EARLY PUBLICATION OPTION:	No	STYLE REQUIREMENTS:	APA
REVIEW PERIOD:	2-3 months	CIRCULATION:	16,000
ACCEPTANCE RATE:	40-50%	REPRINT POLICY:	6 free

JOURNAL TITLE: Canadian Counsellor

MANUSCRIPT ADDRESS: Dr. H. Zingle, Editor
c/o R. Fobert, 1000 Yonge Street
Toronto M4W 2K2, Ontario, Canada

MAJOR CONTENT AREAS: Guidance and counseling

ARTICLES USUALLY ACCEPTED: Not given

TOPICS PREFERRED: Not given

INAPPROPRIATE MANUSCRIPTS: Not given

INDEXED/ABSTRACTED IN: PA

SUBSCRIPTION ADDRESS: Canadian Guidance and Counseling Association
c/o R. Fobert, 1000 Yonge Street
Toronto M4W 2K2, Ontario, Canada

SUBSCRIPTION COST:	$9		
PUBLICATION LAG TIME:	Not given	STYLE SHEET:	Not given
EARLY PUBLICATION OPTION:	Not given	STYLE REQUIREMENTS:	Not given
REVIEW PERIOD:	Not given	CIRCULATION:	1,500
ACCEPTANCE RATE:	Not given	REPRINT POLICY:	Not given

JOURNAL TITLE: Canadian Journal of Behavioral Science

MANUSCRIPT ADDRESS: Department of Psychology
University of British Columbia
Vancouver, B.C. V6T 1W5, Canada

MAJOR CONTENT AREAS: All non-experimental areas

ARTICLES USUALLY ACCEPTED: Applied experimental papers, brief reports, program evaluations

TOPICS PREFERRED: Those with theoretical and/or practical implications

INAPPROPRIATE MANUSCRIPTS: Laboratory experimental studies in the area of learning, perception, etc.

INDEXED/ABSTRACTED IN: PA, AA, CEI, CCSBS, LLBA, SSCI

SUBSCRIPTION ADDRESS: Canadian Psychological Association
1390 Sherbrooke Street West
Montreal, Quebec H3G 1K2, Canada

SUBSCRIPTION COST: $25

PUBLICATION LAG TIME: 6-9 months   STYLE SHEET: Yes

EARLY PUBLICATION OPTION: No   STYLE REQUIREMENTS: APA

REVIEW PERIOD: 3-4 months   CIRCULATION: 1,850

ACCEPTANCE RATE: 10%   REPRINT POLICY: Optional purchase

JOURNAL TITLE: Canadian Journal of Psychology

MANUSCRIPT ADDRESS: Dr. P. C. Dodwell, Editor
Dept. of Psychology, Queen's University
Kingston, Ontario, Canada

MAJOR CONTENT AREAS: Experimental, learning, perception, physiological

ARTICLES USUALLY ACCEPTED: Empirical and theoretical papers in general experimental psychology

TOPICS PREFERRED: Human cognition, perception, and sensation; memory; physiological basis of learning

INAPPROPRIATE MANUSCRIPTS: Applied and clinical papers, social psychology

INDEXED/ABSTRACTED IN: PA, ASW, BI, CEI, CCSBS, CIJE, DSHA, LLBA, PRAJ, SSCI

SUBSCRIPTION ADDRESS: Canadian Psychological Association
Business Office, 1390 Sherbrooke St. W.
Montreal, Quebec H3G 1K2, Canada

SUBSCRIPTION COST: $25

PUBLICATION LAG TIME: 3 months   STYLE SHEET: Yes

EARLY PUBLICATION OPTION: No   STYLE REQUIREMENTS: APA

REVIEW PERIOD: 5 months   CIRCULATION: 1,935

ACCEPTANCE RATE: 25%   REPRINT POLICY: Optional purchase

JOURNAL TITLE: Canadian Psychiatric Association Journal

MANUSCRIPT ADDRESS: 103-225 Lisgar Street
Ottawa, Ontario K2P OC6, Canada

MAJOR CONTENT AREAS: All aspects of clinical and community psychiatry

ARTICLES USUALLY ACCEPTED: Research, review, case studies

TOPICS PREFERRED: None

INAPPROPRIATE MANUSCRIPTS: None

INDEXED/ABSTRACTED IN: PA, BS, CCSBS, IPAPL, LLBA, SSCI

SUBSCRIPTION ADDRESS: Lex Ltd.
2 Tremont Cres.
Don Mills, Ontario, Canada

SUBSCRIPTION COST:	$20		
PUBLICATION LAG TIME:	Variable	STYLE SHEET:	Yes
EARLY PUBLICATION OPTION:	No	STYLE REQUIREMENTS:	Ind. Med.
REVIEW PERIOD:	1-3 months	CIRCULATION:	3,100
ACCEPTANCE RATE:	65%	REPRINT POLICY:	Optional purchase

JOURNAL TITLE: Canadian Psychological Review-Psychologie Canadienne

MANUSCRIPT ADDRESS: Dr. David Gibson, Department of Psychology
University of Calgary
Calgary, Alberta T2N 1N4, Canada

MAJOR CONTENT AREAS: General, critical reviews and theoretical articles in all areas of psychology

ARTICLES USUALLY ACCEPTED: Interpretive, theoretical, discipline bridging and mission scholarships, evaluative reviews, brief comments on psychological affairs

TOPICS PREFERRED: Material of a bridging nature

INAPPROPRIATE MANUSCRIPTS: Program material, descriptive reviews, personal philosophy, metaphysical opinion

INDEXED/ABSTRACTED IN: PA, CCSBS

SUBSCRIPTION ADDRESS: Business Office, Canadian Psychological Assoc.
1390 Sherbrooke St., W.
Montreal, Quebec H3G 1K2, Canada

SUBSCRIPTION COST:	$25		
PUBLICATION LAG TIME:	6 months	STYLE SHEET:	Yes
EARLY PUBLICATION OPTION:	Yes	STYLE REQUIREMENTS:	APA
REVIEW PERIOD:	8 months	CIRCULATION:	3,000
ACCEPTANCE RATE:	30-40%	REPRINT POLICY:	Purchase required

JOURNAL TITLE: Character Potential: A Record of Research

MANUSCRIPT ADDRESS: 207 State Street
Schenectady, NY 12305

MAJOR CONTENT AREAS: Developmental, personality

ARTICLES USUALLY ACCEPTED: Research findings, designs, and philosophy
regarding human potential

TOPICS PREFERRED: Creative approaches to research problems
on development toward an individual's potential

INAPPROPRIATE MANUSCRIPTS: None

INDEXED/ABSTRACTED IN: PA, CCSBS

SUBSCRIPTION ADDRESS: 207 State Street
Schenectady, NY 12305

SUBSCRIPTION COST: $7
PUBLICATION LAG TIME: 1 year
EARLY PUBLICATION OPTION: No
REVIEW PERIOD: 4 weeks
ACCEPTANCE RATE: Usually solicited

STYLE SHEET: Yes
STYLE REQUIREMENTS: Modified AAAS
CIRCULATION: 1,000
REPRINT POLICY: 5-15 free

JOURNAL TITLE: Child Care Quarterly

MANUSCRIPT ADDRESS: Jerome Beker, Ed.D., Editor
5 Cloverdale Lane
Monsey, NY 10952

MAJOR CONTENT AREAS: All areas as they relate to day and residential
child care

ARTICLES USUALLY ACCEPTED: Research, review, theoretical, book review

TOPICS PREFERRED: Practice, supervision, training, and
professional issues in child care

INAPPROPRIATE MANUSCRIPTS: Articles on casework with children, those not
directly related to child care

INDEXED/ABSTRACTED IN: PA, ASW, CCSBS, CIJE, ECEA, SSCI

SUBSCRIPTION ADDRESS: Behavioral Publications
72 Fifth Ave.
New York, NY 10011

SUBSCRIPTION COST: $12.95 individual, $35 institutional
PUBLICATION LAG TIME: 1 year
EARLY PUBLICATION OPTION: Yes
REVIEW PERIOD: 2-3 months
ACCEPTANCE RATE: 45%

STYLE SHEET: Yes
STYLE REQUIREMENTS: APA
CIRCULATION: 2,000
REPRINT POLICY: 1 free copy
of issue

JOURNAL TITLE: Child Development

MANUSCRIPT ADDRESS: W. E. Jeffrey, Ph.D., Editor
Dept. of Psychology, UCLA
Los Angeles, CA 90024

MAJOR CONTENT AREAS: Developmental

ARTICLES USUALLY ACCEPTED: Research, review, theoretical

TOPICS PREFERRED: None

INAPPROPRIATE MANUSCRIPTS: None

INDEXED/ABSTRACTED IN: PA, ASW, AA, BS, CDA, CCSBS, CIJE, DSHA, EI,
ECEA, JHE, LLBA, RHEA, SSCI, WSA

SUBSCRIPTION ADDRESS: The University of Chicago Press
5801 S. Ellis Avenue
Chicago, IL 60637

SUBSCRIPTION COST: $35		
PUBLICATION LAG TIME: 1 year	STYLE SHEET:	Yes
EARLY PUBLICATION OPTION: No	STYLE REQUIREMENTS:	APA
REVIEW PERIOD: 3 months	CIRCULATION:	7,500
ACCEPTANCE RATE: 16%	REPRINT POLICY:	Optional purchase

JOURNAL TITLE: Child Psychiatry and Human Development

MANUSCRIPT ADDRESS: John C. Duffy, U.S. Public Health Service
Commanding Officer, USCG Support Command
Governor's Island, NY 10004

MAJOR CONTENT AREAS: Clinical, developmental, mental retardation

ARTICLES USUALLY ACCEPTED: Clinical articles in child psychiatry

TOPICS PREFERRED: Clinical child psychiatry

INAPPROPRIATE MANUSCRIPTS: Single case studies, reviews of a topic

INDEXED/ABSTRACTED IN: PA, IM, EM, ASW, CDA, BIS, CDA, CCCP, CCSBS,
CIJE, ECEA, PRG, SES, SSCI, WSA

SUBSCRIPTION ADDRESS: Behavioral Publications
72 Fifth Avenue
New York, NY 10011

SUBSCRIPTION COST: $17.50 individual, $40 institutional		
PUBLICATION LAG TIME: 1 year	STYLE SHEET:	No
EARLY PUBLICATION OPTION: Yes	STYLE REQUIREMENTS:	Ind. Med.
REVIEW PERIOD: 2 months	CIRCULATION:	4,000
ACCEPTANCE RATE: 10%	REPRINT POLICY:	Purchase required

JOURNAL TITLE: Child Psychiatry Quarterly

MANUSCRIPT ADDRESS: Dr. Jaya Nagaraja, Professor of Psychiatry
8-2-547/2 7th Rd., Banjara Hills
Hyderabad (AP) India

MAJOR CONTENT AREAS: Child and adolescent psychiatry, developmental psychology

ARTICLES USUALLY ACCEPTED: Research, review, theoretical, book review

TOPICS PREFERRED: Drug addiction, mental retardation, family counseling, clinical work with children

INAPPROPRIATE MANUSCRIPTS: None

INDEXED/ABSTRACTED IN: PA, CCSBS, SSCI

SUBSCRIPTION ADDRESS: 8-2-547/2 7th Rd., Banjara Hills
Hyderabad (AP) India

SUBSCRIPTION COST: $6
PUBLICATION LAG TIME: 3 months   STYLE SHEET: Yes
EARLY PUBLICATION OPTION: Yes   STYLE REQUIREMENTS: IPA
REVIEW PERIOD: 1 month   CIRCULATION: 500
ACCEPTANCE RATE: Not given   REPRINT POLICY: 30 free

JOURNAL TITLE: Child Study Journal

MANUSCRIPT ADDRESS: State University of New York
College at Buffalo, 1300 Elmwood Avenue
Buffalo, New York 14222

MAJOR CONTENT AREAS: Behavior therapy, counseling, developmental, educational, learning, mental retardation, social

ARTICLES USUALLY ACCEPTED: Research, review, theoretical

TOPICS PREFERRED: Educational and psychological implications of research in development

INAPPROPRIATE MANUSCRIPTS: Individual case studies, curriculum studies

INDEXED/ABSTRACTED IN: PA, SA, BS, CDA, CCSBS, CIJE, EI, ECEA, PRG, SSCI

SUBSCRIPTION ADDRESS: State University of New York
College at Buffalo, 1300 Elmwood Avenue
Buffalo, NY 14222

SUBSCRIPTION COST: $6 individual, $12 institutional
PUBLICATION LAG TIME: 12-18 months   STYLE SHEET: Yes
EARLY PUBLICATION OPTION: Yes   STYLE REQUIREMENTS: APA
REVIEW PERIOD: 6-8 months   CIRCULATION: 500
ACCEPTANCE RATE: 25-40%   REPRINT POLICY: 1 free

JOURNAL TITLE: Child Welfare

MANUSCRIPT ADDRESS: 61 Irving Pl.
New York, NY 10003

MAJOR CONTENT AREAS: All areas as applied to child welfare programs and practice

ARTICLES USUALLY ACCEPTED: Research, review, theoretical, book review, program and practice descriptions

TOPICS PREFERRED: Programs, policy, and practice

INAPPROPRIATE MANUSCRIPTS: Material for parents in general; poems

INDEXED/ABSTRACTED IN: ASW, CCSBS, CIJE, EI, ECEA, IBSS, PHRA, PAISB, SSCI, WSA

SUBSCRIPTION ADDRESS: 61 Irving Pl.
New York, NY 10003

SUBSCRIPTION COST:	$8		
PUBLICATION LAG TIME:	9-12 months	STYLE SHEET:	Yes
EARLY PUBLICATION OPTION:	Yes	STYLE REQUIREMENTS:	Own style
REVIEW PERIOD:	1 month	CIRCULATION:	10,000
ACCEPTANCE RATE:	25%	REPRINT POLICY:	5 free copies of issue

JOURNAL TITLE: Children Today

MANUSCRIPT ADDRESS: Office of Child Development
P. O. Box 1182
Washington, DC 20013

MAJOR CONTENT AREAS: Clinical, community, developmental, educational, mental retardation, social, personality

ARTICLES USUALLY ACCEPTED: Descriptions of programs and projects, research reports, theoretical discussions of current issues, short book reviews

TOPICS PREFERRED: Those describing programs to improve the health, education, and welfare of children and families

INAPPROPRIATE MANUSCRIPTS: Case studies involving one or very few subjects

INDEXED/ABSTRACTED IN: PA, ASW, BRI, CINL, CIJE, DSHA, ECA, EI, WSA

SUBSCRIPTION ADDRESS: Superintendent of Documents
U.S. Government Printing Office
Washington, DC 20402

SUBSCRIPTION COST:	$6.10		
PUBLICATION LAG TIME:	2-8 months	STYLE SHEET:	Yes
EARLY PUBLICATION OPTION:	No	STYLE REQUIREMENTS:	MLA
REVIEW PERIOD:	2-4 months	CIRCULATION:	29,000
ACCEPTANCE RATE:	9-10%	REPRINT POLICY:	25 free copies of issue

JOURNAL TITLE: Clinical Social Work Journal

MANUSCRIPT ADDRESS: Mary L. Gottesfeld, Editor
285 West End Avenue
New York, NY 10023

MAJOR CONTENT AREAS: Clinical, social work, psychotherapy

ARTICLES USUALLY ACCEPTED: Research, theoretical, clinical practice

TOPICS PREFERRED: Clinical case material

INAPPROPRIATE MANUSCRIPTS: Education, administration

INDEXED/ABSTRACTED IN: PA, ASW, CDA, CCSBS, PHRA, SLTCPP, SSCI

SUBSCRIPTION ADDRESS: Behavioral Publications
72 Fifth Avenue
New York, NY 10011

SUBSCRIPTION COST: $15 individual, $30 institutional
PUBLICATION LAG TIME: 9 months
EARLY PUBLICATION OPTION: Yes
REVIEW PERIOD: 1 month
ACCEPTANCE RATE: 20%

STYLE SHEET: Yes
STYLE REQUIREMENTS: APA
CIRCULATION: 5,000
REPRINT POLICY: 1 free copy of issue

JOURNAL TITLE: Cognitive Psychology

MANUSCRIPT ADDRESS: Earl Hunt, Editor, Dept. of Psychology
N1-25, University of Washington
Seattle, WA 98195

MAJOR CONTENT AREAS: Experimental, learning

ARTICLES USUALLY ACCEPTED: Research

TOPICS PREFERRED: Cognition

INAPPROPRIATE MANUSCRIPTS: None

INDEXED/ABSTRACTED IN: PA, CCSBS, ISA, LLBA, SSCI

SUBSCRIPTION ADDRESS: Academic Press, Inc.
111 Fifth Avenue
New York, NY 10003

SUBSCRIPTION COST: $22 individual, $44 institutional
PUBLICATION LAG TIME: 5 months
EARLY PUBLICATION OPTION: No
REVIEW PERIOD: 2-3 months
ACCEPTANCE RATE: 15%

STYLE SHEET: No
STYLE REQUIREMENTS: APA
CIRCULATION: 1,777
REPRINT POLICY: 50 free

JOURNAL TITLE: College Student Journal

MANUSCRIPT ADDRESS: Box 566
Chula Vista, California 92010

MAJOR CONTENT AREAS: Counseling, educational, learning, social, college students

ARTICLES USUALLY ACCEPTED: Research, theoretical, book reviews

TOPICS PREFERRED: Studies related to college students

INAPPROPRIATE MANUSCRIPTS: Statistics, philosophy

INDEXED/ABSTRACTED IN: PA, CSPA, CIJE, LLBA, WSA

SUBSCRIPTION ADDRESS: Box 566
Chula Vista, CA 92010

SUBSCRIPTION COST: $7.50 individual, $10 institutional
PUBLICATION LAG TIME: 8-10 months   STYLE SHEET: Yes
EARLY PUBLICATION OPTION: Yes   STYLE REQUIREMENTS: APA
REVIEW PERIOD: 1 month   CIRCULATION: 1,000
ACCEPTANCE RATE: 50%   REPRINT POLICY: Optional purchase

JOURNAL TITLE: Communication

MANUSCRIPT ADDRESS: M. P. Everard, Editor
'Burstalls' Whitwell, Ventnor
Isle of Wight PO38 2QQ, U.K.

MAJOR CONTENT AREAS: Developmental

ARTICLES USUALLY ACCEPTED: Research, review, theoretical, book review, conference reports

TOPICS PREFERRED: Autism and child development from a neurological rather than psychoanalytic point of view

INAPPROPRIATE MANUSCRIPTS: Poetry

INDEXED/ABSTRACTED IN: RHEA

SUBSCRIPTION ADDRESS: The National Society for Autistic Children
1A, Golders Green Road
London NW11 8EA, U.K.

SUBSCRIPTION COST: $5
PUBLICATION LAG TIME: 3-12 months   STYLE SHEET: No
EARLY PUBLICATION OPTION: No   STYLE REQUIREMENTS: Not given
REVIEW PERIOD: 3 weeks   CIRCULATION: 1,750
ACCEPTANCE RATE: Not given   REPRINT POLICY: Some free copies of issue

JOURNAL TITLE: Communication Research

MANUSCRIPT ADDRESS: F. Gerald Kline, Editor
Dept. of Journalism, 2040J LS & A Bldg.
Univ. of Michigan, Ann Arbor, MI 48104

MAJOR CONTENT AREAS: Communication, social

ARTICLES USUALLY ACCEPTED: Research, review, case studies

TOPICS PREFERRED: Explication and testing of models that explain
the processes and outcomes of communication

INAPPROPRIATE MANUSCRIPTS: None

INDEXED/ABSTRACTED IN: PA, APC, CCSBS, ERIC, PHRA, TSI

SUBSCRIPTION ADDRESS: Sage Publications, Inc.
275 South Beverly Drive
Beverly Hills, CA 90212

SUBSCRIPTION COST:	$12 individual, $20 institutional	
PUBLICATION LAG TIME:	6 months	STYLE SHEET: Yes
EARLY PUBLICATION OPTION:	No	STYLE REQUIREMENTS: Sage
REVIEW PERIOD:	4-8 weeks	CIRCULATION: Not given
ACCEPTANCE RATE:	10%	REPRINT POLICY: 25 free

JOURNAL TITLE: Community Mental Health Journal

MANUSCRIPT ADDRESS: Dr. L. Baler, Community Mental Health Journal
University of Michigan School of Public Health
Room 5108 SPHII, Ann Arbor, MI 48104

MAJOR CONTENT AREAS: Community mental health

ARTICLES USUALLY ACCEPTED: Research

TOPICS PREFERRED: Community mental health theory, research, and
practice

INAPPROPRIATE MANUSCRIPTS: None

INDEXED/ABSTRACTED IN: PA, IM, ASW, AHMS, CCCP, MMRI, PHRA, SSCI,
WSA

SUBSCRIPTION ADDRESS: Human Sciences Press
72 Fifth Ave.
New York, NY 10011

SUBSCRIPTION COST:	$30	
PUBLICATION LAG TIME:	1 1/2 - 2 years	STYLE SHEET: Yes
EARLY PUBLICATION OPTION:	Yes	STYLE REQUIREMENTS: APA
REVIEW PERIOD:	3 months	CIRCULATION: 4,250
ACCEPTANCE RATE:	10%	REPRINT POLICY: 50 free

JOURNAL TITLE: Community Mental Health Review

MANUSCRIPT ADDRESS: Harry Gottesfeld, Ph.D., Editor
285 West End Avenue
New York, NY 10023

MAJOR CONTENT AREAS: Community mental health

ARTICLES USUALLY ACCEPTED: Review articles only

TOPICS PREFERRED: Alternatives to hospitalization, mental health
consultation, new mental health roles

INAPPROPRIATE MANUSCRIPTS: None

INDEXED/ABSTRACTED IN: Not yet known (new journal)

SUBSCRIPTION ADDRESS: The Haworth Press
174 Fifth Avenue
New York, NY 10010

SUBSCRIPTION COST: $14 individual, $24 institutional

PUBLICATION LAG TIME:	3-6 months	STYLE SHEET:	Yes
EARLY PUBLICATION OPTION:	No	STYLE REQUIREMENTS:	APA
REVIEW PERIOD:	1 month	CIRCULATION:	1,000
ACCEPTANCE RATE:	Not yet known	REPRINT POLICY:	50 free

JOURNAL TITLE: Comprehensive Psychiatry

MANUSCRIPT ADDRESS: Fritz A. Freyhan, M.D., Editor
2015 R Street, N.W.
Washington, DC 20009

MAJOR CONTENT AREAS: Behavior therapy, clinical, mental retardation,
psychoanalysis, methodology, physiological

ARTICLES USUALLY ACCEPTED: Not given

TOPICS PREFERRED: None

INAPPROPRIATE MANUSCRIPTS: None

INDEXED/ABSTRACTED IN: PA, ASW, CCCP, CCSBS, PRAJ, SSCI

SUBSCRIPTION ADDRESS: Grune & Stratton
111 Fifth Avenue
New York, NY 10003

SUBSCRIPTION COST: $28

PUBLICATION LAG TIME:	3-6 months	STYLE SHEET:	No
EARLY PUBLICATION OPTION:	No	STYLE REQUIREMENTS:	Own style
REVIEW PERIOD:	6 months	CIRCULATION:	2,800
ACCEPTANCE RATE:	Not given	REPRINT POLICY:	Purchase required

JOURNAL TITLE: Constructive Action for Good Health Magazine

MANUSCRIPT ADDRESS: B1104 Ross Towers
710 Lodi Street
Syracuse, NY 13203

MAJOR CONTENT AREAS: Self-help, self-health

ARTICLES USUALLY ACCEPTED: Those showing people how they can help themselves to better health through self-help
methods

TOPICS PREFERRED: Self-help tension reduction; self-health natural
food therapy, exercise, vitamin therapy.

INAPPROPRIATE MANUSCRIPTS: Freudian, behavior modification; those praising
poisonous tranquilizers, ECT, or state hospitals

INDEXED/ABSTRACTED IN: AL

SUBSCRIPTION ADDRESS: B1104 Ross Towers
710 Lodi Street
Syracuse, NY 13203

SUBSCRIPTION COST: $5
PUBLICATION LAG TIME: Several months   STYLE SHEET: Yes (with SSAE)
EARLY PUBLICATION OPTION: No   STYLE REQUIREMENTS: None
REVIEW PERIOD: Several Weeks   CIRCULATION: 500
ACCEPTANCE RATE: 50%   REPRINT POLICY: 1 free

JOURNAL TITLE: Contemporary Drug Problems

MANUSCRIPT ADDRESS: 111 Broadway
New York, NY 10006

MAJOR CONTENT AREAS: All aspects of drug use and abuse

ARTICLES USUALLY ACCEPTED: Research, theoretical

TOPICS PREFERRED: Drug use and abuse, trends, treatment, social
policy

INAPPROPRIATE MANUSCRIPTS: Statistically oriented surveys

INDEXED/ABSTRACTED IN: EM, CCSBS, IPL, IPARL, PAISB, SSCI

SUBSCRIPTION ADDRESS: 95 Morton Street
New York, NY 10014

SUBSCRIPTION COST: $20 individual, $24 institutional
PUBLICATION LAG TIME: 4 months   STYLE SHEET: Yes
EARLY PUBLICATION OPTION: No   STYLE REQUIREMENTS: Own style
REVIEW PERIOD: 45 days   CIRCULATION: 3,000
ACCEPTANCE RATE: 10-15%   REPRINT POLICY: 50 free

JOURNAL TITLE: Contemporary Psychoanalysis

MANUSCRIPT ADDRESS: 20 West 74th Street
New York, NY 10023

MAJOR CONTENT AREAS: Psychoanalysis, psychotherapy, developmental

ARTICLES USUALLY ACCEPTED: Research, practice, psychoanalytic theory,
review essays

TOPICS PREFERRED: Clinical psychoanalysis, psychoanalytic theory

INAPPROPRIATE MANUSCRIPTS: Those not up to professional standards

INDEXED/ABSTRACTED IN: PA, IM, ASW, CCSBS, SSCI

SUBSCRIPTION ADDRESS: Academic Press, Inc.
111 Fifth Avenue
New York, NY 10003

SUBSCRIPTION COST:	$14 individual, $34 institutional		
PUBLICATION LAG TIME:	6-9 months	STYLE SHEET:	Yes
EARLY PUBLICATION OPTION:	Yes	STYLE REQUIREMENTS:	APA
REVIEW PERIOD:	2 months	CIRCULATION:	1,200
ACCEPTANCE RATE:	50%	REPRINT POLICY:	25 free

JOURNAL TITLE: The Cooperator

MANUSCRIPT ADDRESS: 17819 Roscoe Blvd.
Northridge, CA 91324

MAJOR CONTENT AREAS: Psychosynthesis, transpersonal psychology,
that which deals with the whole person.

ARTICLES USUALLY ACCEPTED: Research, poems, theoretical, book review;
primarily an intelligent, but
lay audience

TOPICS PREFERRED: All developments in psychology which deal
with the whole person, spiritual and personal

INAPPROPRIATE MANUSCRIPTS: Papers that are too technical, those with
little understanding of the whole person

INDEXED/ABSTRACTED IN: Not given

SUBSCRIPTION ADDRESS: 17819 Roscoe Blvd.
Northridge, CA 91324

SUBSCRIPTION COST:	$2		
PUBLICATION LAG TIME:	6-12 months	STYLE SHEET:	Yes
EARLY PUBLICATION OPTION:	No	STYLE REQUIREMENTS:	Own style
REVIEW PERIOD:	2 months	CIRCULATION:	1,000-2,000
ACCEPTANCE RATE:	10-20%	REPRINT POLICY:	3 free copies of issue

JOURNAL TITLE: Cornell Journal of Social Relations

MANUSCRIPT ADDRESS: Manuscript Editor, Uris Hall
Cornell University
Ithaca, NY 14853

MAJOR CONTENT AREAS: Almost all areas of psychology and sociology

ARTICLES USUALLY ACCEPTED: Research, review, theoretical, and book review
from advanced graduate students and junior
faculty

TOPICS PREFERRED: Current research in the fields of psychology,
sociology, and arthropology

INAPPROPRIATE MANUSCRIPTS: Poorly written articles

INDEXED/ABSTRACTED IN: PA, SA, BI, CCSBS, IBSS, ILD, IPSA, SSCI

SUBSCRIPTION ADDRESS: Managing Editor, Uris Hall
Cornell University
Ithaca, NY 14853

SUBSCRIPTION COST: $4 ($5 after 1/77)

PUBLICATION LAG TIME: 6-18 months	STYLE SHEET: Yes
EARLY PUBLICATION OPTION: No	STYLE REQUIREMENTS: APA
REVIEW PERIOD: 6 weeks	CIRCULATION: 350
ACCEPTANCE RATE: 35%	REPRINT POLICY: Optional purchase

JOURNAL TITLE: Corrective and Social Psychiatry and Journal
of Behavior Technology Methods and Therapy

MANUSCRIPT ADDRESS: 122 North Cooper
Olathe, KS 66061

MAJOR CONTENT AREAS: Behavior therapy, community, counseling,
organizational, psychotherapy, social

ARTICLES USUALLY ACCEPTED: Research, review, theoretical, book review

TOPICS PREFERRED: Corrections

INAPPROPRIATE MANUSCRIPTS: Long, rambling articles

INDEXED/ABSTRACTED IN: PA, EM, CCSBS

SUBSCRIPTION ADDRESS: 122 North Cooper
Olathe, KS 66061

SUBSCRIPTION COST: $18 individual, $20 institutional

PUBLICATION LAG TIME: 3 months	STYLE SHEET: Yes
EARLY PUBLICATION OPTION: Not given	STYLE REQUIREMENTS: APA
REVIEW PERIOD: 3 months	CIRCULATION: 3,000
ACCEPTANCE RATE: 50%	REPRINT POLICY: Optional purchase

JOURNAL TITLE: The Counseling Psychologist

MANUSCRIPT ADDRESS: Box 1183
Washington University
St. Louis, MO 63130

MAJOR CONTENT AREAS: Counseling, psychotherapy

ARTICLES USUALLY ACCEPTED: Review and theoretical; issues are organized around themes, usually with guest editors and invited articles

TOPICS PREFERRED: Counseling with women, career counseling, assertive training, counseling approaches

INAPPROPRIATE MANUSCRIPTS: Research articles

INDEXED/ABSTRACTED IN: PA, CCSBS, CIJE, EI, SSCI

SUBSCRIPTION ADDRESS: Box 1053
Washington University
St. Louis, MO 63130

SUBSCRIPTION COST: $10 individual, $16 institutional

PUBLICATION LAG TIME: 6 months   STYLE SHEET: Yes

EARLY PUBLICATION OPTION: No   STYLE REQUIREMENTS: APA

REVIEW PERIOD: 3-4 months   CIRCULATION: 4,200

ACCEPTANCE RATE: Not given   REPRINT POLICY: Purchase required

JOURNAL TITLE: Counseling and Values

MANUSCRIPT ADDRESS: Donald A. Biggs
328 Walter Library, University of Minnesota
Minneapolis, MN 55455

MAJOR CONTENT AREAS: Counseling, developmental, educational, personality, psychotherapy

ARTICLES USUALLY ACCEPTED: Research, review, theoretical

TOPICS PREFERRED: The implications of values in counseling

INAPPROPRIATE MANUSCRIPTS: None

INDEXED/ABSTRACTED IN: PA, CPLI, CSPA, CIJE

SUBSCRIPTION ADDRESS: APGA
1607 New Hampshire Avenue, N. W.
Washington, DC 20009

SUBSCRIPTION COST: $10 ($5 for students)

PUBLICATION LAG TIME: 12-16 months   STYLE SHEET: Yes

EARLY PUBLICATION OPTION: No   STYLE REQUIREMENTS: APA

REVIEW PERIOD: 2 months   CIRCULATION: 1,800

ACCEPTANCE RATE: 20%   REPRINT POLICY: Optional purchase

JOURNAL TITLE: Counselor Education and Supervision

MANUSCRIPT ADDRESS: Chris Kehas, Editor
P. O. Box 545
Manchester, NH   03105

MAJOR CONTENT AREAS: Counseling

ARTICLES USUALLY ACCEPTED: Research, theoretical, developmental, and program applications pertinent to counselor education or supervision

TOPICS PREFERRED: Education and supervision of counselors

INAPPROPRIATE MANUSCRIPTS: None

INDEXED/ABSTRACTED IN: PA, CCSBS, CIJE, EI

SUBSCRIPTION ADDRESS: Leola Moore, Subscriptions Manager, APGA
1607 New Hampshire Avenue, N.W.
Washington, DC   20009

SUBSCRIPTION COST: $6

PUBLICATION LAG TIME: Not given	STYLE SHEET:	Not given
EARLY PUBLICATION OPTION: Not given	STYLE REQUIREMENTS:	Own style
REVIEW PERIOD: Up to 3 months	CIRCULATION:	5,000
ACCEPTANCE RATE: Not given	REPRINT POLICY:	10 free

JOURNAL TITLE: The Creative Child and Adult Quarterly

MANUSCRIPT ADDRESS: 8080 Springvalley Drive
Cincinnatti, OH   45236

MAJOR CONTENT AREAS: Counseling, developmental, educational, experimental, gifted & creative individuals

ARTICLES USUALLY ACCEPTED: Research, review, theoretical, book review

TOPICS PREFERRED: Mental health prevention rather than treatment

INAPPROPRIATE MANUSCRIPTS: Those which are not up-to-date in insight or references

INDEXED/ABSTRACTED IN: Not given

SUBSCRIPTION ADDRESS: 8080 Springvalley Drive
Cincinnatti, OH   45236

SUBSCRIPTION COST: $22 ($20 for members)

PUBLICATION LAG TIME: Variable	STYLE SHEET:	Yes (with SSAE)
EARLY PUBLICATION OPTION: No	STYLE REQUIREMENTS:	Modified APA
REVIEW PERIOD: Variable	CIRCULATION:	Not given
ACCEPTANCE RATE: 25%	REPRINT POLICY:	Not given

JOURNAL TITLE: Crime and Delinquency

MANUSCRIPT ADDRESS: NCCD
411 Hackensack Avenue
Hackensack, NJ 07601

MAJOR CONTENT AREAS: Delinquency and juvenile courts, criminal justice

ARTICLES USUALLY ACCEPTED: Research, review, theoretical, book review

TOPICS PREFERRED: Correction, prison, probation, parole, fines, sentencing, law enforcement, criminal justice

INAPPROPRIATE MANUSCRIPTS: Narrow time-bound descriptions of local projects

INDEXED/ABSTRACTED IN: PA, ASW, ACP, BI, CDL, CCSBS, ILP, IPAPL, IPARL, SSCI

SUBSCRIPTION ADDRESS: NCCD
411 Hackensack Avenue
Hackensack, NJ 07601

SUBSCRIPTION COST: $15	
PUBLICATION LAG TIME: 3-24 months	STYLE SHEET: Yes
EARLY PUBLICATION OPTION: No	STYLE REQUIREMENTS: Own style
REVIEW PERIOD: 2-8 weeks	CIRCULATION: 9,000
ACCEPTANCE RATE: 10%	REPRINT POLICY: Optional purchase

JOURNAL TITLE: Criminal Justice and Behavior

MANUSCRIPT ADDRESS: Stanley L. Brodsky, Editor
Dept. of Psychology, Univ. of Alabama
Box 2968, University, AL 35486

MAJOR CONTENT AREAS: Correctional psychology

ARTICLES USUALLY ACCEPTED: Research, review, theoretical, case studies

TOPICS PREFERRED: Processes of behavior change & functioning of clients & employees in the CJ system

INAPPROPRIATE MANUSCRIPTS: None

INDEXED/ABSTRACTED IN: PA, SA, ACP, CDL, CJPI, CCSBS, PHRA, PRG

SUBSCRIPTION ADDRESS: Sage Publications, Inc.
275 South Beverly Drive
Beverly Hills, CA 90212

SUBSCRIPTION COST: $12 individual, $20 institutional	
PUBLICATION LAG TIME: 6 months	STYLE SHEET: Yes
EARLY PUBLICATION OPTION: No	STYLE REQUIREMENTS: Sage
REVIEW PERIOD: 6-8 weeks	CIRCULATION: Not given
ACCEPTANCE RATE: 10%	REPRINT POLICY: 25 free

JOURNAL TITLE: Criminology: An Interdisciplinary Journal

MANUSCRIPT ADDRESS: John Jay College of Criminal Justice
444 West 56th Street
New York, NY 10019

MAJOR CONTENT AREAS: Criminology

ARTICLES USUALLY ACCEPTED: Research, theoretical, review

TOPICS PREFERRED: Research in crime and deviant behavior
which has broad implications

INAPPROPRIATE MANUSCRIPTS: Small studies which have virtually no
generalizability

INDEXED/ABSTRACTED IN: ASW, SA, ACP, CDL, CCSBS, ILP, PHRA, PAISB,
SSCI

SUBSCRIPTION ADDRESS: Sage Publications, Inc.
275 South Beverly Drive
Beverly Hills, CA 90212

SUBSCRIPTION COST: $15 individual, $20 institutional

PUBLICATION LAG TIME: 6-9 months   STYLE SHEET: Yes

EARLY PUBLICATION OPTION: Rarely   STYLE REQUIREMENTS: Sage

REVIEW PERIOD: 4-6 weeks   CIRCULATION: 2,500

ACCEPTANCE RATE: 15-20%   REPRINT POLICY: 20 free

JOURNAL TITLE: Crisis Intervention

MANUSCRIPT ADDRESS: Charles H. Haywood, Ph.D., Editor
3258 Main Street
Buffalo, NY 14214

MAJOR CONTENT AREAS: Behavior therapy, clinical, community,
physiological, social, methodology, evaluation

ARTICLES USUALLY ACCEPTED: Research, review, theoretical, book review,
program descriptions

TOPICS PREFERRED: Crisis and stress research, training,
community-based programs

INAPPROPRIATE MANUSCRIPTS: None

INDEXED/ABSTRACTED IN: PA

SUBSCRIPTION ADDRESS: 3258 Main Street
Buffalo, NY 14214

SUBSCRIPTION COST: $9 individual, $15 institutional

PUBLICATION LAG TIME: 3-6 months   STYLE SHEET: Yes

EARLY PUBLICATION OPTION: Yes   STYLE REQUIREMENTS: APA

REVIEW PERIOD: 3 months   CIRCULATION: 500

ACCEPTANCE RATE: 25%   REPRINT POLICY: 2 free

JOURNAL TITLE: Developmental Medicine and Child Neurology

MANUSCRIPT ADDRESS: 5A Netherhall Gardens
London NW3 5RN, England

MAJOR CONTENT AREAS: Behavior therapy, clinical, community,
developmental, mental retardation, child neurology

ARTICLES USUALLY ACCEPTED: Original articles on all aspects of normal
and abnormal child development

TOPICS PREFERRED: All aspects of normal and disordered child
development

INAPPROPRIATE MANUSCRIPTS: Those which are not clear and concise

INDEXED/ABSTRACTED IN: PA, IM, EM, CCCP, DSHA, LLBA, WSA

SUBSCRIPTION ADDRESS: J. B. Lippincott Co.
East Washington Square
Philadelphia, PA 19105

SUBSCRIPTION COST: $30
PUBLICATION LAG TIME: 6 months   STYLE SHEET: No
EARLY PUBLICATION OPTION: Yes   STYLE REQUIREMENTS: Own style
REVIEW PERIOD: 6 weeks   CIRCULATION: 4,500
ACCEPTANCE RATE: 50%   REPRINT POLICY: 25 free

JOURNAL TITLE: Developmental Psychobiology

MANUSCRIPT ADDRESS: Meyer's Children's Rehabilitation Institute
University of Nebraska Medical Center
444 S. 44th St., Omaha, NE 68131

MAJOR CONTENT AREAS: Comparative, developmental, experimental,
learning, retardation, perception, physiological

ARTICLES USUALLY ACCEPTED: Research (including brief notes), review,
theoretical, book review, announcements

TOPICS PREFERRED: Prenatal, perinatal, & infantile influences on
development; behavior genetics

INAPPROPRIATE MANUSCRIPTS: Behavior of adults without reference to
developmental phenomena

INDEXED/ABSTRACTED IN: PA, IM, BA

SUBSCRIPTION ADDRESS: Wiley-Interscience
605 Third Avenue
New York, NY 10006

SUBSCRIPTION COST: $35
PUBLICATION LAG TIME: 7-10 months   STYLE SHEET: Yes
EARLY PUBLICATION OPTION: No   STYLE REQUIREMENTS: Own style
REVIEW PERIOD: 2-4 months   CIRCULATION: 800
ACCEPTANCE RATE: 60%   REPRINT POLICY: 50 free

JOURNAL TITLE: Developmental Psychology

MANUSCRIPT ADDRESS: Richard D. Odom, Editor, Dept. of Psychology
134 Wesley Hall, Vanderbilt University
Nashville, TN 37240

MAJOR CONTENT AREAS: Developmental

ARTICLES USUALLY ACCEPTED: Research, review, brief reports, monographs

TOPICS PREFERRED: Research in which the developmental
implications are clear and convincing

INAPPROPRIATE MANUSCRIPTS: None

INDEXED/ABSTRACTED IN: PA, BS, CSPA, CCSBS, CIJE, DSHA, LLBA, SSCI,
WSA

SUBSCRIPTION ADDRESS: APA Subscription Office
1200 17th Street, N.W.
Washington, DC 20036

SUBSCRIPTION COST: $30

PUBLICATION LAG TIME:	8 months	STYLE SHEET:	No
EARLY PUBLICATION OPTION:	No	STYLE REQUIREMENTS:	APA
REVIEW PERIOD:	Variable	CIRCULATION:	5,000
ACCEPTANCE RATE:	17%	REPRINT POLICY:	20 free

JOURNAL TITLE: Diseases of the Nervous System

MANUSCRIPT ADDRESS: Hamilton Ford, M.D.
200 University
Galveston, TX 77550

MAJOR CONTENT AREAS: Behavior therapy, clinical, psychoanalysis,
psychotherapy

ARTICLES USUALLY ACCEPTED: Book review, scientific, practical; by
recognized physicians from top sources

TOPICS PREFERRED: Neurology/psychiatry of a very practical
nature

INAPPROPRIATE MANUSCRIPTS: Esoteric material

INDEXED/ABSTRACTED IN: PA, CCCP, CCSBS, DSHA, IPAPL, LLBA

SUBSCRIPTION ADDRESS: Physicians Postgraduate Press
P. O. Box 38293
Memphis, TN 38138

SUBSCRIPTION COST: $15

PUBLICATION LAG TIME:	2-4 months	STYLE SHEET:	Yes
EARLY PUBLICATION OPTION:	Yes	STYLE REQUIREMENTS:	Own style
REVIEW PERIOD:	2 weeks	CIRCULATION:	20,500
ACCEPTANCE RATE:	60%	REPRINT POLICY:	Optional purchase

JOURNAL TITLE: Drug Forum - The Journal of Human Issues

MANUSCRIPT ADDRESS: Baywood Publishing Co.
43 Central Drive
Farmingdale, NY 11735

MAJOR CONTENT AREAS: All areas as related to drug abuse

ARTICLES USUALLY ACCEPTED: Research, review, theoretical, book review
on the psychological, medical, sociological,
and cultural factors in drug abuse

TOPICS PREFERRED: Description and assessment of drug treatment
modalities, legal issues, cultural aspects

INAPPROPRIATE MANUSCRIPTS: None

INDEXED/ABSTRACTED IN: PA, EM, ACP, BA, BIS, CCSBS

SUBSCRIPTION ADDRESS: Baywood Publishing Co.
43 Central Drive
Farmingdale, NY 11735

SUBSCRIPTION COST: $35

PUBLICATION LAG TIME: 9-12 months   STYLE SHEET: Yes
EARLY PUBLICATION OPTION: No   STYLE REQUIREMENTS: APA
REVIEW PERIOD: 4-6 weeks   CIRCULATION: 900
ACCEPTANCE RATE: 50%   REPRINT POLICY: 20 free

JOURNAL TITLE: Drugs in Health Care

MANUSCRIPT ADDRESS: American Society of Hospital Pharmacists
4630 Montgomery Avenue
Washington, DC 20014

MAJOR CONTENT AREAS: Social, economic, and administrative as
related to the drug use process

ARTICLES USUALLY ACCEPTED: Research, demonstration projects, review

TOPICS PREFERRED: The drug use process as a unique area of
health services research and delivery

INAPPROPRIATE MANUSCRIPTS: Drug abuse

INDEXED/ABSTRACTED IN: IPA

SUBSCRIPTION ADDRESS: American Society of Hospital Pharmacists
4630 Montgomery Avenue
Washington, DC 20014

SUBSCRIPTION COST: $15

PUBLICATION LAG TIME: 3-4 months   STYLE SHEET: Yes
EARLY PUBLICATION OPTION: No   STYLE REQUIREMENTS: Ind. Med.
REVIEW PERIOD: 6 weeks   CIRCULATION: 800
ACCEPTANCE RATE: 50%   REPRINT POLICY: 20 free

JOURNAL TITLE: Early Child Development and Care

MANUSCRIPT ADDRESS: Joseph Marcus, MD, Chief Editor
P. O. B. 9082
Jerusalem, 91-090, Israel

MAJOR CONTENT AREAS: All aspects of early child development
and care

ARTICLES USUALLY ACCEPTED: Research, review, theoretical, book
reviews

TOPICS PREFERRED: Not given

INAPPROPRIATE MANUSCRIPTS: Not given

INDEXED/ABSTRACTED IN: BA

SUBSCRIPTION ADDRESS: Gordon and Breach Science Publishers
One Park Avenue
New York, NY 10016

SUBSCRIPTION COST: $21 individual, $38 institutional

PUBLICATION LAG TIME: Not given	STYLE SHEET: Not given
EARLY PUBLICATION OPTION: Not given	STYLE REQUIREMENTS: APA
REVIEW PERIOD: Not given	CIRCULATION: Not given
ACCEPTANCE RATE: Not given	REPRINT POLICY: Optional purchase

JOURNAL TITLE: Education

MANUSCRIPT ADDRESS: Box 566
Chula Vista, CA 92010

MAJOR CONTENT AREAS: Educational, general, learning, mental
retardation

ARTICLES USUALLY ACCEPTED: Research, theoretical, book review

TOPICS PREFERRED: Promising educational innovations

INAPPROPRIATE MANUSCRIPTS: Marriage, sex, family, music

INDEXED/ABSTRACTED IN: BEI, BS, CB, CCSBS, CIJE, EI, GSSRPL, IEA,
JHE, LLBA, RHEA, RICS, WSA

SUBSCRIPTION ADDRESS: Box 566
Chula Vista, CA 92010

SUBSCRIPTION COST: $12

PUBLICATION LAG TIME: 8-10 months	STYLE SHEET: Yes
EARLY PUBLICATION OPTION: Yes	STYLE REQUIREMENTS: APA
REVIEW PERIOD: 1 month	CIRCULATION: 3,500
ACCEPTANCE RATE: 30%	REPRINT POLICY: Optional purchase

JOURNAL TITLE: Education and Training of the Mentally Retarded

MANUSCRIPT ADDRESS: Keystone Learning Center
1834 Meetinghouse Road
Boothwyn, PA 19061

MAJOR CONTENT AREAS: Community, developmental, educational, history
& systems, learning, mental retardation

ARTICLES USUALLY ACCEPTED: Research, program descriptions, instructional
methodology

TOPICS PREFERRED: Programs for the mentally retarded; curriculum
content, methodology, and research; teacher training

INAPPROPRIATE MANUSCRIPTS: Those with a medical orientation

INDEXED/ABSTRACTED IN: ASW, BS, CCSBS, CIJE, DSHA, EI, ECEA, LLBA,
SSCI

SUBSCRIPTION ADDRESS: Keystone Learning Center
1834 Meetinghouse Road
Boothwyn, PA 19061

SUBSCRIPTION COST: $12.50
PUBLICATION LAG TIME: 1 year   STYLE SHEET: Yes
EARLY PUBLICATION OPTION: Yes   STYLE REQUIREMENTS: APA
REVIEW PERIOD: 3 months   CIRCULATION: 10,000
ACCEPTANCE RATE: 40%   REPRINT POLICY: 5 free copies
of issue

JOURNAL TITLE: Educational and Psychological Measurement

MANUSCRIPT ADDRESS: Dr. W. Scott Gehman
Box 6907, College Station
Durham, NC 27708

MAJOR CONTENT AREAS: Individual differences

ARTICLES USUALLY ACCEPTED: Research, theoretical, book review, computer
programs

TOPICS PREFERRED: Problems in the measurement of individual
differences

INAPPROPRIATE MANUSCRIPTS: None

INDEXED/ABSTRACTED IN: PA, BS, CSPA, CCSBS, CIJE, DSHA, EI, ECEA,
IPAPL, IBSS, LLBA, RHEA, SSCI, WSA

SUBSCRIPTION ADDRESS: Box 6907, College Station
Durham, NC 27708

SUBSCRIPTION COST: $16
PUBLICATION LAG TIME: Not given   STYLE SHEET: Not given
EARLY PUBLICATION OPTION: Not given   STYLE REQUIREMENTS: APA
REVIEW PERIOD: Not given   CIRCULATION: Not given
ACCEPTANCE RATE: Not given   REPRINT POLICY: Page charges

JOURNAL TITLE: Educational Psychologist

MANUSCRIPT ADDRESS: Dr. Frank H. Farley, Room 878
1025 W. Johnson St., Univ. of Wisconsin
Madison, WI 53706

MAJOR CONTENT AREAS: Educational

ARTICLES USUALLY ACCEPTED: Theoretical, models, critiques, comments, essays

TOPICS PREFERRED: Essays and theories or models in areas in which psychology makes a contribution to education

INAPPROPRIATE MANUSCRIPTS: Strictly empirical studies

INDEXED/ABSTRACTED IN: PA, IEP

SUBSCRIPTION ADDRESS: Dr. Frank H. Farley, Room 878
1025 W. Johnson St., Univ. of Wisconsin
Madison, WI 53706

SUBSCRIPTION COST: $5 individual, $10 institutional

PUBLICATION LAG TIME: Not known	STYLE SHEET: Yes
EARLY PUBLICATION OPTION: No	STYLE REQUIREMENTS: APA
REVIEW PERIOD: Not known	CIRCULATION: 3,700
ACCEPTANCE RATE: Not known	REPRINT POLICY: Optional purchase

JOURNAL TITLE: Educational Record

MANUSCRIPT ADDRESS: Clifford B. Fair, American Council on Education, One Dupont Circle
Washington, DC 20036

MAJOR CONTENT AREAS: Higher education

ARTICLES USUALLY ACCEPTED: Research, theoretical, book review, personal opinion

TOPICS PREFERRED: Issues affecting higher education

INAPPROPRIATE MANUSCRIPTS: None

INDEXED/ABSTRACTED IN: PA, BS, CSPA, CCSBS, CIJE, EI, EAA, IBSS, LLBA, RHEA, SSCI, WSA, WAH

SUBSCRIPTION ADDRESS: American Council on Education
One Dupont Circle
Washington, DC 20036

SUBSCRIPTION COST: $10

PUBLICATION LAG TIME: 3 months	STYLE SHEET: Yes
EARLY PUBLICATION OPTION: Not given	STYLE REQUIREMENTS: Own style
REVIEW PERIOD: 3 months	CIRCULATION: 10,000
ACCEPTANCE RATE: 15%	REPRINT POLICY: 100 free

JOURNAL TITLE: Educational Technology

MANUSCRIPT ADDRESS: 140 Sylvan Avenue
Englewood Cliffs, NJ 07632

MAJOR CONTENT AREAS: Educational

ARTICLES USUALLY ACCEPTED: Research, review, theoretical, book review

TOPICS PREFERRED: Any aspect of instructional media

INAPPROPRIATE MANUSCRIPTS: None

INDEXED/ABSTRACTED IN: PA, AEI, CCSBS, CIJE, EI, EAA, ECEA, IBSS,
ILD, LLBA, SSCI

SUBSCRIPTION ADDRESS: 140 Sylvan Avenue
Englewood Cliffs, NJ 07632

SUBSCRIPTION COST: $25
PUBLICATION LAG TIME: 6-12 months   STYLE SHEET: Yes
EARLY PUBLICATION OPTION: No   STYLE REQUIREMENTS: Own style
REVIEW PERIOD: 2 weeks   CIRCULATION: 6,500
ACCEPTANCE RATE: 50%   REPRINT POLICY: 2 free copies
of issue

JOURNAL TITLE: Elementary School Guidance and Counseling

MANUSCRIPT ADDRESS: Dr. Robert D. Myrick, Editor
College of Education, University of Florida
Gainesville, FL 32611

MAJOR CONTENT AREAS: Counseling

ARTICLES USUALLY ACCEPTED: Theory into practice, research supporting the
role of the elementary and middle school
counselor, insightful position papers

TOPICS PREFERRED: Counselor role and function, "how to" articles
related to the work of counselors

INAPPROPRIATE MANUSCRIPTS: Term papers, special education articles without
implications for teachers and counselors

INDEXED/ABSTRACTED IN: PA, CIJE, EI

SUBSCRIPTION ADDRESS: Subscriptions Manager, APGA
1607 New Hampshire Avenue, NW
Washington, DC 20009

SUBSCRIPTION COST: $10
PUBLICATION LAG TIME: 6-8 months   STYLE SHEET: Yes
EARLY PUBLICATION OPTION: Yes   STYLE REQUIREMENTS: APA
REVIEW PERIOD: 8-10 weeks   CIRCULATION: 18,000
ACCEPTANCE RATE: 10%   REPRINT POLICY: 3 free copies
of issue

JOURNAL TITLE: Environment and Behavior

MANUSCRIPT ADDRESS: Gary H. Winkel, Editor, Environmental
Psychology Program, City University of New York
33 West 42nd St., New York, NY 10036

MAJOR CONTENT AREAS: Environmental

ARTICLES USUALLY ACCEPTED: Research, theoretical, review

TOPICS PREFERRED: Relationship between the physical environment
and human behavior

INAPPROPRIATE MANUSCRIPTS: None

INDEXED/ABSTRACTED IN: PA, CECD, CCSBS, CIJE, IPARL, PAISB, SSCI

SUBSCRIPTION ADDRESS: Sage Publications, Inc.
275 South Beverly Drive
Beverly Hills, CA 90212

SUBSCRIPTION COST: $12 individual, $20 institutional, $10 student
PUBLICATION LAG TIME: 12 months   STYLE SHEET: Yes
EARLY PUBLICATION OPTION: No   STYLE REQUIREMENTS: Sage
REVIEW PERIOD: 4 months   CIRCULATION: 1,700
ACCEPTANCE RATE: 15%   REPRINT POLICY: 24 free

JOURNAL TITLE: Environmental Psychology and Nonverbal Behavior

MANUSCRIPT ADDRESS: Dr. Randolph M. Lee, Editor
Dept. of Psychology, Trinity College
Hartford, CT 06106

MAJOR CONTENT AREAS: Social, environmental, nonverbal behavior

ARTICLES USUALLY ACCEPTED: Research, theoretical; special sections on
research in progress

TOPICS PREFERRED: Proxemics, kinesics, paralanguage, crowding,
environmental design, behavioral ecology

INAPPROPRIATE MANUSCRIPTS: None

INDEXED/ABSTRACTED IN: PA

SUBSCRIPTION ADDRESS: Behavioral Publications, Inc.
72 Fifth Ave.
New York, NY 10011

SUBSCRIPTION COST: $6.95 individual, $15 institutional
PUBLICATION LAG TIME: 1 year   STYLE SHEET: Yes
EARLY PUBLICATION OPTION: Yes   STYLE REQUIREMENTS: APA
REVIEW PERIOD: 3 months   CIRCULATION: 500
ACCEPTANCE RATE: 20-25%   REPRINT POLICY: Optional
purchase

JOURNAL TITLE: Ergonomics

MANUSCRIPT ADDRESS: Dr. Ivan Brown, MRC Applied Unit
15 Chaucer Road
Cambridge CB2 2EF, England

MAJOR CONTENT AREAS: Applied behavior analysis, engineering,
experimental, learning, system design

ARTICLES USUALLY ACCEPTED: Research and theoretical papers on man-system
interactions, reviews, brief research reports,
book reviews

TOPICS PREFERRED: Decision skills, information processing, stress,
physiological indices of stress, methodology

INAPPROPRIATE MANUSCRIPTS: Sports medicine, applied ergonomics

INDEXED/ABSTRACTED IN: PA, BS, CCBS, EE, ISA, JHE, U, WSA, WTA

SUBSCRIPTION ADDRESS: Taylor & Francis, Ltd. P. O. Box 9137
Church Street Station
New York, NY 10049

SUBSCRIPTION COST: $54.38
PUBLICATION LAG TIME: 10 months
EARLY PUBLICATION OPTION: No
REVIEW PERIOD: 6 weeks
ACCEPTANCE RATE: 65%

STYLE SHEET: Yes
STYLE REQUIREMENTS: Ind. Med.
CIRCULATION: 2,700
REPRINT POLICY: 50 free

JOURNAL TITLE: Ethnology

MANUSCRIPT ADDRESS: Editor, Dept. of Anthropology
University of Pittsburgh
Pittsburgh, PA 15260

MAJOR CONTENT AREAS: Social and cultural anthropology

ARTICLES USUALLY ACCEPTED: Anthropological articles based on field
work

TOPICS PREFERRED: Any type of social and cultural anthropological
data

INAPPROPRIATE MANUSCRIPTS: None

INDEXED/ABSTRACTED IN: ASW, SA, AA, BS, CCSBS, IBSS, IPSA, LLBA,
PRAJ, SSHI, WSA

SUBSCRIPTION ADDRESS: Editor, Dept. of Anthropology
University of Pittsburgh
Pittsburgh, PA 15260

SUBSCRIPTION COST: $10 individual, $15 institutional
PUBLICATION LAG TIME: 1 issue
EARLY PUBLICATION OPTION: No
REVIEW PERIOD: 1-2 months
ACCEPTANCE RATE: 25%

STYLE SHEET: No
STYLE REQUIREMENTS: Own style
CIRCULATION: 4,000
REPRINT POLICY: Optional
purchase

JOURNAL TITLE: Ethos

MANUSCRIPT ADDRESS: Dept. of Anthropology
UCLA
Los Angeles, CA 90024

MAJOR CONTENT AREAS: Cross-cultural psychology and psychiatry

ARTICLES USUALLY ACCEPTED: Research, theoretical

TOPICS PREFERRED: Research demonstrating the relationship
between cultural patterns & individual behavior

INAPPROPRIATE MANUSCRIPTS: None

INDEXED/ABSTRACTED IN: None

SUBSCRIPTION ADDRESS: University of California Press
Univ. of California at Berkeley
Berkeley, CA 94720

SUBSCRIPTION COST: $12 individual, $16 institutional
PUBLICATION LAG TIME: Not given
EARLY PUBLICATION OPTION: No
REVIEW PERIOD: 2 months
ACCEPTANCE RATE: 40%

STYLE SHEET: Yes
STYLE REQUIREMENTS: AAA
CIRCULATION: 600
REPRINT POLICY: 25 free

JOURNAL TITLE: European Journal of Pharmacology

MANUSCRIPT ADDRESS: P. O. Box 5023
Utrecht, The Netherlands

MAJOR CONTENT AREAS: Experimental pharmacology

ARTICLES USUALLY ACCEPTED: Research

TOPICS PREFERRED: Any in the area of experimental pharmacology

INAPPROPRIATE MANUSCRIPTS: Toxicology, drug screening

INDEXED/ABSTRACTED IN: CA, CCSBS

SUBSCRIPTION ADDRESS: North-Holland Publishing Company
P. O. Box 211
Amsterdam, The Netherlands

SUBSCRIPTION COST: $44.80
PUBLICATION LAG TIME: 16 weeks
EARLY PUBLICATION OPTION: No
REVIEW PERIOD: 8 weeks
ACCEPTANCE RATE: 50%

STYLE SHEET: Yes
STYLE REQUIREMENTS: Ind. Med.
CIRCULATION: 1,500
REPRINT POLICY: Optional
purchase

JOURNAL TITLE: The European Journal of Social Psychology

MANUSCRIPT ADDRESS: Psychologisch Laboratorium der Katholieke
Universiteit, Erasmuslaan 16
Nijmegen, The Netherlands

MAJOR CONTENT AREAS: Social

ARTICLES USUALLY ACCEPTED: Research, review, theoretical, book review

TOPICS PREFERRED: None

INAPPROPRIATE MANUSCRIPTS: None

INDEXED/ABSTRACTED IN: PA, CCSBS, LLBA, U

SUBSCRIPTION ADDRESS: Mouton Publishing Co.
Box 482
The Hague, The Netherlands

SUBSCRIPTION COST: $15.50 individual, $23 institutional
PUBLICATION LAG TIME: 1-2 years   STYLE SHEET: Yes
EARLY PUBLICATION OPTION: Yes   STYLE REQUIREMENTS: APA
REVIEW PERIOD: 6-12 months   CIRCULATION: 1,000
ACCEPTANCE RATE: 50%   REPRINT POLICY: 25 free

JOURNAL TITLE: Evaluation Magazine

MANUSCRIPT ADDRESS: 501 Park Avenue
So. Minneapolis, MN 55415

MAJOR CONTENT AREAS: Behavior therapy, clinical, community, systems,
mental retardation, statistics/methodology

ARTICLES USUALLY ACCEPTED: Evaluation of research, findings, and practice;
theory and methodology; notices of publications
and conferences related to evaluation

TOPICS PREFERRED: Mental health evaluation systems and practices
with data, applications of evaluation research

INAPPROPRIATE MANUSCRIPTS: Those unrelated to human services and evaluation

INDEXED/ABSTRACTED IN: GPE

SUBSCRIPTION ADDRESS: 501 Park Avenue
So. Minneapolis, MN 55415

SUBSCRIPTION COST: $3.50 per issue
PUBLICATION LAG TIME: 12 months   STYLE SHEET: Yes
EARLY PUBLICATION OPTION: No   STYLE REQUIREMENTS: Essentially APA
REVIEW PERIOD: 6-8 weeks   CIRCULATION: 21,000
ACCEPTANCE RATE: 50-60%   REPRINT POLICY: Free copies
of issue

JOURNAL TITLE: The Exceptional Child (formerly Slow Learning Child)

MANUSCRIPT ADDRESS: Schonell Educational Research Centre
University of Queensland
St. Lucia 4067, Australia

MAJOR CONTENT AREAS: Behavior therapy, clinical, mental retardation, learning disabilities, special education

ARTICLES USUALLY ACCEPTED: Research, review, theoretical, book review

TOPICS PREFERRED: The exceptional child, theory and practice in special education and related disciplines

INAPPROPRIATE MANUSCRIPTS: None

INDEXED/ABSTRACTED IN: APAIS, AEI, CCSBS, CIJE, DSHA, ECEA

SUBSCRIPTION ADDRESS: The Manager
University of Queensland Press
St. Lucia 4067, Australia

SUBSCRIPTION COST: $13

PUBLICATION LAG TIME: 9 months   STYLE SHEET: Yes

EARLY PUBLICATION OPTION: No   STYLE REQUIREMENTS: APA

REVIEW PERIOD: 3 months   CIRCULATION: 1,500

ACCEPTANCE RATE: 75%   REPRINT POLICY: 12 free

JOURNAL TITLE: Experimental Brain Research

MANUSCRIPT ADDRESS: Depends upon area of research; contact New York office for list of addresses

MAJOR CONTENT AREAS: Neurophysiology, neuropharmacology, neuroanatomy, sensory physiology, neuropsychology

ARTICLES USUALLY ACCEPTED: Research, research notes

TOPICS PREFERRED: Brain research

INAPPROPRIATE MANUSCRIPTS: None

INDEXED/ABSTRACTED IN: Not given

SUBSCRIPTION ADDRESS: Springer-Verlag New York, Inc.
175 Fifth Avenue
New York, NY 10010

SUBSCRIPTION COST: $213.15

PUBLICATION LAG TIME: 3-4 months   STYLE SHEET: Yes

EARLY PUBLICATION OPTION: No   STYLE REQUIREMENTS: Own style

REVIEW PERIOD: Not given   CIRCULATION: Not given

ACCEPTANCE RATE: Not given   REPRINT POLICY: 50 free

JOURNAL TITLE: Existential Psychiatry

MANUSCRIPT ADDRESS: Dr. Jordan Scher, Editor
8 South Michigan Avenue #310
Chicago, IL 60603

MAJOR CONTENT AREAS: Existential psychiatry

ARTICLES USUALLY ACCEPTED: Not given

TOPICS PREFERRED: Not given

INAPPROPRIATE MANUSCRIPTS: Not given

INDEXED/ABSTRACTED IN: IM

SUBSCRIPTION ADDRESS: American Ontoanalytic Association
8 South Michigan Avenue #310
Chicago, IL 60603

SUBSCRIPTION COST: $20

PUBLICATION LAG TIME: Not given	STYLE SHEET: Not given
EARLY PUBLICATION OPTION: Not given	STYLE REQUIREMENTS: Not given
REVIEW PERIOD: Not given	CIRCULATION: 5,000
ACCEPTANCE RATE: Not given	REPRINT POLICY: Not given

JOURNAL TITLE: The Family Coordinator

MANUSCRIPT ADDRESS: Dept. of Child and Family Development
Dawson Hall, University of Gerogia
Athens, GA 30602

MAJOR CONTENT AREAS: Behavior therapy, clinical, community, counseling, educational, psychotherapy, social, general

ARTICLES USUALLY ACCEPTED: Research, review, clinical, theoretical book review

TOPICS PREFERRED: Family life education, marriage and family counseling, services to families

INAPPROPRIATE MANUSCRIPTS: Highly technical research reports which are inappropriate for practitioners

INDEXED/ABSTRACTED IN: PA, ASW, BS, CCSBS, CIJE, ECEA, IBSS, JHE, MMRI, WSA

SUBSCRIPTION ADDRESS: Dept. of Child and Family Development
Dawson Hall, University of Georgia
Athens, GA 30602

SUBSCRIPTION COST: $15
PUBLICATION LAG TIME: 1 year
EARLY PUBLICATION OPTION: No
REVIEW PERIOD: 3 months
ACCEPTANCE RATE: 40%

STYLE SHEET: Yes
STYLE REQUIREMENTS: APA
CIRCULATION: 7,000
REPRINT POLICY: Optional purchase

JOURNAL TITLE: Family Planning Perspectives

MANUSCRIPT ADDRESS: 515 Madison Avenue
New York, NY 10022

MAJOR CONTENT AREAS: Family planning

ARTICLES USUALLY ACCEPTED: Research, review, theoretical, book review

TOPICS PREFERRED: Research in population and fertility control, evaluation of family planning programs & policies

INAPPROPRIATE MANUSCRIPTS: None

INDEXED/ABSTRACTED IN: ASW, CCSBS, PHRA, PAISB

SUBSCRIPTION ADDRESS: 515 Madison Avenue
New York, NY 10022

SUBSCRIPTION COST: $15
PUBLICATION LAG TIME: 4 months
EARLY PUBLICATION OPTION: No
REVIEW PERIOD: 4-5 weeks
ACCEPTANCE RATE: 10%

STYLE SHEET: Yes
STYLE REQUIREMENTS: Own style
CIRCULATION: 29,000
REPRINT POLICY: 50 free if reprinted

JOURNAL TITLE: Family Process

MANUSCRIPT ADDRESS: Box P
Stockbridge, MA 01262

MAJOR CONTENT AREAS: Clinical and psychotherapy as related to family

ARTICLES USUALLY ACCEPTED: Research and theoretical in the field of family therapy and family study

TOPICS PREFERRED: Family therapy and family study

INAPPROPRIATE MANUSCRIPTS: None

INDEXED/ABSTRACTED IN: PA, IM, ASW, SA, BS, CCSBS, DSHA, IBSS, JHE

SUBSCRIPTION ADDRESS: 149 East 78th Street
New York, NY 10021

SUBSCRIPTION COST: $12 individual, $20 institutional
PUBLICATION LAG TIME: 6-20 weeks   STYLE SHEET: Yes
EARLY PUBLICATION OPTION: No   STYLE REQUIREMENTS: Own style
REVIEW PERIOD: 8-10 weeks   CIRCULATION: 5,000
ACCEPTANCE RATE: 17%   REPRINT POLICY: Optional
purchase

JOURNAL TITLE: Family Therapy

MANUSCRIPT ADDRESS: Libra Publishers, Inc.
391 Willets Road
Roslyn Heights, NY 11577

MAJOR CONTENT AREAS: Psychotherapy as related to families

ARTICLES USUALLY ACCEPTED: Research, case studies, review, theoretical

TOPICS PREFERRED: Practical application

INAPPROPRIATE MANUSCRIPTS: None

INDEXED/ABSTRACTED IN: ASW

SUBSCRIPTION ADDRESS: Libra Publishers, Inc.
391 Willets Road
Roslyn Heights, NY 11577

SUBSCRIPTION COST: $16 individual, $20 institutional
PUBLICATION LAG TIME: 4-6 months   STYLE SHEET: Yes
EARLY PUBLICATION OPTION: No   STYLE REQUIREMENTS: APA
REVIEW PERIOD: 3 weeks   CIRCULATION: 1,000
ACCEPTANCE RATE: 30%   REPRINT POLICY: Optional
purchase

JOURNAL TITLE: Genetic Psychology Monographs

MANUSCRIPT ADDRESS: The Managing Editor, The Journal Press
2 Commercial Street, P. O. Box 543
Provincetown, MA 02657

MAJOR CONTENT AREAS: Clinical, developmental, mental retardation, aging

ARTICLES USUALLY ACCEPTED: Developmental and clinical research; new authors should give their credentials

TOPICS PREFERRED: Developmental research

INAPPROPRIATE MANUSCRIPTS: Those not conforming to submission requirements

INDEXED/ABSTRACTED IN: PA, ASW, CCSBS, DSHA, ECEA, JHE, LLBA, PRG

SUBSCRIPTION ADDRESS: The Journal Press
2 Commercial Street, P. O. Box 543
Provincetown, MA 02657

SUBSCRIPTION COST: $30

PUBLICATION LAG TIME: 20 months   STYLE SHEET: Yes

EARLY PUBLICATION OPTION: Yes   STYLE REQUIREMENTS: Journal Press

REVIEW PERIOD: 1 month   CIRCULATION: 1,182

ACCEPTANCE RATE: 40%   REPRINT POLICY: 200 free

JOURNAL TITLE: Geriatrics

MANUSCRIPT ADDRESS: Editorial Department
4015 West 65th Street
Minneapolis, MN 55435

MAJOR CONTENT AREAS: Geriatric medicine

ARTICLES USUALLY ACCEPTED: Research, theoretical and review, all aspects of clinical medicine relating to middle-age and older

TOPICS PREFERRED: Not given

INAPPROPRIATE MANUSCRIPTS: Not given

INDEXED/ABSTRACTED IN: BA, CA, IM, NA, PA

SUBSCRIPTION ADDRESS: Lancet Publications
4015 West 65th Street
Minneapolis, MN 55435

SUBSCRIPTION COST: $21

PUBLICATION LAG TIME: Not given   STYLE SHEET: Not given

EARLY PUBLICATION OPTION: Not given   STYLE REQUIREMENTS: Ind. Med.

REVIEW PERIOD: Not given   CIRCULATION: 51,000

ACCEPTANCE RATE: Not given   REPRINT POLICY: Optional purchase

JOURNAL TITLE: The Gifted Child Quarterly

MANUSCRIPT ADDRESS: National Association for Gifted Children
J. C. Gowan, Editor, 9030 Darby Avenue
Northridge, CA 91324

MAJOR CONTENT AREAS: Educational, psychometrics

ARTICLES USUALLY ACCEPTED: Research, review, theoretical, book review

TOPICS PREFERRED: Giftedness and creativity

INAPPROPRIATE MANUSCRIPTS: Polemics

INDEXED/ABSTRACTED IN: PA, CCSBS, CIJE, EI, ECEA

SUBSCRIPTION ADDRESS: Mrs. Charles Sowell
Rt. 5, Box 630A
Hot Springs, AR 71901

SUBSCRIPTION COST:	$20		
PUBLICATION LAG TIME:	6 months	STYLE SHEET:	No
EARLY PUBLICATION OPTION:	No	STYLE REQUIREMENTS:	APA
REVIEW PERIOD:	1 month	CIRCULATION:	2,500
ACCEPTANCE RATE:	33%	REPRINT POLICY:	Optional purchase

JOURNAL TITLE: The Group Leader's Workshop

MANUSCRIPT ADDRESS: P. O. Box 1254
Berkeley, CA 94701

MAJOR CONTENT AREAS: Group psychotherapy, encounter groups

ARTICLES USUALLY ACCEPTED: Theoretical, case studies

TOPICS PREFERRED: Specific group methods, techniques,
interventions, and exercises

INAPPROPRIATE MANUSCRIPTS: Those which have material which has appeared
in other journals

INDEXED/ABSTRACTED IN: None

SUBSCRIPTION ADDRESS: P. O. Box 1254
Berkeley, CA 94701

SUBSCRIPTION COST:	$35		
PUBLICATION LAG TIME:	8 weeks	STYLE SHEET:	No
EARLY PUBLICATION OPTION:	No	STYLE REQUIREMENTS:	None
REVIEW PERIOD:	6 weeks	CIRCULATION:	4,000
ACCEPTANCE RATE:	30%	REPRINT POLICY:	20 free

JOURNAL TITLE: Group and Organization Studies

MANUSCRIPT ADDRESS: 7596 Eads Avenue
La Jolla, CA 92111

MAJOR CONTENT AREAS: Community, counseling, educational, social,
industrial/organizational, psychotherapy

ARTICLES USUALLY ACCEPTED: Research reviews, book reviews, case and field
studies, cross-cultural studies

TOPICS PREFERRED: Leadership/management, personal growth, affective
education, couples, organizational development

INAPPROPRIATE MANUSCRIPTS: Not yet available (new journal)

INDEXED/ABSTRACTED IN: Will probably appear in: PA, ASW, CCSBS, SSCI

SUBSCRIPTION ADDRESS: 7569 Eads Avenue
La Jolla, CA 92111

SUBSCRIPTION COST: $20, $18 if prepaid
PUBLICATION LAG TIME: 2-3 months   STYLE SHEET: Yes
EARLY PUBLICATION OPTION: No   STYLE REQUIREMENTS: APA
REVIEW PERIOD: 3-4 months   CIRCULATION: Not yet known
ACCEPTANCE RATE: Not yet known   REPRINT POLICY: 3 free copies
of issue

JOURNAL TITLE: Group Process

MANUSCRIPT ADDRESS: Dr. Max Rosenbaum
West Shore Rd, RD #2
Carmel, NY 10512

MAJOR CONTENT AREAS: Clinical, counseling, educational, psychoanalysis,
psychotherapy, social (as applied to group work)

ARTICLES USUALLY ACCEPTED: Program descriptions, review, theoretical,
"reader opinion", research

TOPICS PREFERRED: Group work

INAPPROPRIATE MANUSCRIPTS: None

INDEXED/ABSTRACTED IN: PA

SUBSCRIPTION ADDRESS: Gordon and Breach
One Park Avenue
New York, NY 10016
SUBSCRIPTION COST: $9 individual, $18 institutional
PUBLICATION LAG TIME: 12-18 months   STYLE SHEET: Yes
EARLY PUBLICATION OPTION: No   STYLE REQUIREMENTS: APA
REVIEW PERIOD: 6-9 months   CIRCULATION: Not given
ACCEPTANCE RATE: Not given   REPRINT POLICY: 20-30 free

JOURNAL TITLE: Group Psychotherapy and Psychodrama

MANUSCRIPT ADDRESS: P. O. Box 311
Beacon, NY 12508

MAJOR CONTENT AREAS: Behavior therapy, clinical, community, counseling, methodology, psychotherapy, social
ARTICLES USUALLY ACCEPTED: Review, research, theoretical

TOPICS PREFERRED: Psychodrama, sociometry, group process,
action methods
INAPPROPRIATE MANUSCRIPTS: None

INDEXED/ABSTRACTED IN: PA, ASW

SUBSCRIPTION ADDRESS: Beacon House, Inc.
P. O. Box 311
Beacon, NY 12508

SUBSCRIPTION COST:	$14		
PUBLICATION LAG TIME:	3 months	STYLE SHEET:	Yes
EARLY PUBLICATION OPTION:	No	STYLE REQUIREMENTS:	APA
REVIEW PERIOD:	3 months	CIRCULATION:	1,500
ACCEPTANCE RATE:	25%	REPRINT POLICY:	Optional purchase

JOURNAL TITLE: Groups

MANUSCRIPT ADDRESS: 257 West 86th Street
New York, NY 10024

MAJOR CONTENT AREAS: Behavior therapy, clinical, psychoanalysis, and
psychotherapy as applied to groups
ARTICLES USUALLY ACCEPTED: Research, review, theoretical, case studies

TOPICS PREFERRED: Group and family therapy

INAPPROPRIATE MANUSCRIPTS: None

INDEXED/ABSTRACTED IN: IM

SUBSCRIPTION ADDRESS: 257 West 86th Street
New York, NY 10024

SUBSCRIPTION COST:	$10		
PUBLICATION LAG TIME:	12 months	STYLE SHEET:	Yes
EARLY PUBLICATION OPTION:	No	STYLE REQUIREMENTS:	Ind. Med.
REVIEW PERIOD:	6 months	CIRCULATION:	100
ACCEPTANCE RATE:	75%	REPRINT POLICY:	Optional purchase

JOURNAL TITLE: Groups: A Journal of Group Dynamics
and Psychotherapy
MANUSCRIPT ADDRESS: Samuel Slipp, MD, Editor
823 Park Avenue
New York, NY 10021
MAJOR CONTENT AREAS: Psychoanalysis in groups

ARTICLES USUALLY ACCEPTED: Not given

TOPICS PREFERRED: Group dynamics and psychotherapy

INAPPROPRIATE MANUSCRIPTS: Not given

INDEXED/ABSTRACTED IN: Not given

SUBSCRIPTION ADDRESS: Groups, Jerome Steiner, Editor
211 Central Park West
New York, NY 10024
SUBSCRIPTION COST: $4/issue
PUBLICATION LAG TIME: Not given   STYLE SHEET: Not given
EARLY PUBLICATION OPTION: Not given   STYLE REQUIREMENTS: APA
REVIEW PERIOD: Not given   CIRCULATION: Not given
ACCEPTANCE RATE: Not given   REPRINT POLICY: Not given

JOURNAL TITLE: Handbook of International Sociometry

MANUSCRIPT ADDRESS: Beacon House, Inc.
P. O. Box 311
Beacon, NY 12508

MAJOR CONTENT AREAS: Psychotherapy as applied to groups

ARTICLES USUALLY ACCEPTED: Research, review, theoretical

TOPICS PREFERRED: Sociometry, psychodrama, group psychotherapy, group dynamics

INAPPROPRIATE MANUSCRIPTS: None

INDEXED/ABSTRACTED IN: PA, SA, BS

SUBSCRIPTION ADDRESS: Beacon House, Inc.
P. O. Box 311
Beacon, NY 12508

SUBSCRIPTION COST: $14		
PUBLICATION LAG TIME: 1 year	STYLE SHEET:	Yes
EARLY PUBLICATION OPTION: No	STYLE REQUIREMENTS:	APA
REVIEW PERIOD: 6-8 weeks	CIRCULATION:	500
ACCEPTANCE RATE: Not given	REPRINT POLICY:	Optional purchase

JOURNAL TITLE: Harvard Educational Review

MANUSCRIPT ADDRESS: Longfellow Hall
13 Appian Way
Cambridge, MA 02138

MAJOR CONTENT AREAS: Community, counseling, developmental, educational mental retardation, social, methodology

ARTICLES USUALLY ACCEPTED: Research, review, theoretical, book review

TOPICS PREFERRED: Anything related to issues in education

INAPPROPRIATE MANUSCRIPTS: None

INDEXED/ABSTRACTED IN: PA, ASW, SA, BRD, BRI, BS, CCSBS, CIJE, DSHA, EI, EAA, ECEA, HA, IPAPL, IBSS, ILD, LLBA, PAISB, RHEA, WSA, WAH

SUBSCRIPTION ADDRESS: Longfellow Hall
13 Appian Way
Cambridge, MA 02138

SUBSCRIPTION COST: $14		
PUBLICATION LAG TIME: 4 months	STYLE SHEET:	Yes
EARLY PUBLICATION OPTION: No	STYLE REQUIREMENTS:	APA
REVIEW PERIOD: 1 month	CIRCULATION:	14,000
ACCEPTANCE RATE: 1%	REPRINT POLICY:	25 free

JOURNAL TITLE: Health and Social Service Journal

MANUSCRIPT ADDRESS: 27/29 Furnival Street
London EC4A   1SR, England

MAJOR CONTENT AREAS: Administration, community, family planning, medical social work, health care

ARTICLES USUALLY ACCEPTED: Research, review, theoretical, case studies

TOPICS PREFERRED: Health care and social work administration

INAPPROPRIATE MANUSCRIPTS: "Pop" psychology or psychiatry

INDEXED/ABSTRACTED IN: None

SUBSCRIPTION ADDRESS: 27/29 Furnival Street
London EC4A   1SR, England

SUBSCRIPTION COST: $40
PUBLICATION LAG TIME: 12 weeks
EARLY PUBLICATION OPTION: No
REVIEW PERIOD: 8 weeks
ACCEPTANCE RATE: 20%

STYLE SHEET: No
STYLE REQUIREMENTS: None
CIRCULATION: 11,500
REPRINT POLICY: Optional purchase

JOURNAL TITLE: Health and Social Work

MANUSCRIPT ADDRESS: 2 Park Avenue
New York, NY

MAJOR CONTENT AREAS: Any area related to social work in health care

ARTICLES USUALLY ACCEPTED: Research, review, theoretical, case studies

TOPICS PREFERRED: Any related to social work and health care

INAPPROPRIATE MANUSCRIPTS: Not given

INDEXED/ABSTRACTED IN: ASW

SUBSCRIPTION ADDRESS: 49 Sheridan Avenue
Albany, NY 12210

SUBSCRIPTION COST: $30, $15 to NASW members
PUBLICATION LAG TIME: 3-4 months
EARLY PUBLICATION OPTION: No
REVIEW PERIOD: 3-4 months
ACCEPTANCE RATE: Not given

STYLE SHEET: Yes
STYLE REQUIREMENTS: Chicago
CIRCULATION: Not given
REPRINT POLICY: Optional purchase

JOURNAL TITLE: High School Behavioral Science

MANUSCRIPT ADDRESS: Dr. Robert Mendelsohn
IAPS, Adelphi University
Garden City, NY 11530

MAJOR CONTENT AREAS: Psychology teaching at the pre-college level

ARTICLES USUALLY ACCEPTED: Research, review, theoretical, book review,
program descriptions

TOPICS PREFERRED: Pre-college social science

INAPPROPRIATE MANUSCRIPTS: Social science topics which cannot be related
to the pre-college psychology teacher

INDEXED/ABSTRACTED IN: PA, CIJE

SUBSCRIPTION ADDRESS: Human Sciences Press
72 Fifth Avenue
New York, NY 10011

SUBSCRIPTION COST: $6.95 individual, $15 institutional

PUBLICATION LAG TIME: 6-8 months

STYLE SHEET: Yes

EARLY PUBLICATION OPTION: No

STYLE REQUIREMENTS: APA

REVIEW PERIOD: 3 months

CIRCULATION: 1,000

ACCEPTANCE RATE: 60%

REPRINT POLICY: 1 free

JOURNAL TITLE: Homosexual Counseling Journal

MANUSCRIPT ADDRESS: 30 East 60th Street
Room 708
New York, NY 10022

MAJOR CONTENT AREAS: Counseling (with homosexuals)

ARTICLES USUALLY ACCEPTED: Research, review, theoretical; the emphasis
is on practicality and clinical experience

TOPICS PREFERRED: Counseling with homosexuals and their
families

INAPPROPRIATE MANUSCRIPTS: Those unrelated to counseling with homosexuals

INDEXED/ABSTRACTED IN: PA

SUBSCRIPTION ADDRESS: 30 East 60th Street
Room 708
New York, NY 10022

SUBSCRIPTION COST: $10 individual, $15 institutional

PUBLICATION LAG TIME: 2 months

STYLE SHEET: Yes

EARLY PUBLICATION OPTION: Yes

STYLE REQUIREMENTS: APA

REVIEW PERIOD: 2 months

CIRCULATION: 700

ACCEPTANCE RATE: 20%

REPRINT POLICY: Optional
purchase

JOURNAL TITLE:^x Hospital and Community Psychiatry

MANUSCRIPT ADDRESS: 1700 18th Street, N.W.
Washington, DC 20009

MAJOR CONTENT AREAS: Clinical, community, mental retardation, psychotherapy

ARTICLES USUALLY ACCEPTED: All types that have practical implications for patient care and treatment in mental health facilities

TOPICS PREFERRED: Hospital and community program evaluations, reports of new programs with data

INAPPROPRIATE MANUSCRIPTS: Those duplicating previous research, poor methodology, insufficient general interest

INDEXED/ABSTRACTED IN: PA, IM, ASW, AHMS, CCCP, CCSBS, DSHA, MMRI

SUBSCRIPTION ADDRESS: 1700 18th Street, N.W.
Washington, DC 20009

SUBSCRIPTION COST:	$15 individual, $60 institutional		
PUBLICATION LAG TIME:	9-12 months	STYLE SHEET:	Yes
EARLY PUBLICATION OPTION:	No	STYLE REQUIREMENTS:	Own style
REVIEW PERIOD:	8-10 weeks	CIRCULATION:	18,000
ACCEPTANCE RATE:	33%	REPRINT POLICY:	5 free copies of issue

JOURNAL TITLE: Hospital Progress

MANUSCRIPT ADDRESS: 1438 S. Grand Blvd.
St. Louis, MO 63104

MAJOR CONTENT AREAS: Administration, health care, management

ARTICLES USUALLY ACCEPTED: Research

TOPICS PREFERRED: Management

INAPPROPRIATE MANUSCRIPTS: Self-glorification or commercially-oriented articles; those of local interest only

INDEXED/ABSTRACTED IN: IM, ASW, AHMS, CPLI, CCCP, CCSBS, CINL, HA, HLI, IPARL, MSRS, NSI

SUBSCRIPTION ADDRESS: 1438 S. Grand Blvd.
St. Louis, MO 63104

SUBSCRIPTION COST:	$14		
PUBLICATION LAG TIME:	3 months	STYLE SHEET:	Yes
EARLY PUBLICATION OPTION:	No	STYLE REQUIREMENTS:	Chicago
REVIEW PERIOD:	3 months	CIRCULATION:	15,000
ACCEPTANCE RATE:	25%	REPRINT POLICY:	2 free

JOURNAL TITLE: Hospitals

MANUSCRIPT ADDRESS: American Hospital Association
840 North Lake Shore Drive
Chicago, IL 60611

MAJOR CONTENT AREAS: Health care administration

ARTICLES USUALLY ACCEPTED: Research, review, theoretical

TOPICS PREFERRED: Administratively oriented articles

INAPPROPRIATE MANUSCRIPTS: None

INDEXED/ABSTRACTED IN: ASW, CCCP, CCSBS, HA, JHE

SUBSCRIPTION ADDRESS: American Hospital Association
840 North Lake Shore Drive
Chicago, IL 60611

SUBSCRIPTION COST: $15
PUBLICATION LAG TIME: 6-8 months
EARLY PUBLICATION OPTION: No
REVIEW PERIOD: 4-6 weeks
ACCEPTANCE RATE: Not given

STYLE SHEET: Yes
STYLE REQUIREMENTS: Own style
CIRCULATION: 77,000
REPRINT POLICY: Optional
purchase

JOURNAL TITLE: Human Behavior

MANUSCRIPT ADDRESS: 12031 Wilshire Blvd.
Los Angeles, CA 90025

MAJOR CONTENT AREAS: All

ARTICLES USUALLY ACCEPTED: Those of interest to the general public; a
consumer-type publication

TOPICS PREFERRED: None

INAPPROPRIATE MANUSCRIPTS: Technical or scientific articles

INDEXED/ABSTRACTED IN: PHRA

SUBSCRIPTION ADDRESS: 12031 Wilshire Blvd.
Los Angeles, CA 90025

SUBSCRIPTION COST: $9.80
PUBLICATION LAG TIME: Not given
EARLY PUBLICATION OPTION: No
REVIEW PERIOD: 4-6 weeks
ACCEPTANCE RATE: Not given

STYLE SHEET: No
STYLE REQUIREMENTS: None
CIRCULATION: 80,000
REPRINT POLICY: Optional
purchase

JOURNAL TITLE: Human Development

MANUSCRIPT ADDRESS: Klaus F. Riegel, Dept. of Psychology
University of Michigan
Ann Arbor, MI 48104

MAJOR CONTENT AREAS: Developmental, general, history & systems,
social issues

ARTICLES USUALLY ACCEPTED: Theoretical, review

TOPICS PREFERRED: Theoretical contributions and integrative
reviews

INAPPROPRIATE MANUSCRIPTS: Research reports

INDEXED/ABSTRACTED IN: PA, AA, BEI, BS, CCSBS, CIJE, EI, LLBA, WSA

SUBSCRIPTION ADDRESS: Albert J. Phiebig
P. O. Box 352
White Plains, NY 10602

SUBSCRIPTION COST: $36 individual, $60 institutional

PUBLICATION LAG TIME: 4 months STYLE SHEET: Yes

EARLY PUBLICATION OPTION: No STYLE REQUIREMENTS: APA

REVIEW PERIOD: 6 weeks CIRCULATION: 1,500

ACCEPTANCE RATE: 25% REPRINT POLICY: Optional
purchase

JOURNAL TITLE: Human Factors

MANUSCRIPT ADDRESS: Human Factors Society
Box 1369
Santa Monica, CA 90406

MAJOR CONTENT AREAS: Engineering, experimental, industrial/
organizational, perception, theoretical

ARTICLES USUALLY ACCEPTED: Research, review, theoretical

TOPICS PREFERRED: Those which increase the knowledge of man in
relation to machine and environmental factors

INAPPROPRIATE MANUSCRIPTS: Pure research with no application to man-
machine-environmental systems

INDEXED/ABSTRACTED IN: PA, AHMS, BS, CCSBS, EE, ERA, IPARL

SUBSCRIPTION ADDRESS: The Johns Hopkins University Press
34th and Charles Streets
Baltimore, MD 21218

SUBSCRIPTION COST: $30

PUBLICATION LAG TIME: 6 months STYLE SHEET: Yes

EARLY PUBLICATION OPTION: Yes STYLE REQUIREMENTS: Own style

REVIEW PERIOD: 6 months CIRCULATION: 3,100

ACCEPTANCE RATE: 51% REPRINT POLICY: 50 free

JOURNAL TITLE: Human Organization

MANUSCRIPT ADDRESS: Deward E. Walker, Editor
Institute of Behavioral Science, No. 1
Univ. of Colorado, Boulder, CO 80309
MAJOR CONTENT AREAS: Applied social science

ARTICLES USUALLY ACCEPTED: Research, review, $10 submission fee for
SAA non-members

TOPICS PREFERRED: Applied social science, anthropologicàl
perspective
INAPPROPRIATE MANUSCRIPTS: Not given

INDEXED/ABSTRACTED IN: AA, SSI, SSCI

SUBSCRIPTION ADDRESS: Society for Applied Anthropology
1703 New Hampshire Avenue, N.W.
Washington, DC 2009
SUBSCRIPTION COST: $14 individual, $21 institutional
PUBLICATION LAG TIME: Not given   STYLE SHEET: Not given
EARLY PUBLICATION OPTION: Not given   STYLE REQUIREMENTS: Chicago
REVIEW PERIOD: Not given   CIRCULATION: 3,500
ACCEPTANCE RATE: Not given   REPRINT POLICY: Not given

JOURNAL TITLE: Human Relations

MANUSCRIPT ADDRESS: Eric Trist, Co-ordinating Editor
Wharton School, Univ. of Pennsylvania
Philadelphia, PA 19174
MAJOR CONTENT AREAS: Social science applied to human problems

ARTICLES USUALLY ACCEPTED: Research, review, theoretical, succinct
reports

TOPICS PREFERRED: Not given

INAPPROPRIATE MANUSCRIPTS: Not given

INDEXED/ABSTRACTED IN: BHI, PAISB, PA, SSI

SUBSCRIPTION ADDRESS: Plenum Publishing
227 West 17th Street
New York, NY 10011
SUBSCRIPTION COST: $30 individual, $40 institutional
PUBLICATION LAG TIME: Not given   STYLE SHEET: Not given
EARLY PUBLICATION OPTION: Not given   STYLE REQUIREMENTS: Not given
REVIEW PERIOD: Not given   CIRCULATION: 2,200
ACCEPTANCE RATE: Not given   REPRINT POLICY: 50 free

JOURNAL TITLE: Improving Human Performance Quarterly

MANUSCRIPT ADDRESS: Dr. Jerry Short, Chairman, Editorial Board
School of Education, University of Virginia
Charlottesville, VA 22901

MAJOR CONTENT AREAS: Behavior therapy/applied behavior analysis,
educational

ARTICLES USUALLY ACCEPTED: Research, theoretical

TOPICS PREFERRED: None

INAPPROPRIATE MANUSCRIPTS: None

INDEXED/ABSTRACTED IN: CCSBS, LLBA

SUBSCRIPTION ADDRESS: National Society for Performance and Instruction
Box 266, Rt. 1
Charles Town, WV 25414

SUBSCRIPTION COST: $20 individual, $30 institutional		
PUBLICATION LAG TIME: 6-12 months	STYLE SHEET: No	
EARLY PUBLICATION OPTION: No	STYLE REQUIREMENTS: Own style	
REVIEW PERIOD: 2 months	CIRCULATION: 1,500	
ACCEPTANCE RATE: 70%	REPRINT POLICY: 5 free	

JOURNAL TITLE: Indian Journal of Psychology

MANUSCRIPT ADDRESS: Dr. C. K. Basu, Professor of Psychology
D.E.P.F.E., N.C.E.R.T., Sri Aurobindo Marg
New Delhi-110016, India

MAJOR CONTENT AREAS: Almost all areas

ARTICLES USUALLY ACCEPTED: Research, review, theoretical

TOPICS PREFERRED: Experimental, social, industrial, educational

INAPPROPRIATE MANUSCRIPTS: None

INDEXED/ABSTRACTED IN: PA, BI, IPsA, LLBA, PRG, WSA

SUBSCRIPTION ADDRESS: Shri L.C. Wadhwa, Hony. Asst. Secretary
I.P.A., I.C.S.S.R., IIPA Hostel Building
Indraprastera Estate, New Delhi-110001, India

SUBSCRIPTION COST: $17		
PUBLICATION LAG TIME: 5 months	STYLE SHEET: Yes	
EARLY PUBLICATION OPTION: Yes	STYLE REQUIREMENTS: APA	
REVIEW PERIOD: 8 weeks	CIRCULATION: 1,100	
ACCEPTANCE RATE: 55%	REPRINT POLICY: 10 free	

JOURNAL TITLE: Indian Journal of Social Work

MANUSCRIPT ADDRESS: Editor, Tata Institute of Social Sciences
Sion-Trombay Road
Deonar, Bombay 400 088, India

MAJOR CONTENT AREAS: Social work, psychology/sociology of health
and education, rehabilitation

ARTICLES USUALLY ACCEPTED: Research, review, theoretical, book review,
position papers

TOPICS PREFERRED: Psychiatric social work, psychology and
economics, family and child welfare

INAPPROPRIATE MANUSCRIPTS: Agricultural extension, local sample surveys
of no general interest

INDEXED/ABSTRACTED IN: ASW, IPAPL, SSCI

SUBSCRIPTION ADDRESS: Dept. of Publications, Tata Institute of
Social Sciences, Sion-Trombay Road
Deonar, Bombay 400 088, India

SUBSCRIPTION COST:	$8		
PUBLICATION LAG TIME:	1 year	STYLE SHEET:	Yes
EARLY PUBLICATION OPTION:	No	STYLE REQUIREMENTS:	Own style
REVIEW PERIOD:	9-12 months	CIRCULATION:	1,100
ACCEPTANCE RATE:	40-50%	REPRINT POLICY:	25 free

JOURNAL TITLE: The Individual Psychologist

MANUSCRIPT ADDRESS: Adler-Dreikurs Institute
Div. of Graduate Studies, Bowie State College
Bowie, MD 20715

MAJOR CONTENT AREAS: Counseling, psychotherapy

ARTICLES USUALLY ACCEPTED: Practical articles reflecting Adlerian philosophy;
research articles also accepted if application of
theory is stressed

TOPICS PREFERRED: Individual, family, and group counseling or
therapy with an Adlerian orientation

INAPPROPRIATE MANUSCRIPTS: None

INDEXED/ABSTRACTED IN: PA

SUBSCRIPTION ADDRESS: Circulation Mgr., Adler-Dreikurs Institute
Div. of Graduate Studies, Bowie State College
Bowie, MD 20715

SUBSCRIPTION COST:	$2		
PUBLICATION LAG TIME:	4-10 months	STYLE SHEET:	Yes
EARLY PUBLICATION OPTION:	No	STYLE REQUIREMENTS:	APA
REVIEW PERIOD:	3 months	CIRCULATION:	1,200
ACCEPTANCE RATE:	50%	REPRINT POLICY:	10 free

JOURNAL TITLE: Industrial Gerentology

MANUSCRIPT ADDRESS: The National Council on the Aging
1828 L Street, N.W.
Washington, DC 20036

MAJOR CONTENT AREAS: Industrial as related to middle age and older workers

ARTICLES USUALLY ACCEPTED: Research, review, theoretical, book review, innovative program descriptions

TOPICS PREFERRED: Job redesign, retraining, second careers, retirement policies, pensions and legislation

INAPPROPRIATE MANUSCRIPTS: Topics covered in previous issues

INDEXED/ABSTRACTED IN: PA, EM, CCSBS, CIJE, CLA, PHRA, SSCI, WRA

SUBSCRIPTION ADDRESS: The National Council on the Aging
1828 L Street, N.W.
Washington, DC 20036

SUBSCRIPTION COST: $20

PUBLICATION LAG TIME: 2-6 months   STYLE SHEET: Yes

EARLY PUBLICATION OPTION: No   STYLE REQUIREMENTS: Own style

REVIEW PERIOD: 2-6 months   CIRCULATION: 6,000

ACCEPTANCE RATE: 50%   REPRINT POLICY: 5 free copies of issue

JOURNAL TITLE: Innovations

MANUSCRIPT ADDRESS: American Institutes for Research
P. O. Box 1113
Palo Alto, CA 94302

MAJOR CONTENT AREAS: Behavior therapy, community, counseling, mental retardation, psychotherapy

ARTICLES USUALLY ACCEPTED: Descriptions of practical programs which other mental health caregivers might use

TOPICS PREFERRED: Practical, user-oriented descriptions of programs and practices

INAPPROPRIATE MANUSCRIPTS: Theoretical or philosophical papers

INDEXED/ABSTRACTED IN: Not given

SUBSCRIPTION ADDRESS: P. O. Box 1113
Palo Alto, CA 94302

SUBSCRIPTION COST: No cost

PUBLICATION LAG TIME: 6-9 months   STYLE SHEET: Yes

EARLY PUBLICATION OPTION: No   STYLE REQUIREMENTS: Informal

REVIEW PERIOD: 2-4 weeks   CIRCULATION: 10,000

ACCEPTANCE RATE: 50%   REPRINT POLICY: Optional purchase

JOURNAL TITLE: Intellect

MANUSCRIPT ADDRESS: 1860 Broadway
New York, NY 10023

MAJOR CONTENT AREAS: Educational and social affairs; almost all areas of interest to general public

ARTICLES USUALLY ACCEPTED: Research, review, theoretical, book review

TOPICS PREFERRED: None

INAPPROPRIATE MANUSCRIPTS: Those other than originals

INDEXED/ABSTRACTED IN: CSPA, CCSBS, CIJE, SSCI

SUBSCRIPTION ADDRESS: 1860 Broadway
New York, NY 10023

SUBSCRIPTION COST: Not given		
PUBLICATION LAG TIME: 3 months	STYLE SHEET:	Yes
EARLY PUBLICATION OPTION: No	STYLE REQUIREMENTS:	Own style
REVIEW PERIOD: 4 weeks	CIRCULATION:	8,500
ACCEPTANCE RATE: 15-20%	REPRINT POLICY:	5 free copies of issue

JOURNAL TITLE: Interchange: A Journal of Educational Studies

MANUSCRIPT ADDRESS: O.I.S.E.
252 Bloor Street, West
Toronto, Canada

MAJOR CONTENT AREAS: Educational

ARTICLES USUALLY ACCEPTED: Research, review, theoretical, book review

TOPICS PREFERRED: Educational policy, Canadian education

INAPPROPRIATE MANUSCRIPTS: None

INDEXED/ABSTRACTED IN: PA, CEI, CSPA, CCSBS, CIJE, EAA, ECEA, RHEA

SUBSCRIPTION ADDRESS: O.I.S.E.
252 Bloor Street, West
Toronto, Canada

SUBSCRIPTION COST: $9 individual, $12 institutional		
PUBLICATION LAG TIME: 3 months	STYLE SHEET:	Yes
EARLY PUBLICATION OPTION: No	STYLE REQUIREMENTS:	APA
REVIEW PERIOD: 3 months	CIRCULATION:	2,000
ACCEPTANCE RATE: 15-20%	REPRINT POLICY:	Optional purchase

JOURNAL TITLE: International Archives of Occupational and Environmental Health

MANUSCRIPT ADDRESS: Prof. J.M. Peters, Dept. of Physiology School of Public Health, Harvard University 665 Huntington Ave., Boston, MA 02115

MAJOR CONTENT AREAS: Occupational or ambient environmental problems, methodology

ARTICLES USUALLY ACCEPTED: Review, research, brief communications, documents of international meetings

TOPICS PREFERRED: Morbidity and mortality, estimation of health risks, environmental health effects

INAPPROPRIATE MANUSCRIPTS: None

INDEXED/ABSTRACTED IN: CCCP

SUBSCRIPTION ADDRESS: Springer-Verlag New York, Inc. 175 Fifth Avenue New York, NY 10010

SUBSCRIPTION COST: $149.20

PUBLICATION LAG TIME: 3-4 months   STYLE SHEET: Yes

EARLY PUBLICATION OPTION: No   STYLE REQUIREMENTS: Own style

REVIEW PERIOD: Not given   CIRCULATION: Not given

ACCEPTANCE RATE: Not given   REPRINT POLICY: 50 free

JOURNAL TITLE: International Child Welfare Review

MANUSCRIPT ADDRESS: International Union for Child Welfare P. O. Box 41 1211 Geneva 20, Switzerland

MAJOR CONTENT AREAS: Social work, developmental

ARTICLES USUALLY ACCEPTED: Research, comparative studies of an international scope

TOPICS PREFERRED: Multi-disciplinary approaches to questions about the child, young person, and the family

INAPPROPRIATE MANUSCRIPTS: Medical articles, analyses of a purely national and unidisciplinary nature

INDEXED/ABSTRACTED IN: ASW, ECEA, K

SUBSCRIPTION ADDRESS: International Union for Child Welfare P. O. Box 41 1211 Geneva 20, Switzerland

SUBSCRIPTION COST: $15

PUBLICATION LAG TIME: 3-12 months   STYLE SHEET: No

EARLY PUBLICATION OPTION: Yes   STYLE REQUIREMENTS: None

REVIEW PERIOD: 3 months   CIRCULATION: 5,000

ACCEPTANCE RATE: 50-70%   REPRINT POLICY: Up to 10 free

JOURNAL TITLE: International Journal of the Addictions

MANUSCRIPT ADDRESS: Stanley Einstein, Ph.D.
Institute for the Study of Drug Misuse
111 Fifth Avenue, New York, NY 10011

MAJOR CONTENT AREAS: Addiction, drug misuse

ARTICLES USUALLY ACCEPTED: Research, theoretical, case studies

TOPICS PREFERRED: Studies of addiction and drug misuse

INAPPROPRIATE MANUSCRIPTS: Not given

INDEXED/ABSTRACTED IN: BA, CA, CCCP, IM, PA, SSCI

SUBSCRIPTION ADDRESS: Marcel Dekker Journals
P. O. Box 11305, Church Street Station
New York, NY 10249

SUBSCRIPTION COST: $45 institutional, individual rate on request

PUBLICATION LAG TIME: Not given	STYLE SHEET: Not given
EARLY PUBLICATION OPTION: Not given	STYLE REQUIREMENTS: CA
REVIEW PERIOD: Not given	CIRCULATION: 700
ACCEPTANCE RATE: Not given	REPRINT POLICY: Optional purchase

JOURNAL TITLE: International Journal of Aging and Human Development

MANUSCRIPT ADDRESS: Dr. Robert J. Kastenbaun, Dept. of Psychology
College I, Univ. of Mass., Columbia Point Campus
Dorchester, MA 02125

MAJOR CONTENT AREAS: Gerontology, developmental

ARTICLES USUALLY ACCEPTED: Research, review, theoretical, case history, book review, essay

TOPICS PREFERRED: Molar issues, i.e., implications of gerontological research on knowledge of total development

INAPPROPRIATE MANUSCRIPTS: None

INDEXED/ABSTRACTED IN: CCSBS

SUBSCRIPTION ADDRESS: Baywood Publishing Co., Inc.
43 Central Drive
Farmingdale, NY 11735

SUBSCRIPTION COST: $35

PUBLICATION LAG TIME: 9-12 months	STYLE SHEET: Yes
EARLY PUBLICATION OPTION: No	STYLE REQUIREMENTS: APA
REVIEW PERIOD: 4-6 weeks	CIRCULATION: 1,000
ACCEPTANCE RATE: 50%	REPRINT POLICY: 20 free

JOURNAL TITLE: International Journal of Clinical and Experimental Hypnosis

MANUSCRIPT ADDRESS: Martin T. Orne, M.D., Ph.D., Editor
Institute of Penn. Hospital, 111 N. 49th Street
Philadelphia, PA 19139

MAJOR CONTENT AREAS: Hypnosis

ARTICLES USUALLY ACCEPTED: Clinical and experimental studies, discussions of theory, historical and cultural material, book reviews

TOPICS PREFERRED: Hypnosis in psychology, psychiatry, medicine, and allied areas of science

INAPPROPRIATE MANUSCRIPTS: Single case studies without appropriate literature review

INDEXED/ABSTRACTED IN: PA, IM, EM, CCSBS, DSHA

SUBSCRIPTION ADDRESS: Subscriptions Section
Institute of Penn. Hospital, 111 N. 49th Street
Philadelphia, PA 19139

SUBSCRIPTION COST: $21 individual, $30 institutional

PUBLICATION LAG TIME: 1 year   STYLE SHEET: Yes

EARLY PUBLICATION OPTION: Yes   STYLE REQUIREMENTS: APA

REVIEW PERIOD: 4 months   CIRCULATION: 2,000

ACCEPTANCE RATE: 60%   REPRINT POLICY: Optional purchase

JOURNAL TITLE: International Journal of Criminology and Penology

MANUSCRIPT ADDRESS: Professor W. H. Nagel, Warmondermy 4
4 Oegstgeest
The Netherlands

MAJOR CONTENT AREAS: Social, criminology, penology

ARTICLES USUALLY ACCEPTED: Theoretical, review

TOPICS PREFERRED: Theoretical and comparative issues

INAPPROPRIATE MANUSCRIPTS: None

INDEXED/ABSTRACTED IN: ACP, CCSBS

SUBSCRIPTION ADDRESS: Academic Press, Inc.
111 Fifth Avenue
New York, NY 10003

SUBSCRIPTION COST: $24.50

PUBLICATION LAG TIME: Not given   STYLE SHEET: Yes

EARLY PUBLICATION OPTION: No   STYLE REQUIREMENTS: None

REVIEW PERIOD: Not given   CIRCULATION: 550

ACCEPTANCE RATE: 35%   REPRINT POLICY: 50 free

JOURNAL TITLE: International Journal of Group Psychotherapy

MANUSCRIPT ADDRESS: Box 230
150 Christopher St.
New York, NY 10014

MAJOR CONTENT AREAS: Group psychotherapy, clinical

ARTICLES USUALLY ACCEPTED: Research, clinical

TOPICS PREFERRED: Group psychotherapy

INAPPROPRIATE MANUSCRIPTS: None

INDEXED/ABSTRACTED IN: PA, ASW, BI, CDL, CCSBS, IBSS, LLBA

SUBSCRIPTION ADDRESS: International Universities Press
239 Park Avenue South
New York, NY 10014

SUBSCRIPTION COST: $18.50 individual, $28.50 institutional
PUBLICATION LAG TIME: 1 year   STYLE SHEET: Yes
EARLY PUBLICATION OPTION: No   STYLE REQUIREMENTS: Own style
REVIEW PERIOD: 4 months   CIRCULATION: 5,000
ACCEPTANCE RATE: 25%   REPRINT POLICY: Optional purchase

JOURNAL TITLE: International Journal of Mental Health

MANUSCRIPT ADDRESS: Dr. Gittelman, Editor, Department of Psychiatry
New Jersey College of Medicine, 100 Bergen St.
Newark, NJ 07103

MAJOR CONTENT AREAS: All non-experimental areas plus community and social psychiatry, epidemiology

ARTICLES USUALLY ACCEPTED: Research, review, theoretical, book review; unsolicited papers only if related to the theme of the particular issue

TOPICS PREFERRED: Those pertaining to public mental health care

INAPPROPRIATE MANUSCRIPTS: None

INDEXED/ABSTRACTED IN: PA, IM, CCSBS

SUBSCRIPTION ADDRESS: International Arts & Science Press
901 N. Broadway
New York, NY 10003

SUBSCRIPTION COST: $20 individual, $40 institutional
PUBLICATION LAG TIME: 1 year   STYLE SHEET: Yes
EARLY PUBLICATION OPTION: No   STYLE REQUIREMENTS: APA
REVIEW PERIOD: 1-2 months   CIRCULATION: 1,200
ACCEPTANCE RATE: Usually solicited   REPRINT POLICY: 20 free

JOURNAL TITLE: International Journal of Offender Therapy
and Comparative Criminology
MANUSCRIPT ADDRESS: 199 Gloucester Place
London NW1 6BU, England

MAJOR CONTENT AREAS: Offender therapy

ARTICLES USUALLY ACCEPTED: Clinical articles preferred; research, review,
and theoretical also accepted

TOPICS PREFERRED: Treatment techniques

INAPPROPRIATE MANUSCRIPTS: None

INDEXED/ABSTRACTED IN: PA, ASW, SA, ACP, CCSBS, ICS, LLBA

SUBSCRIPTION ADDRESS: 199 Gloucester Place
London NW1 6BU,-England

SUBSCRIPTION COST:	$20		
PUBLICATION LAG TIME:	1-2 years	STYLE SHEET:	Yes
EARLY PUBLICATION OPTION:	No	STYLE REQUIREMENTS:	Own style
REVIEW PERIOD:	1-2 months	CIRCULATION:	3,000
ACCEPTANCE RATE:	25%	REPRINT POLICY:	10 free copies of issue

JOURNAL TITLE: International Journal of Psychiatry in
Medicine
MANUSCRIPT ADDRESS: Dr. Don R. Lipsitt, Mt. Auburn Hospital
330 Mt. Auburn Street
Cambridge, MA 02138
MAJOR CONTENT AREAS: Behavior therapy, clinical, counseling,
personality, psychotherapy
ARTICLES USUALLY ACCEPTED: Research, review, theoretical, case studies

TOPICS PREFERRED: Psychosocial aspects of patient care, the
teaching of psychiatry, case studies
INAPPROPRIATE MANUSCRIPTS: None

INDEXED/ABSTRACTED IN: PA, IM, EM, ASW, CCCP, CCSBS

SUBSCRIPTION ADDRESS: Baywood Publishing Co.
43 Central Drive
Farmingdale, NY 11735

SUBSCRIPTION COST:	$35		
PUBLICATION LAG TIME:	3-6 months	STYLE SHEET:	Yes
EARLY PUBLICATION OPTION:	No	STYLE REQUIREMENTS:	Own style
REVIEW PERIOD:	3-6 months	CIRCULATION:	800
ACCEPTANCE RATE:	30%	REPRINT POLICY:	20 free

JOURNAL TITLE: International Journal of Psycho-Analysis

MANUSCRIPT ADDRESS: Joseph Sandler, Editor
35 Circus Road
London, NW8 9JG, England

MAJOR CONTENT AREAS: Psychoanalysis

ARTICLES USUALLY ACCEPTED: Theory and practice, book reviews

TOPICS PREFERRED: Not given

INAPPROPRIATE MANUSCRIPTS: Not given

INDEXED/ABSTRACTED IN: Not given

SUBSCRIPTION ADDRESS: Bailliere Tindall
7 & 8 Henrietta Street
London, WC2E 8QE, England

SUBSCRIPTION COST: $35	
PUBLICATION LAG TIME: Not given	STYLE SHEET: Not given
EARLY PUBLICATION OPTION: Not given	STYLE REQUIREMENTS: Not given
REVIEW PERIOD: Not given	CIRCULATION: Not given
ACCEPTANCE RATE: Not given	REPRINT POLICY: 50 free offprints

JOURNAL TITLE: International Journal of Psychoanalytic
Psychotherapy

MANUSCRIPT ADDRESS: Robert Langs, M.D.
70 Glen Cove Road
Roslyn Heights, NY 11577

MAJOR CONTENT AREAS: Clinical, psychoanalysis, psychotherapy

ARTICLES USUALLY ACCEPTED: Research, review, theoretical, book review as
related to psychoanalytic psychotherapy

TOPICS PREFERRED: Psychoanalysis, applied analysis, analytic-
oriented therapy

INAPPROPRIATE MANUSCRIPTS: None

INDEXED/ABSTRACTED IN: CCSBS

SUBSCRIPTION ADDRESS: Jason Aaronson, Inc.
59 Fourth Ave.
New York, NY 10003

SUBSCRIPTION COST: $20	
PUBLICATION LAG TIME: 5-12 months	STYLE SHEET: Yes
EARLY PUBLICATION OPTION: No	STYLE REQUIREMENTS: Chicago
REVIEW PERIOD: 2-4 weeks	CIRCULATION: 5,000
ACCEPTANCE RATE: 80%	REPRINT POLICY: Optional purchase

JOURNAL TITLE: International Journal of Social Psychiatry

MANUSCRIPT ADDRESS: Prof. Marvin K. Opler, Department of Anthropology & Psychiatry, State Univ. of N.Y., 4242 Ridge Lea Rd., Buffalo, NY 14226

MAJOR CONTENT AREAS: Behavior therapy, clinical, community, psychotherapy, social

ARTICLES USUALLY ACCEPTED: Research, review, theoretical, book review, clinical

TOPICS PREFERRED: Psycho-social psychotherapy, community psychotherapy

INAPPROPRIATE MANUSCRIPTS: None

INDEXED/ABSTRACTED IN: PA, ASW, BI, BS, CCSBS, IBSS, PRAJ, WSA

SUBSCRIPTION ADDRESS: 18 Park Avenue
London NW11 7SJ, England

SUBSCRIPTION COST: $15 individual, $20 institutional
PUBLICATION LAG TIME: 5 months
EARLY PUBLICATION OPTION: No
REVIEW PERIOD: 5 weeks
ACCEPTANCE RATE: 50%

STYLE SHEET: No
STYLE REQUIREMENTS: APA
CIRCULATION: 2,500
REPRINT POLICY: 1 free copy of issue

JOURNAL TITLE: International Journal of Sport Psychology

MANUSCRIPT ADDRESS: Edizioni Luigi Pozzi s.p.a.
Via Panama 68-00198 Roma, Italy

MAJOR CONTENT AREAS: Sport psychology

ARTICLES USUALLY ACCEPTED: Research, review

TOPICS PREFERRED: Sport psychology

INAPPROPRIATE MANUSCRIPTS: None

INDEXED/ABSTRACTED IN: PA

SUBSCRIPTION ADDRESS: Edizioni Luigi Pozzi s.p.a.
Via Panama 68-00198 Roma, Italy

SUBSCRIPTION COST: $10 individual, $15 institutional
PUBLICATION LAG TIME: 4-6 months
EARLY PUBLICATION OPTION: No
REVIEW PERIOD: 4-6 months
ACCEPTANCE RATE: 60%

STYLE SHEET: Yes
STYLE REQUIREMENTS: Ind. Med.
CIRCULATION: 1,000
REPRINT POLICY: 20 free

JOURNAL TITLE: International Journal of Symbology

MANUSCRIPT ADDRESS: Dr. R. A. Craddick, Dept. of Psychology
Georgia State University, University Plaza
Atlanta, GA   30303

MAJOR CONTENT AREAS: Clinical, educational, perception, personality,
psychoanalysis, psychotherapy

ARTICLES USUALLY ACCEPTED: Research, review, theoretical, book review,
as related to the investigation of symbols

TOPICS PREFERRED: Any topic, including religion, art, literature,
or architeture, if related to symbols

INAPPROPRIATE MANUSCRIPTS: Those unrelated to symbols

INDEXED/ABSTRACTED IN: PA, CCSBS, LLBA

SUBSCRIPTION ADDRESS: Dr. R. A. Craddick, Dept. of Psychology
Georgia State University, University Plaza
Atlanta, GA   30303

SUBSCRIPTION COST: $11 individual, $20 institutional

PUBLICATION LAG TIME: 3-12 months   STYLE SHEET: Yes

EARLY PUBLICATION OPTION: No   STYLE REQUIREMENTS: Own style

REVIEW PERIOD: 2 months   CIRCULATION: 310

ACCEPTANCE RATE: 70%   REPRINT POLICY: 50 free

JOURNAL TITLE: International Migration Review

MANUSCRIPT ADDRESS: 209 Flagg Place
Staten Island, NY   10304

MAJOR CONTENT AREAS: Comparative, history & systems, industrial/
organizational, social

ARTICLES USUALLY ACCEPTED: Theoretical, research, documentation, book
review

TOPICS PREFERRED: Sociological, demographic, historical, and
legislative aspects of human migration

INAPPROPRIATE MANUSCRIPTS: None

INDEXED/ABSTRACTED IN: SA, AA, BS, CCSBS, HA, IBSS, LLBA, PHRA

SUBSCRIPTION ADDRESS: Center for Migration Studies
209 Flagg Place
Staten Island, NY   10304

SUBSCRIPTION COST: $14.50 individual, $19.50 institutional

PUBLICATION LAG TIME: Varies   STYLE SHEET: Yes

EARLY PUBLICATION OPTION: No   STYLE REQUIREMENTS: Own style

REVIEW PERIOD: 3-5 months   CIRCULATION: 2,300

ACCEPTANCE RATE: 30%   REPRINT POLICY: Purchase
required

JOURNAL TITLE:	International Social Science Journal
MANUSCRIPT ADDRESS:	UNESCO Place de Fontenoy 75700 Paris, France
MAJOR CONTENT AREAS:	All social sciences
ARTICLES USUALLY ACCEPTED:	Only those relating to the main theme of an issue; most are solicited
TOPICS PREFERRED:	Comparative or transnational research, methodological or theoretical innovations
INAPPROPRIATE MANUSCRIPTS:	Those not related to issue themes
INDEXED/ABSTRACTED IN:	ASW, AA, AI, APAIS, BEI, CCSBS, EAA, HA, IPAPL, ILD, IPSA, JHE, LLBA, PRAJ, PAISB, RHEA, SSHI
SUBSCRIPTION ADDRESS:	Sales Division of UNESCO Place de Fontenoy 75700 Paris, France
SUBSCRIPTION COST:	52 French francs
PUBLICATION LAG TIME:	6-12 months
EARLY PUBLICATION OPTION:	No
REVIEW PERIOD:	2-3 weeks
ACCEPTANCE RATE:	Usually solicited

STYLE SHEET:	Yes
STYLE REQUIREMENTS:	Own style
CIRCULATION:	10,000
REPRINT POLICY:	25 free

JOURNAL TITLE: Journal of Abnormal Child Psychology

MANUSCRIPT ADDRESS: P. O. Box 248074
Coral Gables, FL   33124

MAJOR CONTENT AREAS: Behavior therapy, clinical, counseling,
developmental, psychotherapy

ARTICLES USUALLY ACCEPTED: Research, review, theoretical

TOPICS PREFERRED: Empirical studies related to deviant
children

INAPPROPRIATE MANUSCRIPTS: None

INDEXED/ABSTRACTED IN: PA, CDA, CCSBS

SUBSCRIPTION ADDRESS: Plenum Press
227 West 17th Street
New York, NY   10011

SUBSCRIPTION COST: $16 individual, $32 institutional
PUBLICATION LAG TIME: 1 year   STYLE SHEET: Yes
EARLY PUBLICATION OPTION: No   STYLE REQUIREMENTS: APA
REVIEW PERIOD: 2 months   CIRCULATION: 1,000
ACCEPTANCE RATE: 50%   REPRINT POLICY: Optional
purchase

JOURNAL TITLE: Journal of Abnormal Psychology

MANUSCRIPT ADDRESS: Leonard D. Eron, Editor, Dept. of Psychology
Box 4348, Univ. of Illinois at Chicago Circle
Chicago, IL   60680

MAJOR CONTENT AREAS: All areas related to the etiology, development, and course of disordered behavior

ARTICLES USUALLY ACCEPTED: Research and theoretical in the broad field of
abnormal behavior, its determinants, and its
correlates

TOPICS PREFERRED: Any in the area of abnormal behavior

INAPPROPRIATE MANUSCRIPTS: None

INDEXED/ABSTRACTED IN: PA, ASW, CSPA, CCSBS, CIJE, DSHA, ECEA, LLBA,
RHEA, WSA

SUBSCRIPTION ADDRESS: APA Subscription Office
1200 17th Street, N.W.
Washington, DC   20036

SUBSCRIPTION COST: $25
PUBLICATION LAG TIME: 11 months   STYLE SHEET: No
EARLY PUBLICATION OPTION: No   STYLE REQUIREMENTS: APA
REVIEW PERIOD: Variable   CIRCULATION: 6,500
ACCEPTANCE RATE: 25%   REPRINT POLICY: 20 free

JOURNAL TITLE: Journal of Advertising Research

MANUSCRIPT ADDRESS: 3 East 54th Street
New York, NY 10022

MAJOR CONTENT AREAS: Advertising research

ARTICLES USUALLY ACCEPTED: Research

TOPICS PREFERRED: Measurement of advertising effects, interactions of price and advertising, media & copy research
INAPPROPRIATE MANUSCRIPTS: Public opinion studies, studies of small samples with students
INDEXED/ABSTRACTED IN: PA, ADPA, BS, BPI, CCSBS, EE, JHE, MDA, TC, TMA

SUBSCRIPTION ADDRESS: 3 East 54th Street
New York, NY 10022

SUBSCRIPTION COST: $30 (students and professors $20)
PUBLICATION LAG TIME: Up to 9 months   STYLE SHEET: Yes
EARLY PUBLICATION OPTION: No   STYLE REQUIREMENTS: Chicago
REVIEW PERIOD: 6 months   CIRCULATION: 4,100
ACCEPTANCE RATE: Not given   REPRINT POLICY: 10 free copies
of issue

JOURNAL TITLE: The Journal of Aesthetic Education

MANUSCRIPT ADDRESS: 288B, School of Education
University of Illinois
Urbana, IL 61801
MAJOR CONTENT AREAS: Psychology of art and education

ARTICLES USUALLY ACCEPTED: Research, theoretical, review

TOPICS PREFERRED: Aesthetic interest and public policy, the aesthetic import of the new communications media
INAPPROPRIATE MANUSCRIPTS: No particular topics

INDEXED/ABSTRACTED IN: PA, AES, CCSBS, CIJE, PI

SUBSCRIPTION ADDRESS: University of Illinois Press
Urbana, IL 61801

SUBSCRIPTION COST: $10
PUBLICATION LAG TIME: Variable   STYLE SHEET: Yes
EARLY PUBLICATION OPTION: No   STYLE REQUIREMENTS: Own style
REVIEW PERIOD: 1 month   CIRCULATION: Not given
ACCEPTANCE RATE: Not known   REPRINT POLICY: Optional
purchase

JOURNAL TITLE: Journal of Alcohol and Drug Education

MANUSCRIPT ADDRESS: Box 6109
University of Alabama
University, AL   35486

MAJOR CONTENT AREAS: Methodology, alcohol and drug use

ARTICLES USUALLY ACCEPTED: Research, theoretical, book review, reports
of community and school education programs
on alcohol and drugs

TOPICS PREFERRED: Studies on drinking styles and patterns,
education and prevention

INAPPROPRIATE MANUSCRIPTS: Psychological studies on alcoholism, physiology
of drugs and alcohol

INDEXED/ABSTRACTED IN: CCSBS, CIJE

SUBSCRIPTION ADDRESS: 3500 N. Logan
Lansing, MI   48914

SUBSCRIPTION COST: $4
PUBLICATION LAG TIME: 4 months
EARLY PUBLICATION OPTION: No
REVIEW PERIOD: 6 weeks
ACCEPTANCE RATE: Not given

STYLE SHEET: Yes
STYLE REQUIREMENTS: APA
CIRCULATION: 672
REPRINT POLICY: 4 free copies
of issue

JOURNAL TITLE: The Journal of Alcoholism

MANUSCRIPT ADDRESS: Medical Council on Alcoholism
8 Bourdon Street
London W1X 9HY, England

MAJOR CONTENT AREAS: Alcoholism

ARTICLES USUALLY ACCEPTED: Research, review, theoretical, case
studies

TOPICS PREFERRED: All aspects (including legal) of research
and treatment with alcoholics

INAPPROPRIATE MANUSCRIPTS: None

INDEXED/ABSTRACTED IN: CCSBS

SUBSCRIPTION ADDRESS: B. Edsall and Co., Ltd.
36 Eccleston Square
London SW1V 1PF, England

SUBSCRIPTION COST: $15
PUBLICATION LAG TIME: 6 months
EARLY PUBLICATION OPTION: Yes
REVIEW PERIOD: 3 months
ACCEPTANCE RATE: 75%

STYLE SHEET: Yes
STYLE REQUIREMENTS: Ind. Med.
CIRCULATION: 23,000
REPRINT POLICY: 25 free

JOURNAL TITLE: Journal of Altered States of Consciousness

MANUSCRIPT ADDRESS: 43 Central Drive
Farmingdale, NY 11735

MAJOR CONTENT AREAS: Altered states of consciousness

ARTICLES USUALLY ACCEPTED: Research, review, theoretical, book review,
case studies

TOPICS PREFERRED: None

INAPPROPRIATE MANUSCRIPTS: None

INDEXED/ABSTRACTED IN: Not given

SUBSCRIPTION ADDRESS: 43 Central Drive
Farmingdale, NY 11735

SUBSCRIPTION COST: $27.50
PUBLICATION LAG TIME: Not given
EARLY PUBLICATION OPTION: No
REVIEW PERIOD: 6 weeks
ACCEPTANCE RATE: 30%

STYLE SHEET: Yes
STYLE REQUIREMENTS: Not given
CIRCULATION: 600
REPRINT POLICY: Not given

JOURNAL TITLE: Journal of the American Academy of Child
Psychiatry

MANUSCRIPT ADDRESS: 333 Cedar Street
New Haven, CT 06510

MAJOR CONTENT AREAS: Behavior therapy, community, developmental,
mental retardation, psychoanalysis, psychotherapy

ARTICLES USUALLY ACCEPTED: Research, review, theoretical

TOPICS PREFERRED: Clinical and basic research related to child
psychiatry

INAPPROPRIATE MANUSCRIPTS: Anecdotal case studies

INDEXED/ABSTRACTED IN: PA, CCSBS, IPAPL, LLBA

SUBSCRIPTION ADDRESS: Journals Dept., Yale University Press
92-A Yale Station
New Haven, CT 06520

SUBSCRIPTION COST: $17.50
PUBLICATION LAG TIME: 9 months
EARLY PUBLICATION OPTION: Yes
REVIEW PERIOD: 3 months
ACCEPTANCE RATE: 18%

STYLE SHEET: Yes
STYLE REQUIREMENTS: Own style
CIRCULATION: 3,300
REPRINT POLICY: Optional
purchase

JOURNAL TITLE: Journal of the American Academy of Psychoanalysis

MANUSCRIPT ADDRESS: American Academy of Psychoanalysis
40 Gramercy Park North
New York, NY 10010

MAJOR CONTENT AREAS: Psychoanalysis

ARTICLES USUALLY ACCEPTED: Any articles of interest to the readership, primarily psychoanalysts

TOPICS PREFERRED: Theoretical and clinical psychoanalysis

INAPPROPRIATE MANUSCRIPTS: Those at a level more appropriate to the general public

INDEXED/ABSTRACTED IN: IM, CCSBS

SUBSCRIPTION ADDRESS: John Wiley and Sons
604 Third Avenue
New York, NY 10016

SUBSCRIPTION COST:	$25		
PUBLICATION LAG TIME:	3-8 months	STYLE SHEET:	Yes
EARLY PUBLICATION OPTION:	No	STYLE REQUIREMENTS:	Own style
REVIEW PERIOD:	6 weeks	CIRCULATION:	3,000
ACCEPTANCE RATE:	25%	REPRINT POLICY:	20 free

JOURNAL TITLE: Journal of the American Geriatrics Society

MANUSCRIPT ADDRESS: 10 Columbus Circle
New York, NY 10019

MAJOR CONTENT AREAS: General psychiatry

ARTICLES USUALLY ACCEPTED: Research, review, theoretical, case studies

TOPICS PREFERRED: Clinical health care of the aged

INAPPROPRIATE MANUSCRIPTS: Windy dissertations from the "fringes"

INDEXED/ABSTRACTED IN: IM, ASW, AHMS, BIS, CCCP, CCSBS, LLBA, WAH

SUBSCRIPTION ADDRESS: Publications Office
10 Columbus Circle
New York, NY 10019

SUBSCRIPTION COST:	$25		
PUBLICATION LAG TIME:	5 months	STYLE SHEET:	Yes
EARLY PUBLICATION OPTION:	No	STYLE REQUIREMENTS:	Own style
REVIEW PERIOD:	1 month	CIRCULATION:	10,000
ACCEPTANCE RATE:	50%	REPRINT POLICY:	Optional purchase

JOURNAL TITLE: Journal of the American Psychoanalytic Association

MANUSCRIPT ADDRESS: 23 The Hemlocks
Roslyn Estates, NY 11576

MAJOR CONTENT AREAS: Clinical, developmental, experimental, personality, psychoanalysis, psychotherapy

ARTICLES USUALLY ACCEPTED: Clinical, theoretical, research, review, book review

TOPICS PREFERRED: Psychoanalysis and articles from psychiatry and behavioral sciences relevant to psychoanalysis

INAPPROPRIATE MANUSCRIPTS: Statistical, social, and political surveys

INDEXED/ABSTRACTED IN: PA, ASW, BI, CCSBS, IPARL, LLBA, PRAJ

SUBSCRIPTION ADDRESS: International Universities Press, inc.
239 Park Avenue South
New York, NY 10003

SUBSCRIPTION COST: $22 individual, $30 institutional

PUBLICATION LAG TIME: 9-12 months   STYLE SHEET: Yes

EARLY PUBLICATION OPTION: Yes   STYLE REQUIREMENTS: Own style

REVIEW PERIOD: 3 months   CIRCULATION: 5,500

ACCEPTANCE RATE: 33%   REPRINT POLICY: Optional purchase

JOURNAL TITLE: Journal of the American Society of Psychosomatic Dentistry and Medicine

MANUSCRIPT ADDRESS: Leo Wollman, M.D., Ph.D., Executive Director
2802 Mermaid Avenue
Brooklyn, NY 11224

MAJOR CONTENT AREAS: Behavior therapy, clinical, perception, psychotherapy, personality

ARTICLES USUALLY ACCEPTED: Research, review, theoretical

TOPICS PREFERRED: Psychosomatics, hypnosis, psychotherapy, parapsychology

INAPPROPRIATE MANUSCRIPTS: Very few

INDEXED/ABSTRACTED IN: PA, IM, IPAPL

SUBSCRIPTION ADDRESS: Leo Wollman, M.D., Ph.D., Executive Director
2802 Mermaid Avenue
Brooklyn, NY 11224

SUBSCRIPTION COST: $20

PUBLICATION LAG TIME: 6 months   STYLE SHEET: Yes

EARLY PUBLICATION OPTION: Yes   STYLE REQUIREMENTS: Ind. Med.

REVIEW PERIOD: A few days   CIRCULATION: 400

ACCEPTANCE RATE: 70%   REPRINT POLICY: 30 free

JOURNAL TITLE: Journal of the American Society for Psychical Research

MANUSCRIPT ADDRESS: 5 West 73rd Street
New York, NY 10023

MAJOR CONTENT AREAS: Parapsychology

ARTICLES USUALLY ACCEPTED: Research, review, theoretical, book review

TOPICS PREFERRED: Only those dealing with parapsychology

INAPPROPRIATE MANUSCRIPTS: None

INDEXED/ABSTRACTED IN: PA, CCSBS, MHBRI, SSCI

SUBSCRIPTION ADDRESS: 5 West 73rd Street
New York, NY 10023

SUBSCRIPTION COST: $20 individual, $12 institutional
PUBLICATION LAG TIME: 1 year   STYLE SHEET: Yes
EARLY PUBLICATION OPTION: No   STYLE REQUIREMENTS: Modified APA
REVIEW PERIOD: 8-10 weeks   CIRCULATION: 3,000
ACCEPTANCE RATE: 20%   REPRINT POLICY: 100 free

JOURNAL TITLE: The Journal of Analytical Psychology

MANUSCRIPT ADDRESS: 30 Devonshire Place
London W.I., England

MAJOR CONTENT AREAS: Psychotherapy and other areas as related to
Jungian psychology

ARTICLES USUALLY ACCEPTED: Clinical and theoretical articles on
analytical psychology

TOPICS PREFERRED: All aspects of Jungian psychology and related
fields

INAPPROPRIATE MANUSCRIPTS: Non-Jungian material

INDEXED/ABSTRACTED IN: PA, BI, CCSBS, WMP

SUBSCRIPTION ADDRESS: 30 Devonshire Place
London W.I., England

SUBSCRIPTION COST: $12
PUBLICATION LAG TIME: 4-18 months   STYLE SHEET: Yes
EARLY PUBLICATION OPTION: No   STYLE REQUIREMENTS: Own style
REVIEW PERIOD: Not given   CIRCULATION: 1,200
ACCEPTANCE RATE: 50%   REPRINT POLICY: 50 free

JOURNAL TITLE: Journal of Applied Behavior Analysis

MANUSCRIPT ADDRESS: W. Stewart Agras, Editor, Dept. of Psychiatry and Behavioral Sciences, Stanford Univ. School of Medicine, Stanford, CA 94305

MAJOR CONTENT AREAS: Behavior therapy, clinical, community, counseling, education, industrial, learning, methodology

ARTICLES USUALLY ACCEPTED: Reports of experimental research involving applications of the experimental analysis of behavior, technical articles

TOPICS PREFERRED: Intensive or between group analyses of behavior change procedure

INAPPROPRIATE MANUSCRIPTS: Case studies

INDEXED/ABSTRACTED IN: PA, CCSBS, DSHA, ECEA, LLBA

SUBSCRIPTION ADDRESS: Mary Louise Wright, Business Manager Dept. of Human Development, Univ. of Kansas Lawrence, KS 66045

SUBSCRIPTION COST: $10 individual, $18 institutional

PUBLICATION LAG TIME: 9-12 months   STYLE SHEET: Yes

EARLY PUBLICATION OPTION: No   STYLE REQUIREMENTS: Modified APA

REVIEW PERIOD: 2 months   CIRCULATION: 7,500

ACCEPTANCE RATE: 25%   REPRINT POLICY: 50 free

JOURNAL TITLE: The Journal of Applied Behavioral Science

MANUSCRIPT ADDRESS: P. O. Box 9155 Rosslyn Station Arlington, VA 22209

MAJOR CONTENT AREAS: Applied behavior analysis, behavioral science applied to social policy, organizations

ARTICLES USUALLY ACCEPTED: Research, theoretical, case studies

TOPICS PREFERRED: Rigorous research and application of applied behavioral science to a sufficiently large sample

INAPPROPRIATE MANUSCRIPTS: Management, consumerism, religion, Skinner's behaviorism, psychotherapy

INDEXED/ABSTRACTED IN: PA, ASW, AA, BS, CSPA, CDL, CCSBS, CIJE, EE, EI, EAA, ERA, ECEA, IPAPL, IBSS, LLBA, PRA, PHRA, RHEA

SUBSCRIPTION ADDRESS: P. O. Box 9155 Rosslyn Station Arlington, VA 22209

SUBSCRIPTION COST: $19

PUBLICATION LAG TIME: 1 year   STYLE SHEET: Yes

EARLY PUBLICATION OPTION: No   STYLE REQUIREMENTS: APA

REVIEW PERIOD: 1-3 months   CIRCULATION: 6,500

ACCEPTANCE RATE: 10%   REPRINT POLICY: Optional purchase

JOURNAL TITLE: Journal of Applied Psychology

MANUSCRIPT ADDRESS: Edwin A. Fleishman, Editor, Amer. Institutes for Research, 3301 New Mexico Avenue, N.W. Washington, DC 20016

MAJOR CONTENT AREAS: Applied, industrial/ organizational

ARTICLES USUALLY ACCEPTED: Research, occasional theoretical of interest to psychologists in such settings as universities, industry, government, etc.

TOPICS PREFERRED: None

INAPPROPRIATE MANUSCRIPTS: Those dealing with clinical psychology

INDEXED/ABSTRACTED IN: PA, BS, CSPA, CCSBS, CIJE, EE, EAA, EI, ERA, IPARL, JHE, LLBA, PMA, PHRA, RHEA

SUBSCRIPTION ADDRESS: APA Subscription Office 1200 17th Street, N.W. Washington, DC 20036

SUBSCRIPTION COST: $25

PUBLICATION LAG TIME: 11 months

EARLY PUBLICATION OPTION: No

REVIEW PERIOD: Variable

ACCEPTANCE RATE: 25%

STYLE SHEET: No

STYLE REQUIREMENTS: APA

CIRCULATION: 6,100

REPRINT POLICY: 20 free

JOURNAL TITLE: Journal of Applied Rehabilitation Counseling

MANUSCRIPT ADDRESS: Education Building 440 Austin, TX 78712

MAJOR CONTENT AREAS: Rehabilitation

ARTICLES USUALLY ACCEPTED: All types of articles relevant to rehabilitation counseling

TOPICS PREFERRED: Counseling the disabled

INAPPROPRIATE MANUSCRIPTS: Descriptions of rehabilitation counselor training programs

INDEXED/ABSTRACTED IN: ECEA

SUBSCRIPTION ADDRESS: NRCA 1522 K Street Washington, DC 20005

SUBSCRIPTION COST: $8

PUBLICATION LAG TIME: 3 months

EARLY PUBLICATION OPTION: No

REVIEW PERIOD: 3 months

ACCEPTANCE RATE: 30%

STYLE SHEET: Yes

STYLE REQUIREMENTS: APA

CIRCULATION: 9,500

REPRINT POLICY: 5 free

JOURNAL TITLE: Journal of Applied Social Psychology

MANUSCRIPT ADDRESS: Dr. Peter Suedfeld, Editor, Dept. of Psychology Univ. of British Columbia, 2075 Westbrook Pl. Vancouver, B.C. V6T 1W5, Canada

MAJOR CONTENT AREAS: Social

ARTICLES USUALLY ACCEPTED: Research, theoretical, review, applications based on research

TOPICS PREFERRED: Any research in social psychology of actual or potential applicable value

INAPPROPRIATE MANUSCRIPTS: Research in education

INDEXED/ABSTRACTED IN: PA, EM, CSPA, CCSBS, CIJE, WSA

SUBSCRIPTION ADDRESS: Scripta Publishing Co. 1511 K Street, N.W. Washington, DC 20005

SUBSCRIPTION COST: $18 individual, $36 institutional

PUBLICATION LAG TIME: 1 year

EARLY PUBLICATION OPTION: No

REVIEW PERIOD: 3 months

ACCEPTANCE RATE: 15-20%

STYLE SHEET: No

STYLE REQUIREMENTS: APA

CIRCULATION: Not given

REPRINT POLICY: Not given

JOURNAL TITLE: Journal of the Association for the Study of Perception

MANUSCRIPT ADDRESS: Association for the Study of Perception Box 744 DeKalb, IL 60115

MAJOR CONTENT AREAS: Experimental, perception, learning

ARTICLES USUALLY ACCEPTED: Research, theoretical, and review on all topics dealing directly with perception as a primary input process

TOPICS PREFERRED: All areas of perception; learning problems of children

INAPPROPRIATE MANUSCRIPTS: Personal experience stories with no research documentation

INDEXED/ABSTRACTED IN: CCSBS, CIJE, EI, ECEA

SUBSCRIPTION ADDRESS: Association for the Study of Perception Box 744 DeKalb, IL 60115

SUBSCRIPTION COST: $5

PUBLICATION LAG TIME: 6-12 months

EARLY PUBLICATION OPTION: No

REVIEW PERIOD: 3-6 months

ACCEPTANCE RATE: 50%

STYLE SHEET: Yes

STYLE REQUIREMENTS: APA

CIRCULATION: 400

REPRINT POLICY: Optional purchase

JOURNAL TITLE: Journal of Autism and Childhood
Schizophrenia

MANUSCRIPT ADDRESS: Dept. of Psychiatry, School of Medicine
University of North Carolina
Chapel Hill, NC 27514

MAJOR CONTENT AREAS: Behavior therapy, clinical, community,
counseling, developmental, psychoanalysis

ARTICLES USUALLY ACCEPTED: Research, review, theoretical, book review

TOPICS PREFERRED: Autism, childhood schizophrenia, and related
developmental disabilities

INAPPROPRIATE MANUSCRIPTS: None

INDEXED/ABSTRACTED IN: PA, IM, CCSBS, CIJE, DSHA, ECEA, LLBA

SUBSCRIPTION ADDRESS: Plenum Publishing Corp.
227 W. 17th Street
New York, NY 10011

SUBSCRIPTION COST: $17.50 individual, $32 institutional

PUBLICATION LAG TIME:	4-6 months	STYLE SHEET:	Yes
EARLY PUBLICATION OPTION:	Yes	STYLE REQUIREMENTS:	APA
REVIEW PERIOD:	4-8 weeks	CIRCULATION:	2,500
ACCEPTANCE RATE:	70%	REPRINT POLICY:	Optional purchase

JOURNAL TITLE: Journal of Behavior Therapy and Experimental
Psychiatry

MANUSCRIPT ADDRESS: Dr. Joseph Wolpe, Editor
Temple U. Medical School, Eastern Pa. Psychiatric
Institute, Henry Avenue, Philadelphia, PA 19129

MAJOR CONTENT AREAS: Behavior therapy/applied behavior analysis,
experimental psychiatry

ARTICLES USUALLY ACCEPTED: Research, case reports; should have follow-up
data of at least six months' duration

TOPICS PREFERRED: New methods, target behaviors, or populations;
observations of considerable interest

INAPPROPRIATE MANUSCRIPTS: Smoking, eating, and addictive behaviors with
less than one year follow-up

INDEXED/ABSTRACTED IN: PA, IM, CCSBS, LLBA, PRG

SUBSCRIPTION ADDRESS: Pergamon Press, Inc.
Maxwell House, Fairview Park
Elmsford, NY 10523

SUBSCRIPTION COST: $25 individual, $55 institutional

PUBLICATION LAG TIME:	3 months	STYLE SHEET:	Yes
EARLY PUBLICATION OPTION:	No	STYLE REQUIREMENTS:	APA
REVIEW PERIOD:	3-5 months	CIRCULATION:	4,200
ACCEPTANCE RATE:	25-35%	REPRINT POLICY:	Optional purchase

JOURNAL TITLE: Journal of Biological Psychology/The Worm Runner's Digest

MANUSCRIPT ADDRESS: Box 644
Ann Arbor, MI   48107

MAJOR CONTENT AREAS: Behavior therapy, comparative, experimental, learning, physiological, general, history

ARTICLES USUALLY ACCEPTED: For JBP, primarily research; for Digest, poems, spoofs, cartoons, fun articles, or satires on science and education.

TOPICS PREFERRED: Memory transfer, behavior modification

INAPPROPRIATE MANUSCRIPTS: No specific topics, just anything boring or trivial

INDEXED/ABSTRACTED IN: PA, SA, LLBA

SUBSCRIPTION ADDRESS: Box 644
Ann Arbor, MI   48107

SUBSCRIPTION COST:	$5		
PUBLICATION LAG TIME:	6-9 months	STYLE SHEET:	Yes
EARLY PUBLICATION OPTION:	No	STYLE REQUIREMENTS:	APA
REVIEW PERIOD:	2-4 months	CIRCULATION:	1,200
ACCEPTANCE RATE:	50%	REPRINT POLICY:	100 free from JBP

JOURNAL TITLE: Journal of Black Psychology

MANUSCRIPT ADDRESS: Dr. William David Smith, Editor
116 Old Commons, University of Cincinnati
Cincinnati, OH   45221

MAJOR CONTENT AREAS: All areas related to black psychology

ARTICLES USUALLY ACCEPTED: Research, review, theoretical, book review

TOPICS PREFERRED: Black psychology

INAPPROPRIATE MANUSCRIPTS: None

INDEXED/ABSTRACTED IN: Not given

SUBSCRIPTION ADDRESS: P. O. Box 2929
Washington, DC   20002

SUBSCRIPTION COST:	$10 individual, $15 institutional		
PUBLICATION LAG TIME:	2-4 weeks	STYLE SHEET:	No
EARLY PUBLICATION OPTION:	No	STYLE REQUIREMENTS:	Own style
REVIEW PERIOD:	2-3 months	CIRCULATION:	2,500
ACCEPTANCE RATE:	30%	REPRINT POLICY:	2 free

JOURNAL TITLE: Journal of Black Studies

MANUSCRIPT ADDRESS: Molefi K. Asante, Editor
Dept. of Black Studies, State University of N.Y.
Buffalo, NY 14226

MAJOR CONTENT AREAS: Social work practice, health care, social activism

ARTICLES USUALLY ACCEPTED: Research

TOPICS PREFERRED: Social science perspectives on the Afro-American world

INAPPROPRIATE MANUSCRIPTS: None

INDEXED/ABSTRACTED IN: ASW, SA, AES, CCSBS, CIJE, MA, PHRA

SUBSCRIPTION ADDRESS: Sage Publications, Inc.
275 South Beverly Drive
Beverly Hills, CA 90212

SUBSCRIPTION COST: $20
PUBLICATION LAG TIME: 6-24 months
EARLY PUBLICATION OPTION: No
REVIEW PERIOD: 6-8 weeks
ACCEPTANCE RATE: 10%

STYLE SHEET: Yes
STYLE REQUIREMENTS: Sage
CIRCULATION: 1,352
REPRINT POLICY: 5 free

JOURNAL TITLE: Journal of Child Psychology and Psychiatry

MANUSCRIPT ADDRESS: N. Garmezy, Dept. of Psychology
Elliott Hall, University of Minnesota
Minneapolis, MN 55455

MAJOR CONTENT AREAS: All areas of psychology and psychiatry as related to children

ARTICLES USUALLY ACCEPTED: Research, review, theoretical, case studies

TOPICS PREFERRED: Child psychology and psychiatry

INAPPROPRIATE MANUSCRIPTS: None

INDEXED/ABSTRACTED IN: BEI, CCSBS, RHEA, WSA

SUBSCRIPTION ADDRESS: Pergamon Press
Headington Hill Hall
Oxford OX3 OBW, England

SUBSCRIPTION COST: $25 individual, $40 institutional
PUBLICATION LAG TIME: 9-12 months
EARLY PUBLICATION OPTION: No
REVIEW PERIOD: 3 months
ACCEPTANCE RATE: Not given

STYLE SHEET: No
STYLE REQUIREMENTS: Own style
CIRCULATION: 4,300
REPRINT POLICY: Voluntary page charge

JOURNAL TITLE: Journal of Child Psychotherapy

MANUSCRIPT ADDRESS: Burgh House
New End Square
London NW3, U.K.

MAJOR CONTENT AREAS: Clinical, psychoanalysis, psychotherapy

ARTICLES USUALLY ACCEPTED: Research, review, theoretical, case studies

TOPICS PREFERRED: Detailed psychoanalytic case studies with children revealing psychodynamic insights

INAPPROPRIATE MANUSCRIPTS: Behavior therapy, case studies which would involve breach of confidence if published

INDEXED/ABSTRACTED IN: PA, ASW, BEI, CDA

SUBSCRIPTION ADDRESS: The Distribution Secretary
Burgh House, New End Square
London NW3, U.K.

SUBSCRIPTION COST: $7.50 individual, $6 institutional
PUBLICATION LAG TIME: Annual publication   STYLE SHEET: Yes
EARLY PUBLICATION OPTION: No   STYLE REQUIREMENTS: Own style
REVIEW PERIOD: Not given   CIRCULATION: 1,000
ACCEPTANCE RATE: 90%   REPRINT POLICY: Optional purchase

JOURNAL TITLE: Journal of Chronic Diseases

MANUSCRIPT ADDRESS: Dept. of Medicine, Northwestern University
303 E. Chicago Avenue
Chicago, IL 60611

MAJOR CONTENT AREAS: Clinical, community, health care

ARTICLES USUALLY ACCEPTED: Research, review, theoretical, book review, case studies

TOPICS PREFERRED: Biostatistics, epidemiology, chronic diseases

INAPPROPRIATE MANUSCRIPTS: None

INDEXED/ABSTRACTED IN: IM, ASW, AHMS, CCCP, IPAPL, WAH

SUBSCRIPTION ADDRESS: Pergamon Press, Ltd.
Headington Hill Hall
Oxford OX3 OBW, England

SUBSCRIPTION COST: $25 individual, $60 institutional
PUBLICATION LAG TIME: 3-5 months   STYLE SHEET: Yes
EARLY PUBLICATION OPTION: No   STYLE REQUIREMENTS: Ind. Med.
REVIEW PERIOD: 3-5 months   CIRCULATION: 3,500
ACCEPTANCE RATE: 40%   REPRINT POLICY: Optional purchase

JOURNAL TITLE: Journal of Clinical Psychology

MANUSCRIPT ADDRESS: Vladimir Pishkin
VA Hospital, 921 Northeast 13th Street
Oklahoma City, OK 73104

MAJOR CONTENT AREAS: Clinical

ARTICLES USUALLY ACCEPTED: Research

TOPICS PREFERRED: Psychodynamics and psychopathology,
psychodiagnostic processes, drug and alcohol abuse

INAPPROPRIATE MANUSCRIPTS: None

INDEXED/ABSTRACTED IN: PA, IM, ASW, CSPA, CCSBS, CIJE, IPARL, LLBA,
WSA

SUBSCRIPTION ADDRESS: 4 Conant Square
Brandon, VT 05733

SUBSCRIPTION COST:	$20 individual, $25 institutional		
PUBLICATION LAG TIME:	6-9 months	STYLE SHEET:	Yes
EARLY PUBLICATION OPTION:	No	STYLE REQUIREMENTS:	APA
REVIEW PERIOD:	3 weeks	CIRCULATION:	2,766
ACCEPTANCE RATE:	35%	REPRINT POLICY:	Optional purchase

JOURNAL TITLE: Journal of Clinical Child Psychology

MANUSCRIPT ADDRESS: Diane J. Willis, Ph.D., Editor
1100 N.E. 13th
Oklahoma City, OK 73117

MAJOR CONTENT AREAS: Clinical, developmental

ARTICLES USUALLY ACCEPTED: Research, theoretical, and advocacy
articles which are problem oriented

TOPICS PREFERRED: Research with practical application to
problems of children

INAPPROPRIATE MANUSCRIPTS: Lengthy statistical articles with no
application to practical work for children

INDEXED/ABSTRACTED IN: PA, CCSBS

SUBSCRIPTION ADDRESS: Diane J. Willis, Ph.D., Editor
1100 N.E. 13th
Oklahoma City, OK 73117

SUBSCRIPTION COST:	$9		
PUBLICATION LAG TIME:	2-3 months	STYLE SHEET:	Yes
EARLY PUBLICATION OPTION:	Yes	STYLE REQUIREMENTS:	APA
REVIEW PERIOD:	1 month	CIRCULATION:	1,500
ACCEPTANCE RATE:	Not given	REPRINT POLICY:	2 free

JOURNAL TITLE: Journal of College Student Personnel

MANUSCRIPT ADDRESS: Albert B. Hood, Editor
W112 East Hall, University of Iowa
Iowa City, IO 52242

MAJOR CONTENT AREAS: Counseling, developmental, educational, and
personality as related to college students

ARTICLES USUALLY ACCEPTED: Research, review, theoretical

TOPICS PREFERRED: College counseling and student personnel
administration

INAPPROPRIATE MANUSCRIPTS: Speeches and papers not written for scholarly
journals

INDEXED/ABSTRACTED IN: PA, CSPA, CCSBS, CIJE, EAA, EI, WSA

SUBSCRIPTION ADDRESS: American Personnel and Guidance Association
1607 New Hampshire Ave., N. W.
Washington, D.C. 20009

SUBSCRIPTION COST: $15
PUBLICATION LAG TIME: 4-6 months   STYLE SHEET: Yes
EARLY PUBLICATION OPTION: No   STYLE REQUIREMENTS: APA
REVIEW PERIOD: 2-3 months   CIRCULATION: 10,000
ACCEPTANCE RATE: 35%   REPRINT POLICY: 50 free

JOURNAL TITLE: Journal of Communication

MANUSCRIPT ADDRESS: George Gerbner, Editor, The Annenberg School
of Communications, University of Pennsylvania
3620 Walnut, Philadelphia, PA 19174

MAJOR CONTENT AREAS: Communications

ARTICLES USUALLY ACCEPTED: Research reports, book reviews

TOPICS PREFERRED: Speech communications, mass communication,
interpersonal and group communication

INAPPROPRIATE MANUSCRIPTS: None

INDEXED/ABSTRACTED IN: PA, BS, CCSBS, CIJE, DSHA, EI, HA, ISA, IBSS,
LLBA

SUBSCRIPTION ADDRESS: Journal of Communication
P. O. Box 13358
Philadelphia, PA 19101

SUBSCRIPTION COST: $15
PUBLICATION LAG TIME: 6-12 months   STYLE SHEET: No
EARLY PUBLICATION OPTION: No   STYLE REQUIREMENTS: Own style
REVIEW PERIOD: 3-6 months   CIRCULATION: 6,500
ACCEPTANCE RATE: 10%   REPRINT POLICY: Optional
purchase

JOURNAL TITLE: Journal of Communication Disorders

MANUSCRIPT ADDRESS: Professor R. W. Rieber
John Jay College, 444 West 56th Street
New York, NY 10019

MAJOR CONTENT AREAS: Behavior therapy, clinical, mental retardation, psychotherapy

ARTICLES USUALLY ACCEPTED: Research, review, theoretical, case studies

TOPICS PREFERRED: Anatomical, psychodynamic, diagnostic, and therapeutic aspects of communication disorders

INAPPROPRIATE MANUSCRIPTS: None

INDEXED/ABSTRACTED IN: PA, BS, CCCP, CCSBS, DSHA, LLBA

SUBSCRIPTION ADDRESS: American Elsevier Publishing Co.
52 Vanderbilt Avenue
New York, NY 10017

SUBSCRIPTION COST: $18 individual, $35 institutional
PUBLICATION LAG TIME: 9 months   STYLE SHEET: Yes
EARLY PUBLICATION OPTION: No   STYLE REQUIREMENTS: APA
REVIEW PERIOD: 4-5 months   CIRCULATION: 1,000
ACCEPTANCE RATE: Not given   REPRINT POLICY: Purchase required

JOURNAL TITLE: Journal of Community Health

MANUSCRIPT ADDRESS: Robert Kane, M.D., Editor
Dept. of Family & Community Medicine,
Univ. of Utah, Salt Lake City, UT 84132

MAJOR CONTENT AREAS: Community

ARTICLES USUALLY ACCEPTED: Research, evaluation, review, policy issues

TOPICS PREFERRED: Project evaluations

INAPPROPRIATE MANUSCRIPTS: Health education

INDEXED/ABSTRACTED IN: IM, CCCP, CCSBS, SSCI

SUBSCRIPTION ADDRESS: Human Sciences Press
72 Fifth Avenue
New York, NY 10011

SUBSCRIPTION COST: $15 individual, $30 institutional
PUBLICATION LAG TIME: 6 months   STYLE SHEET: Yes
EARLY PUBLICATION OPTION: No   STYLE REQUIREMENTS: Own style
REVIEW PERIOD: 1-3 months   CIRCULATION: 1,500
ACCEPTANCE RATE: 40%   REPRINT POLICY: Optional purchase

JOURNAL TITLE: Journal of Community Psychology

MANUSCRIPT ADDRESS: Box 319
George Peabody College
Nashville, TN 37203

MAJOR CONTENT AREAS: Community

ARTICLES USUALLY ACCEPTED: Research, theoretical

TOPICS PREFERRED: Community psychology

INAPPROPRIATE MANUSCRIPTS: None

INDEXED/ABSTRACTED IN: PA

SUBSCRIPTION ADDRESS: 4 Conant Square
Brandon, VT 05733

SUBSCRIPTION COST: $15 individual, $25 institutional
PUBLICATION LAG TIME: 4-6 months   STYLE SHEET: Yes
EARLY PUBLICATION OPTION: Not given   STYLE REQUIREMENTS: APA
REVIEW PERIOD: 2 months   CIRCULATION: 1,000
ACCEPTANCE RATE: 40%   REPRINT POLICY: Purchase
required

JOURNAL TITLE: Journal of Comparative and Physiological
Psychology

MANUSCRIPT ADDRESS: Garth J. Thomas, Editor, Center for Brain Resear
Medical Center, University of Rochester
Rochester, NY 14642

MAJOR CONTENT AREAS: Comparative, physiological

ARTICLES USUALLY ACCEPTED: Research, monographs

TOPICS PREFERRED: Experimental reports that elucidate physiological or biological mechanisms of behavior

INAPPROPRIATE MANUSCRIPTS: None

INDEXED/ABSTRACTED IN: PA, DSHA, LLBA

SUBSCRIPTION ADDRESS: APA Subscription Office
1200 17th Street, N.W.
Washington, DC 20036

SUBSCRIPTION COST: $45
PUBLICATION LAG TIME: 12 months   STYLE SHEET: No
EARLY PUBLICATION OPTION: No   STYLE REQUIREMENTS: APA
REVIEW PERIOD: Variable   CIRCULATION: 2,900
ACCEPTANCE RATE: 49%   REPRINT POLICY: 20 free

JOURNAL TITLE: Journal of Conflict Resolution

MANUSCRIPT ADDRESS: 124 Prospect Street
New Haven, CT 06511

MAJOR CONTENT AREAS: Community, history & systems, social, war
and peace within nations, personality

ARTICLES USUALLY ACCEPTED: Empirical research or rigorous theoretical

TOPICS PREFERRED: Quantitative research in political science,
formal theory, experimental psychology

INAPPROPRIATE MANUSCRIPTS: Historical descriptive articles

INDEXED/ABSTRACTED IN: PA, ASW, BS, CCSBS, EAA, HA, IPAPL, IBSS, IPSA,
PRAJ, SSHI

SUBSCRIPTION ADDRESS: Sage Publications
275 South Beverly Drive
Beverly Hills, CA 90212

SUBSCRIPTION COST: $14.40 individual, $24 institutional
PUBLICATION LAG TIME: 4 months   STYLE SHEET: Yes
EARLY PUBLICATION OPTION: No   STYLE REQUIREMENTS: Sage
REVIEW PERIOD: 3 months   CIRCULATION: 3,000
ACCEPTANCE RATE: 15-20%   REPRINT POLICY: 24 free

JOURNAL TITLE: Journal of Consulting and Clinical Psychology

MANUSCRIPT ADDRESS: Brendon A. Maher, Editor, 1120 William James Hall
Harvard University, 33 Kirkland Street
Cambridge, MA 02138

MAJOR CONTENT AREAS: Clinical, personality (if related to problems
in clinical)

ARTICLES USUALLY ACCEPTED: Research, case study, and occasional theoretical
papers on diagnosis and treatment in disordered
behavior and populations of clinical interest

TOPICS PREFERRED: Any related to clinical and consulting issues

INAPPROPRIATE MANUSCRIPTS: None

INDEXED/ABSTRACTED IN: PA, ASW, CSPA, CCSBS, CIJE, ECEA, LLBA, WSA

SUBSCRIPTION ADDRESS: APA Subscription Office
1200 17th Street, N.W.
Washington, DC 20036

SUBSCRIPTION COST: $30
PUBLICATION LAG TIME: 9 months   STYLE SHEET: No
EARLY PUBLICATION OPTION: No   STYLE REQUIREMENTS: APA
REVIEW PERIOD: Variable   CIRCULATION: 8,400
ACCEPTANCE RATE: 21%   REPRINT POLICY: 20 free

JOURNAL TITLE: Journal of Consumer Research

MANUSCRIPT ADDRESS: 201 Vance Hall
Wharton School
Philadelphia, PA 19174

MAJOR CONTENT AREAS: Industrial organizational, personality, social, methodology, consumer behavior

ARTICLES USUALLY ACCEPTED: Research, review, theoretical

TOPICS PREFERRED: Interdisciplinary research on consumer behavior

INAPPROPRIATE MANUSCRIPTS: None

INDEXED/ABSTRACTED IN: PA, CCSBS

SUBSCRIPTION ADDRESS: 222 S. Riverside Plaza
Chicago, IL 60606

SUBSCRIPTION COST: $12.50 members, $25 non-members
PUBLICATION LAG TIME: 9-12 months   STYLE SHEET: Yes
EARLY PUBLICATION OPTION: No   STYLE REQUIREMENTS: Chicago
REVIEW PERIOD: 3-6 months   CIRCULATION: 4,000
ACCEPTANCE RATE: 15-20%   REPRINT POLICY: Optional purchase

JOURNAL TITLE: Journal of Contemporary Psychotherapy

MANUSCRIPT ADDRESS: 97-29 64th Road
Forest Hills, NY 11374

MAJOR CONTENT AREAS: Behavior therapy, psychoanalysis, psychotherapy

ARTICLES USUALLY ACCEPTED: Theoretical, research, book review

TOPICS PREFERRED: New techniques and innovations, controversial issues

INAPPROPRIATE MANUSCRIPTS: Those which are inordinately statistical and dull

INDEXED/ABSTRACTED IN: PA, ASW, CCSBS

SUBSCRIPTION ADDRESS: 97-29 64th Road
Forest Hills, NY 11374

SUBSCRIPTION COST: $5
PUBLICATION LAG TIME: 3-10 months   STYLE SHEET: Yes
EARLY PUBLICATION OPTION: No   STYLE REQUIREMENTS: APA
REVIEW PERIOD: 2 months   CIRCULATION: 2,000
ACCEPTANCE RATE: 20%   REPRINT POLICY: 3 free copies of issue

JOURNAL TITLE: Journal of Counseling Psychology

MANUSCRIPT ADDRESS: Ralph F. Berdie, Editor, 408 Morrill Hall
University of Minnesota
Minneapolis, MN 55455

MAJOR CONTENT AREAS: Counseling

ARTICLES USUALLY ACCEPTED: Research, theoretical, and practice concerning
counseling and related activities; occasional
research and test review articles

TOPICS PREFERRED: Developmental aspects of counseling; diagnostic,
group, remedial, and therapeutic approaches

INAPPROPRIATE MANUSCRIPTS: None

INDEXED/ABSTRACTED IN: PA, ASW, BRI, BS, CSPA, CCSBS, CIJE, DSHA,
EI, ERA, PMA, RHEA, WSA

SUBSCRIPTION ADDRESS: APA Subscription Office
1200 17th Street, N.W.
Washington, DC 20036

SUBSCRIPTION COST: $20

PUBLICATION LAG TIME: 11 months   STYLE SHEET: No

EARLY PUBLICATION OPTION: No   STYLE REQUIREMENTS: APA

REVIEW PERIOD: Variable   CIRCULATION: 7,400

ACCEPTANCE RATE: 21%   REPRINT POLICY: 20 free

JOURNAL TITLE: Journal of Creative Behavior

MANUSCRIPT ADDRESS: Creative Education Foundation, Inc.
1300 Elmwood Avenue, Chase Hall
Buffalo, NY 14222

MAJOR CONTENT AREAS: Personality

ARTICLES USUALLY ACCEPTED: Research, review, theoretical

TOPICS PREFERRED: Creativity and problem-solving

INAPPROPRIATE MANUSCRIPTS: None

INDEXED/ABSTRACTED IN: PA, BS, CCSBS, CIJE, DSHA, EE, EI, EAA, ECEA,
LLBA, RHEA

SUBSCRIPTION ADDRESS: Creative Education Foundation, Inc.
1300 Elmwood Avenue, Chase Hall
Buffalo, NY 14222

SUBSCRIPTION COST: $9

PUBLICATION LAG TIME: 6 months   STYLE SHEET: Yes

EARLY PUBLICATION OPTION: No   STYLE REQUIREMENTS: APA

REVIEW PERIOD: 6 months   CIRCULATION: 5,000

ACCEPTANCE RATE: 30-40%   REPRINT POLICY: 2 free copies
of issue

JOURNAL TITLE: Journal of Cross-Cultural Psychology

MANUSCRIPT ADDRESS: Dept. of Psychology
Western Washington State College
Bellingham, WA 98225

MAJOR CONTENT AREAS: Almost all areas, provided that the cross-cultured method is employed

ARTICLES USUALLY ACCEPTED: Research, review, book review (by invitation)

TOPICS PREFERRED: Psychological variables as they are affected by culture

INAPPROPRIATE MANUSCRIPTS: Subcultural data with no comparison involving one or more additional cultures

INDEXED/ABSTRACTED IN: PA, AA, CCSBS, CIJE

SUBSCRIPTION ADDRESS: Sage Publications
275 South Beverly Drive
Beverly Hills, CA 90212

SUBSCRIPTION COST: $12 individual, $20 institutional
PUBLICATION LAG TIME: 6 months   STYLE SHEET: Yes
EARLY PUBLICATION OPTION: No   STYLE REQUIREMENTS: APA, Sage
REVIEW PERIOD: 6 weeks   CIRCULATION: 1,200
ACCEPTANCE RATE: 15%   REPRINT POLICY: 24 free

JOURNAL TITLE: Journal of Drug Education

MANUSCRIPT ADDRESS: Baywood Publishing Co., Inc.
43 Central Drive
Farmingdale, NY 11735

MAJOR CONTENT AREAS: Drug education

ARTICLES USUALLY ACCEPTED: Research, review, theoretical

TOPICS PREFERRED: Any in the area of drug education

INAPPROPRIATE MANUSCRIPTS: None

INDEXED/ABSTRACTED IN: PA, EM, ACP, BIS, CIJE

SUBSCRIPTION ADDRESS: Baywood Publishing Co., Inc.
43 Central Drive
Farmingdale, NY 11735

SUBSCRIPTION COST: $35
PUBLICATION LAG TIME: 9-12 months   STYLE SHEET: Yes
EARLY PUBLICATION OPTION: No   STYLE REQUIREMENTS: APA
REVIEW PERIOD: 4-6 weeks   CIRCULATION: 1,200
ACCEPTANCE RATE: 50%   REPRINT POLICY: 20 free

JOURNAL TITLE: Journal of Drug Issues

MANUSCRIPT ADDRESS: Richard L. Rachin, Editor
P. O. Box 4021
Tallahassee, FL 32303

MAJOR CONTENT AREAS: Drugs

ARTICLES USUALLY ACCEPTED: Reports of research completed and in
progress, articles on drug issues

TOPICS PREFERRED: Topical drug issues

INAPPROPRIATE MANUSCRIPTS: None

INDEXED/ABSTRACTED IN: PA, EM, ASW, CCSBS, HB, IPA, SSCI

SUBSCRIPTION ADDRESS: P. O. Box 4021
Tallahassee, FL 32303

SUBSCRIPTION COST:	$25		
PUBLICATION LAG TIME:	Up to 18 months	STYLE SHEET:	Yes
EARLY PUBLICATION OPTION:	Yes	STYLE REQUIREMENTS:	Own style
REVIEW PERIOD:	6 weeks	CIRCULATION:	Not given
ACCEPTANCE RATE:	33%	REPRINT POLICY:	2 free copies of issue

JOURNAL TITLE: Journal of Education for Social Work

MANUSCRIPT ADDRESS: 345 East 46th Street
New York, NY 10017

MAJOR CONTENT AREAS: Social work education

ARTICLES USUALLY ACCEPTED: Research, theoretical, program descriptions

TOPICS PREFERRED: Social work education

INAPPROPRIATE MANUSCRIPTS: Social work practice

INDEXED/ABSTRACTED IN: ASW, CCSBS, CIJE

SUBSCRIPTION ADDRESS: None - membership publication only

SUBSCRIPTION COST:	None		
PUBLICATION LAG TIME:	16-20 months	STYLE SHEET:	Yes
EARLY PUBLICATION OPTION:	Yes	STYLE REQUIREMENTS:	Chicago
REVIEW PERIOD:	2-3 months	CIRCULATION:	6,000
ACCEPTANCE RATE:	15-20%	REPRINT POLICY:	Optional purchase

JOURNAL TITLE: Journal of Educational Measurement

MANUSCRIPT ADDRESS: Richard M. Jaeger, Editor
FAO 295, University of South Florida
Tampa, FL 33620

MAJOR CONTENT AREAS: Educational

ARTICLES USUALLY ACCEPTED: Original research on theory or practice in educational measurement

TOPICS PREFERRED: Any topic within the broad area of applied educational measurement

INAPPROPRIATE MANUSCRIPTS: Purely statistical articles, statements of opinic articles on educational psychology

INDEXED/ABSTRACTED IN: PA, BS, CSPA, CCSBS, CIJE, EI, JHE, LLBA

SUBSCRIPTION ADDRESS: 206 South Kedzie Hall
Michigan State University
East Lansing, MI 48824

SUBSCRIPTION COST:	$15		
PUBLICATION LAG TIME:	11 months	STYLE SHEET:	No
EARLY PUBLICATION OPTION:	No	STYLE REQUIREMENTS:	APA
REVIEW PERIOD:	3 months	CIRCULATION:	3,300
ACCEPTANCE RATE:	12%	REPRINT POLICY:	Optional purchase

JOURNAL TITLE: Journal of Educational Psychology

MANUSCRIPT ADDRESS: Joanna Williams, Editor, P.O. Box 51
Teachers College, Columbia University
New York, NY 10027

MAJOR CONTENT AREAS: Educational

ARTICLES USUALLY ACCEPTED: Research and theoretical dealing with problems of learning and teaching and with the psychological development of the individual

TOPICS PREFERRED: Studies of the more complex types of behavior, especially related to educational settings

INAPPROPRIATE MANUSCRIPTS: None

INDEXED/ABSTRACTED IN: PA, BS, CSPA, CCSBS, CIJE, DSHA, EI, EAA, ECEA, JHE, LLBA, RHEA

SUBSCRIPTION ADDRESS: APA Subscription Office
1200 17th Street, N.W.
Washington, DC 20036

SUBSCRIPTION COST:	$30		
PUBLICATION LAG TIME:	11 months	STYLE SHEET:	No
EARLY PUBLICATION OPTION:	No	STYLE REQUIREMENTS:	APA
REVIEW PERIOD:	Variable	CIRCULATION:	6,500
ACCEPTANCE RATE:	26%	REPRINT POLICY:	20 free

JOURNAL TITLE: Journal of Educational Research

MANUSCRIPT ADDRESS: 4000 Albemarle Street, N.W.
Washington, DC 20016

MAJOR CONTENT AREAS: Educational

ARTICLES USUALLY ACCEPTED: Research

TOPICS PREFERRED: New guidelines are being established; consult journal

INAPPROPRIATE MANUSCRIPTS: Reviews of the literature

INDEXED/ABSTRACTED IN: PA, BS, CSPA, CCSBS, CIJE, EI, EAA, DSHA, IPAPL, IBSS, JHE, LLBA, RHEA, WSA, WAH

SUBSCRIPTION ADDRESS: 4000 Albemarle Street, N.W.
Washington, DC 20016

SUBSCRIPTION COST: $15
PUBLICATION LAG TIME: 3 months
EARLY PUBLICATION OPTION: No
REVIEW PERIOD: 3 months
ACCEPTANCE RATE: 15%

STYLE SHEET: Yes
STYLE REQUIREMENTS: Chicago
CIRCULATION: 6,400
REPRINT POLICY: Optional purchase

JOURNAL TITLE: Journal of Employment Counseling

MANUSCRIPT ADDRESS: David P. Meyer, Ph.D., Editor
School of Education, Oakland University
Rochester, MI 48063

MAJOR CONTENT AREAS: Counseling

ARTICLES USUALLY ACCEPTED: Research, review, theoretical, book review; most readers work in agencies with disadvantaged populations

TOPICS PREFERRED: Process evaluation of counseling, new counseling techniques

INAPPROPRIATE MANUSCRIPTS: Those dealing with school problems, processes, and populations

INDEXED/ABSTRACTED IN: PA, CCSBS, CIJE

SUBSCRIPTION ADDRESS: APGA
1607 New Hampshire Avenue, N.W.
Washington, DC 20009

SUBSCRIPTION COST: $10
PUBLICATION LAG TIME: 9-12 months
EARLY PUBLICATION OPTION: Yes
REVIEW PERIOD: 10 weeks
ACCEPTANCE RATE: 50%

STYLE SHEET: Yes
STYLE REQUIREMENTS: APA
CIRCULATION: 1,700
REPRINT POLICY: 5 free copies of issue

JOURNAL TITLE: Journal of the Experimental Analysis of Behavior

MANUSCRIPT ADDRESS: M. D. Zeiler
Dept. of Psychology, Emory University
Atlanta, GA 30322

MAJOR CONTENT AREAS: Comparative, experimental, learning, physiological

ARTICLES USUALLY ACCEPTED: Primarily research, occasionally review and theoretical

TOPICS PREFERRED: Operant conditioning

INAPPROPRIATE MANUSCRIPTS: Large group studies

INDEXED/ABSTRACTED IN: PA, CCSBS, DSHA, IPARL, LLBA

SUBSCRIPTION ADDRESS: Kay Dinsmoor
Dept. of Psychology, Indiana University
Bloomington, IN 47401

SUBSCRIPTION COST: $10 individual, $26 institutional

PUBLICATION LAG TIME: 3-6 months

EARLY PUBLICATION OPTION: No

REVIEW PERIOD: 2 months

ACCEPTANCE RATE: 50%

STYLE SHEET: Yes

STYLE REQUIREMENTS: APA

CIRCULATION: 4,047

REPRINT POLICY: 50 free

JOURNAL TITLE: Journal of Experimental Child Psychology

MANUSCRIPT ADDRESS: David S. Palermo, Editor
441 Moore Bldg., Pennsylvania State University
University Park, PA 16802

MAJOR CONTENT AREAS: Developmental, experimental, learning, mental retardation, perception, social

ARTICLES USUALLY ACCEPTED: Research, review, theoretical

TOPICS PREFERRED: Those which can be investigated empirically, allowing expansion of our psychological knowledge

INAPPROPRIATE MANUSCRIPTS: None

INDEXED/ABSTRACTED IN: PA, ASW, BS, CDA, CCSBS, CIJE, DSHA, EI, IBSS, LLBA

SUBSCRIPTION ADDRESS: Academic Press, Inc.
111 Fifth Avenue
New York, NY 10003

SUBSCRIPTION COST: $33.50

PUBLICATION LAG TIME: 6-12 months

EARLY PUBLICATION OPTION: No

REVIEW PERIOD: 4-8 weeks

ACCEPTANCE RATE: 25-30%

STYLE SHEET: Yes

STYLE REQUIREMENTS: APA

CIRCULATION: 1,200

REPRINT POLICY: 50 free

JOURNAL TITLE: The Journal of Experimental Education

MANUSCRIPT ADDRESS: John Schmid
University of Northern Colorado
Greeley, CO 80631

MAJOR CONTENT AREAS: Educational

ARTICLES USUALLY ACCEPTED: Research

TOPICS PREFERRED: Experimental education

INAPPROPRIATE MANUSCRIPTS: None

INDEXED/ABSTRACTED IN: PA, BS, CSPA, CCSBS, CIJE, DSHA, EI, EAA,
ECEA, JHE, LLBA, RHEA, WSA

SUBSCRIPTION ADDRESS: 4000 Albemarle Street, N.W.
Suite 302
Washington, DC 20016

SUBSCRIPTION COST: $10 individual, $12 institutional		
PUBLICATION LAG TIME: 18 months	STYLE SHEET:	Yes
EARLY PUBLICATION OPTION: Yes	STYLE REQUIREMENTS:	APA
REVIEW PERIOD: 3 months	CIRCULATION:	2,000
ACCEPTANCE RATE: 50%	REPRINT POLICY:	3 free

JOURNAL TITLE: Journal of Experimental Psychology: Animal
Behavior Processes

MANUSCRIPT ADDRESS: Allan R. Wagner, Editor
Dept. of Psychology, Yale University
New Haven, CT 06510

MAJOR CONTENT AREAS: Experimental, perception, learning

ARTICLES USUALLY ACCEPTED: Research on the basic mechanisms of perception,
learning, motivation, and performance, especially
as revealed in the behavior of infrahuman animals

TOPICS PREFERRED: None

INAPPROPRIATE MANUSCRIPTS: None

INDEXED/ABSTRACTED IN: PA, CIJE, DSHA, JHE, LLBA, RHEA

SUBSCRIPTION ADDRESS: APA Subscription Office
1200 17th Street, N.W.
Washington, DC 20036

SUBSCRIPTION COST: $16		
PUBLICATION LAG TIME: 7 months	STYLE SHEET:	No
EARLY PUBLICATION OPTION: No	STYLE REQUIREMENTS:	APA
REVIEW PERIOD: Variable	CIRCULATION:	4,100
ACCEPTANCE RATE: 20%	REPRINT POLICY:	20 free

JOURNAL TITLE: Journal of Experimental Psychology: General

MANUSCRIPT ADDRESS: Gregory A. Kimble, Editor
Dept of Psychology, University of Colorado
Boulder, CO 80302

MAJOR CONTENT AREAS: Experimental, general

ARTICLES USUALLY ACCEPTED: Research in any experimental area resulting in
a long, integrative report in an area of interest
to the entire community of experimental psychologi

TOPICS PREFERRED: Any in the experimental area

INAPPROPRIATE MANUSCRIPTS: None

INDEXED/ABSTRACTED IN: PA, CCSBS, CIJE, DSHA, JHE, LLBA, RHEA

SUBSCRIPTION ADDRESS: APA Subscription Office
1200 17th Street, N.W.
Washington, DC 20036

SUBSCRIPTION COST:	$16		
PUBLICATION LAG TIME:	8 months	STYLE SHEET:	No
EARLY PUBLICATION OPTION:	No	STYLE REQUIREMENTS:	APA
REVIEW PERIOD:	Variable	CIRCULATION:	4,300
ACCEPTANCE RATE:	44%	REPRINT POLICY:	20 free

JOURNAL TITLE: Journal of Experimental Psychology: Human
Learning and Memory

MANUSCRIPT ADDRESS: Lyle E. Bourne, Jr., Editor
Dept. of Psychology, University of Colorado
Boulder, CO 80302

MAJOR CONTENT AREAS: Experimental, learning

ARTICLES USUALLY ACCEPTED: Research on fundamental acquisition, retention,
and transfer processes in human behavior

TOPICS PREFERRED: None

INAPPROPRIATE MANUSCRIPTS: None

INDEXED/ABSTRACTED IN: PA, CCSBS, CIJE, DSHA, JHE, LLBA, RHEA

SUBSCRIPTION ADDRESS: APA Subscription Office
1200 17th Street, N.W.
Washington, DC 20036

SUBSCRIPTION COST:	$28		
PUBLICATION LAG TIME:	9 months	STYLE SHEET:	No
EARLY PUBLICATION OPTION:	No	STYLE REQUIREMENTS:	APA
REVIEW PERIOD:	Variable	CIRCULATION:	4,400
ACCEPTANCE RATE:	23%	REPRINT POLICY:	20 free

JOURNAL TITLE: Journal of Experimental Psychology: Human Perception and Performance

MANUSCRIPT ADDRESS: Michael I. Posner, Editor
Dept. of Psychology, University of Oregon
Eugene, OR 97403

MAJOR CONTENT AREAS: Experimental, perception

ARTICLES USUALLY ACCEPTED: Research designed to foster understanding of information-processing operations and their relation to experience and performance

TOPICS PREFERRED: Information-processing

INAPPROPRIATE MANUSCRIPTS: None

INDEXED/ABSTRACTED IN: PA, CCSBS, CIJE, DSHA, JHE, LLBA, RHEA

SUBSCRIPTION ADDRESS: APA Subscription Office
1200 17th Street, N.W.
Washington, DC 20036

SUBSCRIPTION COST: $16
PUBLICATION LAG TIME: 9 months
EARLY PUBLICATION OPTION: No
REVIEW PERIOD: Variable
ACCEPTANCE RATE: 18%

STYLE SHEET: No
STYLE REQUIREMENTS: APA
CIRCULATION: 4,400
REPRINT POLICY: 20 free

JOURNAL TITLE: Journal of Experimental Social Psychology

MANUSCRIPT ADDRESS: A. Doob, Editor
Dept. of Psychology, University of Toronto
Toronto, Ontario, Canada

MAJOR CONTENT AREAS: Social

ARTICLES USUALLY ACCEPTED: Research, review, theoretical, methodological notes

TOPICS PREFERRED: None

INAPPROPRIATE MANUSCRIPTS: None

INDEXED/ABSTRACTED IN: PA, CSPA, CCSBS, CIJE, WSA

SUBSCRIPTION ADDRESS: Academic Press
111 Fifth Avenue
New York, NY 10003

SUBSCRIPTION COST: $40
PUBLICATION LAG TIME: 8 months
EARLY PUBLICATION OPTION: No
REVIEW PERIOD: 6 weeks
ACCEPTANCE RATE: 15%

STYLE SHEET: No
STYLE REQUIREMENTS: APA
CIRCULATION: Not given
REPRINT POLICY: Optional purchase

JOURNAL TITLE: Journal of Extension

MANUSCRIPT ADDRESS: Jerry Parsons, Editor
310 Poe Hall, North Carolina State University
Raleigh, NC 27606

MAJOR CONTENT AREAS: Adult education

ARTICLES USUALLY ACCEPTED: Research emphasizing how to apply the results, program descriptions, personal opinions

TOPICS PREFERRED: Those that will help adult educators with action programs

INAPPROPRIATE MANUSCRIPTS: Detailed methodology and research techniques

INDEXED/ABSTRACTED IN: ASW, CCSBS, CIJE, PHRA

SUBSCRIPTION ADDRESS: 605 Extension Building
432 N. Lake Street
Madison, WI 53706

SUBSCRIPTION COST: $9 individual, $4.50 institutional

PUBLICATION LAG TIME: 1 year   STYLE SHEET: Yes
EARLY PUBLICATION OPTION: No   STYLE REQUIREMENTS: Chicago
REVIEW PERIOD: 2 months   CIRCULATION: 7,200
ACCEPTANCE RATE: 50%   REPRINT POLICY: 5 free

JOURNAL TITLE: Journal of Family Counseling

MANUSCRIPT ADDRESS: The Editor
Box 2124 Hillside Manor
New Hyde Park, NY 11040

MAJOR CONTENT AREAS: Behavior therapy, clinical, counseling, couple and family therapy methodology

ARTICLES USUALLY ACCEPTED: Applied research, methodology, applied theory; book reviews should be sent to Dr. Sauber, Review Editor, 17 Friendship St., Newport, RI 02840

TOPICS PREFERRED: New modalities in family therapy

INAPPROPRIATE MANUSCRIPTS: Sex therapy, "Ann Landers" type articles, pep talks to improve marriage, out-of-date articles

INDEXED/ABSTRACTED IN: PA, ASW

SUBSCRIPTION ADDRESS: Transaction, Inc.
Rutgers University
New Brunswick, NJ 08903

SUBSCRIPTION COST: $8 individual, $14 institutional

PUBLICATION LAG TIME: 3-4 months   STYLE SHEET: Yes
EARLY PUBLICATION OPTION: Yes   STYLE REQUIREMENTS: APA,Chicago
REVIEW PERIOD: 3-4 months   CIRCULATION: 2,500
ACCEPTANCE RATE: 60%   REPRINT POLICY: 2 free copies of issue

JOURNAL TITLE: The Journal of Family Practice

MANUSCRIPT ADDRESS: Department of Family Practice
School of Medicine, University of California
Davis, CA 95616

MAJOR CONTENT AREAS: Behavioral science in family practice,
clinical research

ARTICLES USUALLY ACCEPTED: Research, clinical, educational

TOPICS PREFERRED: Behavioral science in family practice

INAPPROPRIATE MANUSCRIPTS: Excessively general ones that do not
present data or relate to a clinical context

INDEXED/ABSTRACTED IN: IM

SUBSCRIPTION ADDRESS: Appleton-Century-Crofts
292 Madison Avenue
New York, NY 10017

SUBSCRIPTION COST:	$25		
PUBLICATION LAG TIME:	4-6 months	STYLE SHEET:	Yes
EARLY PUBLICATION OPTION:	Yes	STYLE REQUIREMENTS:	Ind. Med.
REVIEW PERIOD:	8 weeks	CIRCULATION:	70,000
ACCEPTANCE RATE:	50%	REPRINT POLICY:	50 free

JOURNAL TITLE: The Journal of General Psychology

MANUSCRIPT ADDRESS: The Managing Editor, The Journal Press
2 Commercial St., P. O. Box 543
Provincetown, MA 02657

MAJOR CONTENT AREAS: Comparative, engineering, general, history,
learning, perception, physiological, psychometrics

ARTICLES USUALLY ACCEPTED: Primarily research; new authors should submit
their credentials

TOPICS PREFERRED: Comparative, physiological, and general
psychology

INAPPROPRIATE MANUSCRIPTS: Essays more suitable for popular magazines,
articles not conforming to submission requirements

INDEXED/ABSTRACTED IN: PA, CCSBS, CIJE, DSHA, LLBA, PRG, WSA, WAH

SUBSCRIPTION ADDRESS: The Journal Press
2 Commercial St., P. O. Box 543
Provincetown, MA 02657

SUBSCRIPTION COST:	$30		
PUBLICATION LAG TIME:	16 months	STYLE SHEET:	Yes
EARLY PUBLICATION OPTION:	No	STYLE REQUIREMENTS:	Journal Press
REVIEW PERIOD:	1 month	CIRCULATION:	1,693
ACCEPTANCE RATE:	40%	REPRINT POLICY:	100 free

JOURNAL TITLE: Journal of Genetic Psychology

MANUSCRIPT ADDRESS: The Managing Editor, The Journal Press
2 Commercial Street, P. O. Box 543
Provincetown, MA 02657

MAJOR CONTENT AREAS: Clinical, developmental, mental retardation

ARTICLES USUALLY ACCEPTED: Developmental research, clinical articles;
new authors should submit their credentials

TOPICS PREFERRED: Aging

INAPPROPRIATE MANUSCRIPTS: Those not conforming to submission
requirements

INDEXED/ABSTRACTED IN: PA, ASW, BI, BS, CSPA, CCSBS, CIJE, DSHA,
ECEA, IBSS, LLBA, PRG, RHEA, WSA

SUBSCRIPTION ADDRESS: The Journal Press
2 Commercial Street, P. O. Box 543
Provincetown, MA 02657

SUBSCRIPTION COST: $30
PUBLICATION LAG TIME: 19 months   STYLE SHEET: Yes
EARLY PUBLICATION OPTION: No   STYLE REQUIREMENTS: Journal Press
REVIEW PERIOD: 1 month   CIRCULATION: 1,616
ACCEPTANCE RATE: 40%   REPRINT POLICY: 100 free

JOURNAL TITLE: Journal of Gerontology

MANUSCRIPT ADDRESS: Harold Brody, Ph.D., M.D., Dept of Anatomical
Sciences, State Univ. of NY at Buffalo,
317 Farber Hall, Buffalo, NY 14214

MAJOR CONTENT AREAS: All areas of gerontology

ARTICLES USUALLY ACCEPTED: Research, review, book review

TOPICS PREFERRED: Experimental material in gerontology from
psychology, social gerontology, & medicine

INAPPROPRIATE MANUSCRIPTS: Non-experimental material, non-aging
research

INDEXED/ABSTRACTED IN: PA, IM, ASW, BI, BA, CCSBS, ERA, JHE, PAISB

SUBSCRIPTION ADDRESS: Gerontological Society
Suite 520, One Dupont Circle
Washington, DC 20036

SUBSCRIPTION COST: $30
PUBLICATION LAG TIME: 4-6 months   STYLE SHEET: Yes
EARLY PUBLICATION OPTION: No   STYLE REQUIREMENTS: Own style
REVIEW PERIOD: 2-4 weeks   CIRCULATION: 6,400
ACCEPTANCE RATE: 30-40%   REPRINT POLICY: Optional
purchase

JOURNAL TITLE: Journal of Geriatric Psychiatry

MANUSCRIPT ADDRESS: 90 Forest Avenue
West Newton, MA 02165

MAJOR CONTENT AREAS: Geriatrics, behavior therapy, psychoanalysis, psychotherapy

ARTICLES USUALLY ACCEPTED: Research, review, theoretical

TOPICS PREFERRED: Geriatrics

INAPPROPRIATE MANUSCRIPTS: None

INDEXED/ABSTRACTED IN: IM, CCSBS, LLBA

SUBSCRIPTION ADDRESS: 239 Park Avenue South
New York, NY 10003

SUBSCRIPTION COST: $12 individual, $20 institutional
PUBLICATION LAG TIME: Less than 1 year   STYLE SHEET: Yes
EARLY PUBLICATION OPTION: No   STYLE REQUIREMENTS: Own style
REVIEW PERIOD: 2-3 months   CIRCULATION: 1,500
ACCEPTANCE RATE: 30-40%   REPRINT POLICY: purchase required

JOURNAL TITLE: Journal of Graphonanalysis

MANUSCRIPT ADDRESS: 325 West Jackson Blvd.
Chicago, IL 60606

MAJOR CONTENT AREAS: All areas as related to graphoanalysis

ARTICLES USUALLY ACCEPTED: Research, theoretical

TOPICS PREFERRED: None

INAPPROPRIATE MANUSCRIPTS: None

INDEXED/ABSTRACTED IN: Not given

SUBSCRIPTION ADDRESS: 325 West Jackson Blvd.
Chicago, IL 60606

SUBSCRIPTION COST: $10 (members only)
PUBLICATION LAG TIME: 2 months   STYLE SHEET: Not given
EARLY PUBLICATION OPTION: No   STYLE REQUIREMENTS: APA
REVIEW PERIOD: 1 month   CIRCULATION: 50,000
ACCEPTANCE RATE: Not given   REPRINT POLICY: Not given

JOURNAL TITLE: Journal on the Handicapped Child

MANUSCRIPT ADDRESS: West Virginia Commission on Mental Retardation
State Capitol
Charleston, WV 25305

MAJOR CONTENT AREAS: Counseling, developmental, educational, mental
retardation, recreation, community

ARTICLES USUALLY ACCEPTED: Issues are devoted to special topics; publication
restricted to West Virginia writers about West
Virginia programs for the handicapped

TOPICS PREFERRED: Those of interest to special education people

INAPPROPRIATE MANUSCRIPTS: Topics other than MR, DD, or other handicaps

INDEXED/ABSTRACTED IN: None

SUBSCRIPTION ADDRESS: No subscription

SUBSCRIPTION COST: No charge
PUBLICATION LAG TIME: 2 months
EARLY PUBLICATION OPTION: Yes
REVIEW PERIOD: 2 weeks
ACCEPTANCE RATE: 75%

STYLE SHEET: No
STYLE REQUIREMENTS: APA
CIRCULATION: 2,200
REPRINT POLICY: 2-10 free

JOURNAL TITLE: Journal of Health and Social Behavior

MANUSCRIPT ADDRESS: Mary E. W. Goss, Editor
Dept. of Public Health, Cornell Univ.
Medical College, Ithaca, NY 10021

MAJOR CONTENT AREAS: Social, personality

ARTICLES USUALLY ACCEPTED: Research, theoretical

TOPICS PREFERRED: Social factors relating to health and illness;
health occupations, organizations and institutions

INAPPROPRIATE MANUSCRIPTS: None

INDEXED/ABSTRACTED IN: PA, IM, EM, ASW, AHMS, BI, BIS, BS, CSPA,
CCSBS, ECEA, IBSS, SSHI, WSA

SUBSCRIPTION ADDRESS: American Sociological Association
1722 N Street, N. W.
Washington, DC 20036

SUBSCRIPTION COST: $12 individual, $16 institutional
PUBLICATION LAG TIME: 9-12 months
EARLY PUBLICATION OPTION: No
REVIEW PERIOD: 3 months
ACCEPTANCE RATE: 16%

STYLE SHEET: Yes
STYLE REQUIREMENTS: APA, ASA
CIRCULATION: 2,000
REPRINT POLICY: 1 free copy
of issue

JOURNAL TITLE: Journal of the History of the Behavioral Sciences

MANUSCRIPT ADDRESS: Barbara Ross, Editor, Psychology Dept. I Univ. of Massachusetts, Harbor Campus Boston, MA 02125

MAJOR CONTENT AREAS: History

ARTICLES USUALLY ACCEPTED: Book reviews by senior men in their disciplines, historical studies

TOPICS PREFERRED: None

INAPPROPRIATE MANUSCRIPTS: No particular type; if received, an appropriate journal is recommended

INDEXED/ABSTRACTED IN: PA, SA, AA, BI, BS, CCSBS, HA, PRG

SUBSCRIPTION ADDRESS: 4 Conant Square Brandon, VT 05733

SUBSCRIPTION COST:	$15 individual, $25 institutional		
PUBLICATION LAG TIME:	9 months	STYLE SHEET:	Yes
EARLY PUBLICATION OPTION:	Yes	STYLE REQUIREMENTS:	Chicago
REVIEW PERIOD:	2-4 months	CIRCULATION:	971
ACCEPTANCE RATE:	40-50%	REPRINT POLICY:	Optional purchase

JOURNAL TITLE: Journal of Homosexuality

MANUSCRIPT ADDRESS: Charles Silverstein, Ph.D., Director Institute for Human Identity, 490 West End Ave. New York, NY 10024

MAJOR CONTENT AREAS: All areas as related to homosexuality, including legal and social aspects

ARTICLES USUALLY ACCEPTED: Research, review, theoretical, practice

TOPICS PREFERRED: Social and personality

INAPPROPRIATE MANUSCRIPTS: Poems, personal accounts, single psychoanalytic case studies, those with poor methodology

INDEXED/ABSTRACTED IN: PA, SA, CCSBS, PRG

SUBSCRIPTION ADDRESS: The Haworth Press 174 Fifth Avenue New York, NY 10010

SUBSCRIPTION COST:	$15 individual, $30 institutional		
PUBLICATION LAG TIME:	6-9 months	STYLE SHEET:	Yes
EARLY PUBLICATION OPTION:	Yes	STYLE REQUIREMENTS:	APA
REVIEW PERIOD:	2-8 weeks	CIRCULATION:	4,000
ACCEPTANCE RATE:	5%	REPRINT POLICY:	50 free

JOURNAL TITLE: Journal of Human Stress

MANUSCRIPT ADDRESS: 82 Cochituate Road
Framingham, MA 01701

MAJOR CONTENT AREAS: Behavior therapy, clinical, experimental,
physiological, methodology as related to stress

ARTICLES USUALLY ACCEPTED: Original research on human stress with hard
data

TOPICS PREFERRED: Human stress

INAPPROPRIATE MANUSCRIPTS: Animal studies

INDEXED/ABSTRACTED IN: IM (applied for)

SUBSCRIPTION ADDRESS: 82 Cochituate Road
Framingham, MA 01701

SUBSCRIPTION COST: $9
PUBLICATION LAG TIME: 3 months
EARLY PUBLICATION OPTION: No
REVIEW PERIOD: 3-8 weeks
ACCEPTANCE RATE: Not given

STYLE SHEET: Yes
STYLE REQUIREMENTS: Ind. Med.
CIRCULATION: 9,000
REPRINT POLICY: 25 free copies
of issue

JOURNAL TITLE: Journal of Humanistic Psychology

MANUSCRIPT ADDRESS: Suite 205
1314 Westwood Blvd.
Los Angeles, CA 90024

MAJOR CONTENT AREAS: Clinical, personality, psychotherapy

ARTICLES USUALLY ACCEPTED: Experiential, theoretical, research; also
personal essays, reports of applications,
humanistic analyses of contemporary culture

TOPICS PREFERRED: Authenticity, encounter, self-actualization,
being-motivation, personal growth, love, identity

INAPPROPRIATE MANUSCRIPTS: None

INDEXED/ABSTRACTED IN: PA, BI, CCSBS, CIJE, LLBA, PRAJ, PHRA

SUBSCRIPTION ADDRESS: 325 Ninth Street
San Francisco, CA 94103

SUBSCRIPTION COST: $10 individual, $14 institutional
PUBLICATION LAG TIME: 1-2 years
EARLY PUBLICATION OPTION: Yes
REVIEW PERIOD: 1-12 weeks
ACCEPTANCE RATE: 10%

STYLE SHEET: Yes
STYLE REQUIREMENTS: APA
CIRCULATION: 500
REPRINT POLICY: 100 free

JOURNAL TITLE: Journal of Individual Psychology

MANUSCRIPT ADDRESS: Dr. Guy J. Manaster
College of Education, University of Texas
Austin, TX 78712

MAJOR CONTENT AREAS: All areas as related to Adlerian psychology

ARTICLES USUALLY ACCEPTED: Research, review, theoretical, book review

TOPICS PREFERRED: Adlerian case histories, literary criticism,
psychohistory, testing Adlerian hypotheses

INAPPROPRIATE MANUSCRIPTS: Although not inappropriate, too many papers
on birth order are received

INDEXED/ABSTRACTED IN: PA, ASW, CSPA, CCSBS, IBSS, PRAJ

SUBSCRIPTION ADDRESS: Dr. H. L. Ansbacher
John Dewey Hall, University of Vermont
Burlington, VT 05401

SUBSCRIPTION COST: $7

PUBLICATION LAG TIME: Less than 1 year   STYLE SHEET: No

EARLY PUBLICATION OPTION: No   STYLE REQUIREMENTS: APA

REVIEW PERIOD: 2-3 months   CIRCULATION: 1,800

ACCEPTANCE RATE: 35%   REPRINT POLICY: Optional
purchase

JOURNAL TITLE: Journal of Instructional Psychology

MANUSCRIPT ADDRESS: P. O. Box 5630
Milwaukee, WI 53211

MAJOR CONTENT AREAS: Educational, learning, mental retardation

ARTICLES USUALLY ACCEPTED: Research, theoretical

TOPICS PREFERRED: Bilingual and multiculture issues

INAPPROPRIATE MANUSCRIPTS: Clinical reports

INDEXED/ABSTRACTED IN: PA

SUBSCRIPTION ADDRESS: P. O. Box 5630
Milwaukee, WI 53211

SUBSCRIPTION COST: $7.50 individual, $10 institutional

PUBLICATION LAG TIME: 6-12 months   STYLE SHEET: Yes

EARLY PUBLICATION OPTION: No   STYLE REQUIREMENTS: APA

REVIEW PERIOD: 2 months   CIRCULATION: 150

ACCEPTANCE RATE: 50%   REPRINT POLICY: 3 free copies
of issue

JOURNAL TITLE: Journal of Jewish Communal Service

MANUSCRIPT ADDRESS: 33 West 60th Street
New York, NY 10023

MAJOR CONTENT AREAS: Behavior therapy, psychotherapy, social work

ARTICLES USUALLY ACCEPTED: Research, theoretical, practice

TOPICS PREFERRED: Practice in clinical and community work

INAPPROPRIATE MANUSCRIPTS: Those written as class assignments by graduate students

INDEXED/ABSTRACTED IN: ASW, IPAPL, IBSS, PAISB, WAH

SUBSCRIPTION ADDRESS: 15 East 26th Street
New York, NY 10010

SUBSCRIPTION COST: $9.50
PUBLICATION LAG TIME: 6 months
EARLY PUBLICATION OPTION: Yes
REVIEW PERIOD: 3-4 months
ACCEPTANCE RATE: 15%

STYLE SHEET: Yes
STYLE REQUIREMENTS: Chicago
CIRCULATION: 2,900
REPRINT POLICY: 3 free

JOURNAL TITLE: Journal of Learning Disabilities

MANUSCRIPT ADDRESS: P.E. Lane, Editor
101 E. Ontario Street
Chicago, IL 60611

MAJOR CONTENT AREAS: Behavior therapy, clinical, counseling, developmental, educational, learning, methodolog

ARTICLES USUALLY ACCEPTED: Review, research, clinical application, theoretical, book review, viewpoint, program description

TOPICS PREFERRED: Language and learning disorders, intervention techniques

INAPPROPRIATE MANUSCRIPTS: Statistical manipulations with diagnostic test results which do not help LD children

INDEXED/ABSTRACTED IN: PA, EM, BA, BRI, CDA, CCSBS, CIJE, DSHA, EI, ECEA, LLBA, PRG, RL

SUBSCRIPTION ADDRESS: Circulation Dept.
101 E. Ontario St.
Chicago, IL 60611

SUBSCRIPTION COST: $12
PUBLICATION LAG TIME: 6-8 months
EARLY PUBLICATION OPTION: No
REVIEW PERIOD: 3 months
ACCEPTANCE RATE: 20%

STYLE SHEET: Yes
STYLE REQUIREMENTS: APA
CIRCULATION: 18,000
REPRINT POLICY: 5 free copies of issue

JOURNAL TITLE: Journal of Leisure Research

MANUSCRIPT ADDRESS: Dr. Arlin Epperson, Editor, Dept. of RPA
School of Pub. Com. Serv., 606 Clark Hall
Univ. of Mo., Columbia, MO 65201

MAJOR CONTENT AREAS: Leisure, outdoor recreation, and related
topics

ARTICLES USUALLY ACCEPTED: Research, model development, research notes,
solicited book review

TOPICS PREFERRED: Methodology, behavioral research, park and
resources management, administration

INAPPROPRIATE MANUSCRIPTS: Sports and sport psychology

INDEXED/ABSTRACTED IN: PA, CCSBS, CIJE, EI

SUBSCRIPTION ADDRESS: National Recreation and Park Association
1601 North Kent St.
Arlington, VA 22209

SUBSCRIPTION COST: $10		
PUBLICATION LAG TIME: 3-6 months	STYLE SHEET: Yes	
EARLY PUBLICATION OPTION: No	STYLE REQUIREMENTS: Chicago	
REVIEW PERIOD: 2-3 months	CIRCULATION: 1,700	
ACCEPTANCE RATE: 25-40%	REPRINT POLICY: 2 free	

JOURNAL TITLE: Journal of Marketing

MANUSCRIPT ADDRESS: Suite 605
One Gateway Center
Newton, MA 02158

MAJOR CONTENT AREAS: Marketing, management

ARTICLES USUALLY ACCEPTED: Research, theoretical, marketing applications

TOPICS PREFERRED: Application of marketing theory to business
problems

INAPPROPRIATE MANUSCRIPTS: Reinventing the wheel

INDEXED/ABSTRACTED IN: PA, ADPA, BI, BRI, BS, BPI, CCSBS, CICF, EE,
IPAPL, IBSS, ILD, JEL, JHE, MA, MI, MDA,
PAISB, TC, TMA

SUBSCRIPTION ADDRESS: American Marketing Association
225 South Riverside Plaza
Chicago, IL 60606

SUBSCRIPTION COST: $18 individual, $30 institutional		
PUBLICATION LAG TIME: 3-6 months	STYLE SHEET: Yes	
EARLY PUBLICATION OPTION: No	STYLE REQUIREMENTS: Chicago	
REVIEW PERIOD: 3 months	CIRCULATION: 20,000	
ACCEPTANCE RATE: 15%	REPRINT POLICY: Optional purchase	

JOURNAL TITLE: Journal of Marketing Research

MANUSCRIPT ADDRESS: Harper Boyd, Jr., Editor
College of Business Admin., Univ. of Arkansas
Fayetteville, AR 72701

MAJOR CONTENT AREAS: Marketing research

ARTICLES USUALLY ACCEPTED: Research, theoretical, and computer abstracts
in the field of marketing research

TOPICS PREFERRED: Methodology and the philosophical, conceptual,
and technical problems of research in marketing

INAPPROPRIATE MANUSCRIPTS: None

INDEXED/ABSTRACTED IN: PA, BS, BPI, CCSBS, CICF, EE, JEL, JHE, MI,
TC

SUBSCRIPTION ADDRESS: American Marketing Association
222 South Riverside Plaza
Chicago, IL 60606

SUBSCRIPTION COST: $18
PUBLICATION LAG TIME: 3 months
EARLY PUBLICATION OPTION: No
REVIEW PERIOD: 3 months
ACCEPTANCE RATE: 30%

STYLE SHEET: Yes
STYLE REQUIREMENTS: Own style
CIRCULATION: 12,000
REPRINT POLICY: Optional
purchase

JOURNAL TITLE: Journal of Marriage and the Family

MANUSCRIPT ADDRESS: Felix M. Berardo, Ph.D., Editor
Dept. of Sociology, University of Florida
Gainesville, FL 32611

MAJOR CONTENT AREAS: Community, developmental, social

ARTICLES USUALLY ACCEPTED: Original theory, research, interpretation,
and critical discussion of materials related
to marriage and the family

TOPICS PREFERRED: Theoretical and research articles on marriage
and family variables

INAPPROPRIATE MANUSCRIPTS: Clinical diagnoses, polemic essays, primarily
medical articles

INDEXED/ABSTRACTED IN: PA, ASW, SA, APAIS, BRI, BS, CSPA, CCSBS,
CIJE, EI, ECEA, GSSRPL, IBSS, IBSSSCA, JHE,
SSHI, WSA

SUBSCRIPTION ADDRESS: National Council on Family Relations
1219 University Avenue Southeast
Minneapolis, MN 55414

SUBSCRIPTION COST: $20
PUBLICATION LAG TIME: 6-7 months
EARLY PUBLICATION OPTION: Yes
REVIEW PERIOD: 8-10 weeks
ACCEPTANCE RATE: 13%

STYLE SHEET: No
STYLE REQUIREMENTS: APA
CIRCULATION: 11,000
REPRINT POLICY: Optional
purchase

JOURNAL TITLE: Journal of Marriage and Family Counseling

MANUSCRIPT ADDRESS: William C. Nichols, Ed.D., Editor
Sandels Building, Florida State University
Tallahassee, FL 32306

MAJOR CONTENT AREAS: Psychotherapy, marriage & family therapy counseling

ARTICLES USUALLY ACCEPTED: Clinical, research, theoretical

TOPICS PREFERRED: Marriage and family therapy and related areas

INAPPROPRIATE MANUSCRIPTS: Academic materials, materials from non-clinicians, individual psychotherapy

INDEXED/ABSTRACTED IN: PA, ASW, SA

SUBSCRIPTION ADDRESS: 225 Yale Avenue
Claremont, CA 91711

SUBSCRIPTION COST: $15 individual, $25 institutional
PUBLICATION LAG TIME: 3 months (minimum) STYLE SHEET: Yes
EARLY PUBLICATION OPTION: No STYLE REQUIREMENTS: APA
REVIEW PERIOD: 2-3 months CIRCULATION: 5,500
ACCEPTANCE RATE: 30% REPRINT POLICY: Optional purchase

JOURNAL TITLE: Journal of Mathematical Psychology

MANUSCRIPT ADDRESS: Dr. William H. Batchelder, Editor
School of Social Sciences, Univ. of California
Irvine, CA 92664

MAJOR CONTENT AREAS: Most experimental areas without a major application of mathematical formalism

ARTICLES USUALLY ACCEPTED: Theoretical and empirical research in all areas of mathematical psychology

TOPICS PREFERRED: Mathematical models, foundations of psychological measurement

INAPPROPRIATE MANUSCRIPTS: Expansive, quasi-philosophical, mathematical schemes from non-professional psychologists

INDEXED/ABSTRACTED IN: PA, BI, BA, CCSBS, LLBA, SSCI

SUBSCRIPTION ADDRESS: Academic Press, Inc.
111 Fifth Avenue
New York, NY 10003

SUBSCRIPTION COST: $16.50 individual, $33 institutional
PUBLICATION LAG TIME: 6-12 months STYLE SHEET: Yes
EARLY PUBLICATION OPTION: No STYLE REQUIREMENTS: APA
REVIEW PERIOD: 2-5 months CIRCULATION: 1,200
ACCEPTANCE RATE: 30-40% REPRINT POLICY: 50 free

JOURNAL TITLE: Journal of Mental Deficiency Research

MANUSCRIPT ADDRESS: Dr. B. W. Richards, Editor
St. Lawrence's Hospital
Caterham, Surrey CR3 5YA, England

MAJOR CONTENT AREAS: Mental retardation, behavior therapy, developmental

ARTICLES USUALLY ACCEPTED: Research, case studies

TOPICS PREFERRED: Mental deficiency research

INAPPROPRIATE MANUSCRIPTS: None

INDEXED/ABSTRACTED IN: PA, EM, BEI, CCSBS, CIJE, ECEA, LLBA

SUBSCRIPTION ADDRESS: National Society for Mentally Handicapped
Children, Pembridge Hall, 17 Pembridge Square
London W2 4EP, England

SUBSCRIPTION COST:	$30		
PUBLICATION LAG TIME:	3-6 months	STYLE SHEET:	Yes
EARLY PUBLICATION OPTION:	No	STYLE REQUIREMENTS:	Own style
REVIEW PERIOD:	1 month	CIRCULATION:	1,000
ACCEPTANCE RATE:	75%	REPRINT POLICY:	50 free

JOURNAL TITLE: Journal of Mental Health

MANUSCRIPT ADDRESS: Room 426, Colorado Building
1341 G Street, N.W.
Washington, DC 20005

MAJOR CONTENT AREAS: Neurotics Anonymous

ARTICLES USUALLY ACCEPTED: Only those submitted by members of Neurotics
Anonymous or those about the program

TOPICS PREFERRED: Treatment of mental illness

INAPPROPRIATE MANUSCRIPTS: None

INDEXED/ABSTRACTED IN: PA

SUBSCRIPTION ADDRESS: Room 426 Colorado Building
1341 G Street, N.W.
Washington, DC 20005

SUBSCRIPTION COST:	$4		
PUBLICATION LAG TIME:	N/A	STYLE SHEET:	N/A
EARLY PUBLICATION OPTION:	N/A	STYLE REQUIREMENTS:	None
REVIEW PERIOD:	N/A	CIRCULATION:	1,000
ACCEPTANCE RATE:	N/A	REPRINT POLICY:	3 free

JOURNAL TITLE: Journal of Mental Health Administration

MANUSCRIPT ADDRESS: Dr. Warren A. Thompson, Missouri Institute of Psychiatry, 5400 Arsenal Street St. Louis, MO 63139

MAJOR CONTENT AREAS: Organizational, mental health administration

ARTICLES USUALLY ACCEPTED: Applied research with direct application to administration in mental health and related human service delivery systems

TOPICS PREFERRED: Administration in mental health, developmental disabilities, and community mental health

INAPPROPRIATE MANUSCRIPTS: Clinical topics

INDEXED/ABSTRACTED IN: Not given

SUBSCRIPTION ADDRESS: AMHA 4131 North Grand River Avenue, Suite 3 Lansing, MI 48906

SUBSCRIPTION COST: $10

PUBLICATION LAG TIME: 10 months   STYLE SHEET: Not given

EARLY PUBLICATION OPTION: Not given   STYLE REQUIREMENTS: Not given

REVIEW PERIOD: 8 months   CIRCULATION: 2,000

ACCEPTANCE RATE: 20%   REPRINT POLICY: 5 free

JOURNAL TITLE: Journal of Motor Behavior

MANUSCRIPT ADDRESS: Dr. Richard A. Schmidt, Editor, Dept of Physical Education, University of Southern California Los Angeles, CA 90007

MAJOR CONTENT AREAS: Educational, engineering, experimental, industrial, learning, social

ARTICLES USUALLY ACCEPTED: Research, review, theoretical

TOPICS PREFERRED: Motor performance and learning

INAPPROPRIATE MANUSCRIPTS: Eye movement work

INDEXED/ABSTRACTED IN: PA, CCSBS, LLBA

SUBSCRIPTION ADDRESS: Journal Publishing Affiliates 727 De La Guerra Plaza Santa Barbara, CA 93101

SUBSCRIPTION COST: $10 individual, $25 institutional

PUBLICATION LAG TIME: 3-4 months   STYLE SHEET: No

EARLY PUBLICATION OPTION: No   STYLE REQUIREMENTS: APA

REVIEW PERIOD: 8-10 weeks   CIRCULATION: 1,000

ACCEPTANCE RATE: 50%   REPRINT POLICY: Optional purchase

JOURNAL TITLE: Journal of Multivariate Experimental
         Personality and Clinical Psychology
MANUSCRIPT ADDRESS: Dr. Charles Burdsal, Editor
         Dept. of Psychology #34, Wichita State Univ.
         Wichita, KS 67208
MAJOR CONTENT AREAS: Personality, clinical

ARTICLES USUALLY ACCEPTED: Research, review, theoretical, and
         occasional book review

TOPICS PREFERRED: Personality and clinical articles utilizing
         multivariate methodology
INAPPROPRIATE MANUSCRIPTS: Literature reviews not related to multivariates

INDEXED/ABSTRACTED IN: PA (applied for)

SUBSCRIPTION ADDRESS: Dr. Charles Burdsal, Editor
         Dept. of Psychology #34, Wichita State Univ.
         Wichita, KS 67208
SUBSCRIPTION COST: $16
PUBLICATION LAG TIME: 6-12 months   STYLE SHEET: Yes
EARLY PUBLICATION OPTION: No   STYLE REQUIREMENTS: APA
REVIEW PERIOD: 6 weeks   CIRCULATION: 250
ACCEPTANCE RATE: 50%   REPRINT POLICY: 50 free

JOURNAL TITLE: Journal of Music Therapy

MANUSCRIPT ADDRESS: P. O. Box 610
         Lawrence, KS 66044

MAJOR CONTENT AREAS: All areas as related to music therapy

ARTICLES USUALLY ACCEPTED: Research, theoretical, clinical

TOPICS PREFERRED: Music therapy

INAPPROPRIATE MANUSCRIPTS: None

INDEXED/ABSTRACTED IN: PA, BI, DSHA, ECEA, HLI, MI, SLTCPP

SUBSCRIPTION ADDRESS: P. O. Box 610
         Lawrence, KS 66044

SUBSCRIPTION COST: $7
PUBLICATION LAG TIME: Variable   STYLE SHEET: Yes
EARLY PUBLICATION OPTION: No   STYLE REQUIREMENTS: APA
REVIEW PERIOD: 2-3 months   CIRCULATION: 2,700
ACCEPTANCE RATE: 75%   REPRINT POLICY: 3 free

JOURNAL TITLE: Journal of Nervous and Mental Disease

MANUSCRIPT ADDRESS: Institute of Psychiatry and Human Behavior
645 West Redwood
Baltimore, MD 21201

MAJOR CONTENT AREAS: All areas of clinical psychiatry

ARTICLES USUALLY ACCEPTED: Research, review

TOPICS PREFERRED: Research on the scientific basis of clinical psychiatry

INAPPROPRIATE MANUSCRIPTS: Neurology, neurosurgery, detailed statistical studies

INDEXED/ABSTRACTED IN: PA, IM, ASW, BI, CCCP, CCSBS, CIJE, ECEA, DSHA, IPAPL, LLBA, WSA, WAH

SUBSCRIPTION ADDRESS: Williams & Wilkins Co.
428 East Preston St.
Baltimore, MD 21202

SUBSCRIPTION COST:	$35 individual, $45 institutional		
PUBLICATION LAG TIME:	8 months	STYLE SHEET:	Yes
EARLY PUBLICATION OPTION:	No	STYLE REQUIREMENTS:	Own style
REVIEW PERIOD:	4-5 months	CIRCULATION:	2,700
ACCEPTANCE RATE:	35%	REPRINT POLICY:	Purchase required

JOURNAL TITLE: Journal of Neurology, Neurosurgery, & Psychiatry

MANUSCRIPT ADDRESS: British Medical Association
B.M.A. House, Tavistock Square
London WC1H 9JR, England

MAJOR CONTENT AREAS: Clinical, experimental, mental retardation, psychoanalysis, psychotherapy

ARTICLES USUALLY ACCEPTED: Research, review

TOPICS PREFERRED: Neurology, neurosurgery, psychiatry

INAPPROPRIATE MANUSCRIPTS: None

INDEXED/ABSTRACTED IN: PA, CCCP, DSHA, LLBA

SUBSCRIPTION ADDRESS: British Medical Association
B.M.A. House, Tavistock Square
London WC1H 9JR, England

SUBSCRIPTION COST:	$65.50		
PUBLICATION LAG TIME:	6 months	STYLE SHEET:	Yes
EARLY PUBLICATION OPTION:	Yes	STYLE REQUIREMENTS:	Ind. Med.
REVIEW PERIOD:	1 month	CIRCULATION:	6,000
ACCEPTANCE RATE:	50%	REPRINT POLICY:	25 free

JOURNAL TITLE: Journal of Neurophysiology

MANUSCRIPT ADDRESS: American Physiological Association
9650 Rockville Pike
Bethesda, MD 20014

MAJOR CONTENT AREAS: Experimental, physiological

ARTICLES USUALLY ACCEPTED: Research

TOPICS PREFERRED: Those dealing with the function of the
nervous system

INAPPROPRIATE MANUSCRIPTS: None

INDEXED/ABSTRACTED IN: PA, BA, LLBA

SUBSCRIPTION ADDRESS: American Physiological Association
9650 Rockville Pike
Bethesda, MD 20014

SUBSCRIPTION COST: $50

PUBLICATION LAG TIME: 6-12 months   STYLE SHEET: Yes

EARLY PUBLICATION OPTION: No   STYLE REQUIREMENTS: Own style

REVIEW PERIOD: 3-6 months   CIRCULATION: 2,700

ACCEPTANCE RATE: 65%   REPRINT POLICY: Optional
purchase

JOURNAL TITLE: Journal of Non-White Concerns in Personnel
and Guidance

MANUSCRIPT ADDRESS: Maggie Martin, Editor, Counseling Center
Univ. of Michigan-Dearborn, 4901 Evergreen Rd.
Dearborn, MI 48128

MAJOR CONTENT AREAS: Counseling, educational, social

ARTICLES USUALLY ACCEPTED: Research, theoretical, book review

TOPICS PREFERRED: Counseling minorities, career guidance models,
abuse and misuse of standardized testing

INAPPROPRIATE MANUSCRIPTS: Program descriptions, those that tell what is
wrong but do not suggest new approaches

INDEXED/ABSTRACTED IN: CIJE

SUBSCRIPTION ADDRESS: APGA
1607 New Hampshire Avenue, N.W.
Washington, DC 20009

SUBSCRIPTION COST: $10

PUBLICATION LAG TIME: 6-9 months   STYLE SHEET: Yes

EARLY PUBLICATION OPTION: No   STYLE REQUIREMENTS: APA

REVIEW PERIOD: 3-6 months   CIRCULATION: 2,000

ACCEPTANCE RATE: 40%   REPRINT POLICY: 6 free

JOURNAL TITLE: Journal of Occupational Psychology

MANUSCRIPT ADDRESS: Prof. B. Shackel, Dept. of Human Sciences
Loughborough University of Technology
Leicestershire, England

MAJOR CONTENT AREAS: Engineering, organizational, industrial

ARTICLES USUALLY ACCEPTED: Research, review, theoretical, technical
notes, case studies

TOPICS PREFERRED: All areas of psychology in relation to human
occupations and organizations

INAPPROPRIATE MANUSCRIPTS: Those poorly written

INDEXED/ABSTRACTED IN: PA, CCSBS

SUBSCRIPTION ADDRESS: Cambridge University Press
32 East 57th Street
New York, NY 10022

SUBSCRIPTION COST:	$31 individual, $39 institutional		
PUBLICATION LAG TIME:	6-8 months	STYLE SHEET:	Yes
EARLY PUBLICATION OPTION:	No	STYLE REQUIREMENTS:	BPA
REVIEW PERIOD:	3-4 months	CIRCULATION:	1,500
ACCEPTANCE RATE:	35-40%	REPRINT POLICY:	50 free

JOURNAL TITLE: Journal of Operational Psychiatry

MANUSCRIPT ADDRESS: A. Favazza, M.D., Editor
Dept. of Psychiatry, Univ. of Missouri
Medical Center, Columbia, MO 65201

MAJOR CONTENT AREAS: All areas of psychiatry

ARTICLES USUALLY ACCEPTED: Research, review; a letter of inquiry should
be sent prior to submitting article

TOPICS PREFERRED: Interdisciplinary articles, large scale reviews
with competent bibliographies

INAPPROPRIATE MANUSCRIPTS: Position papers, anecdotal material, articles
with a narrow focus

INDEXED/ABSTRACTED IN: PA, SA

SUBSCRIPTION ADDRESS: 803 Stadium Road
Columbia, MO 65201

SUBSCRIPTION COST:	No charge		
PUBLICATION LAG TIME:	6 months	STYLE SHEET:	No
EARLY PUBLICATION OPTION:	No	STYLE REQUIREMENTS:	JAMA
REVIEW PERIOD:	3-4 weeks	CIRCULATION:	5,000
ACCEPTANCE RATE:	Not given	REPRINT POLICY:	Optional purchase

JOURNAL TITLE: Journal of Orgonomy

MANUSCRIPT ADDRESS: Box 565, Ansonia Station
New York, NY 10023

MAJOR CONTENT AREAS: Medical orgonomy, psychiatric orgone therapy

ARTICLES USUALLY ACCEPTED: Research, review, theoretical, book review on
any aspect of orgonomy

TOPICS PREFERRED: Orgonomic medicine, sociopolitics, or
psychiatry; sex-economic counseling and education

INAPPROPRIATE MANUSCRIPTS: Those with a mystical approach to life energy

INDEXED/ABSTRACTED IN: REAPP

SUBSCRIPTION ADDRESS: Box 565, Ansonia Station
New York, NY 10023

SUBSCRIPTION COST: $10 individual, $9 institutional
PUBLICATION LAG TIME: 5-6 months   STYLE SHEET: Yes
EARLY PUBLICATION OPTION: No   STYLE REQUIREMENTS: Chicago
REVIEW PERIOD: 1-8 weeks   CIRCULATION: 1,500
ACCEPTANCE RATE: 50%   REPRINT POLICY: 2 free copies
of issue

JOURNAL TITLE: Journal of the Otto Rank Association

MANUSCRIPT ADDRESS: 58 E. Court Street
Doylestown, PA 18901

MAJOR CONTENT AREAS: Counseling, educational, general, history,
psychoanalysis, psychotherapy, social

ARTICLES USUALLY ACCEPTED: Any article exploring the concepts of
Otto Rank

TOPICS PREFERRED: Those in literature or psychology which explore
Rank's concepts

INAPPROPRIATE MANUSCRIPTS: None

INDEXED/ABSTRACTED IN: PA, CCSBS

SUBSCRIPTION ADDRESS: 58 E. Court Street
Doylestown, PA 18901

SUBSCRIPTION COST: $10
PUBLICATION LAG TIME: 6 months   STYLE SHEET: Yes
EARLY PUBLICATION OPTION: No   STYLE REQUIREMENTS: None
REVIEW PERIOD: 1 month   CIRCULATION: 500
ACCEPTANCE RATE: Not given   REPRINT POLICY: Optional
purchase

JOURNAL TITLE: Journal of Parapsychology

MANUSCRIPT ADDRESS: Box 6847 College Station
Durham, NC 27708

MAJOR CONTENT AREAS: Parapsychology

ARTICLES USUALLY ACCEPTED: Research, theoretical if based on research,
occasional survey; book review by invitation

TOPICS PREFERRED: New research in parapsychology

INAPPROPRIATE MANUSCRIPTS: Ghosts, hauntings, survival after death,
unsupported theories about ESP

INDEXED/ABSTRACTED IN: PA, CCSBS

SUBSCRIPTION ADDRESS: Box 6847 College Station
Durham, NC 27708

SUBSCRIPTION COST: $10		
PUBLICATION LAG TIME: 3-6 weeks	STYLE SHEET: No	
EARLY PUBLICATION OPTION: No	STYLE REQUIREMENTS: APA, Chicago	
REVIEW PERIOD: 3-4 weeks	CIRCULATION: 1,650	
ACCEPTANCE RATE: 33%	REPRINT POLICY: 25 free	

JOURNAL TITLE: The Journal of Pastoral Care

MANUSCRIPT ADDRESS: Dr. Luberta McCabe, Managing Editor
61 Lexington Avenue
Cambridge, MA 02138

MAJOR CONTENT AREAS: Clinical, counseling, psychotherapy

ARTICLES USUALLY ACCEPTED: Research, review, theoretical

TOPICS PREFERRED: Pastoral care, chaplaincy, ministry theory,
pastoral counseling, psychotherapy, theology

INAPPROPRIATE MANUSCRIPTS: None

INDEXED/ABSTRACTED IN: PA, HLI, IRPL, RTA

SUBSCRIPTION ADDRESS: Business Office, Association for Clinical
Pastoral Education, Suite 450, 475 Riverside Dr.
New York, NY 10027

SUBSCRIPTION COST: $8		
PUBLICATION LAG TIME: 6 months-3 years	STYLE SHEET: Yes	
EARLY PUBLICATION OPTION: No	STYLE REQUIREMENTS: Chicago	
REVIEW PERIOD: 2-3 months	CIRCULATION: 8,500	
ACCEPTANCE RATE: 20-25%	REPRINT POLICY: Optional purchase	

JOURNAL TITLE: Journal of Pediatrics

MANUSCRIPT ADDRESS: 3300 Henry Avenue
Philadelphia, PA 19129

MAJOR CONTENT AREAS: Behavior therapy, clinical, developmental,
mental retardation as related to pediatrics

ARTICLES USUALLY ACCEPTED: Research

TOPICS PREFERRED: Any aspect of clinical pediatrics

INAPPROPRIATE MANUSCRIPTS: None

INDEXED/ABSTRACTED IN: IM, ASW, BS, CCCP, CIJE, DSHA, ECEA, JHE,
WAH

SUBSCRIPTION ADDRESS: C.V. Mosby Company
11830 Westline Industrial Drive
St. Louis, MO 63141

SUBSCRIPTION COST:	$18.50 individual, $27.50 institutional		
PUBLICATION LAG TIME:	6-8 months	STYLE SHEET:	No
EARLY PUBLICATION OPTION:	Yes	STYLE REQUIREMENTS:	Ind. Med.
REVIEW PERIOD:	4-6 weeks	CIRCULATION:	24,822
ACCEPTANCE RATE:	46%	REPRINT POLICY:	Optional purchase

JOURNAL TITLE: Journal of Personality

MANUSCRIPT ADDRESS: Philip R. Costanzo, Editor
P. O. Box GM, Duke Station
Durham, NC 27706

MAJOR CONTENT AREAS: Personality

ARTICLES USUALLY ACCEPTED: Empirical articles on personality

TOPICS PREFERRED: Experimental personality, developmental and
social as related to personality

INAPPROPRIATE MANUSCRIPTS: Inconclusive brief reports, theoretical articles
not related to empirical findings

INDEXED/ABSTRACTED IN: PA, IM, ASW, BA, BS, CSPA, CCSBS, DSHA, EI,
ECEA, LLBA, WSA

SUBSCRIPTION ADDRESS: Duke University Press
P. O. Box 6697, College Station
Durham, NC 27708

SUBSCRIPTION COST:	$15		
PUBLICATION LAG TIME:	1 year	STYLE SHEET:	Yes
EARLY PUBLICATION OPTION:	No	STYLE REQUIREMENTS:	APA
REVIEW PERIOD:	4 months	CIRCULATION:	2,219
ACCEPTANCE RATE:	10%	REPRINT POLICY:	Optional purchase

JOURNAL TITLE: Journal of Personality Assessment

MANUSCRIPT ADDRESS: 7840 S.W. 51st Avenue
Portland, OR 92719

MAJOR CONTENT AREAS: Clinical, counseling, personality

ARTICLES USUALLY ACCEPTED: Research, review, theoretical, book review, case studies

TOPICS PREFERRED: None

INAPPROPRIATE MANUSCRIPTS: None

INDEXED/ABSTRACTED IN: PA, BI, CCSBS, DSHA, ECEA, LLBA, WSA

SUBSCRIPTION ADDRESS: 1070 East Angeleno Avenue
Burbank, CA 91501

SUBSCRIPTION COST:	$18		
PUBLICATION LAG TIME:	1 year	STYLE SHEET:	No
EARLY PUBLICATION OPTION:	No	STYLE REQUIREMENTS:	APA
REVIEW PERIOD:	2-3 weeks	CIRCULATION:	2,700
ACCEPTANCE RATE:	Not given	REPRINT POLICY:	Optional purchase

JOURNAL TITLE: Journal of Personality and Social Psychology

MANUSCRIPT ADDRESS: John T. Lanzetta, Editor
Dept of Psychology, Dartmouth College
Hanover, NH 03755

MAJOR CONTENT AREAS: Social, personality

ARTICLES USUALLY ACCEPTED: Research on social motivation, attitudes, social interaction, communication processes, group behavior, person perception, conformity

TOPICS PREFERRED: None

INAPPROPRIATE MANUSCRIPTS: None

INDEXED/ABSTRACTED IN: PA, ASW, BS, CSPA, CCSBS, CIJE, DSHA, EAA, ECEA, IPARL, IBSS, IPSA, LLBA, PMA, RHEA, WSA

SUBSCRIPTION ADDRESS: APA Subscription Office
1200 17th Street, N.W.
Washington, DC 20036

SUBSCRIPTION COST:	$60		
PUBLICATION LAG TIME:	16 months	STYLE SHEET:	No
EARLY PUBLICATION OPTION:	No	STYLE REQUIREMENTS:	APA
REVIEW PERIOD:	Variable	CIRCULATION:	6,100
ACCEPTANCE RATE:	13%	REPRINT POLICY:	20 free

JOURNAL TITLE: Journal of Personalized Instruction

MANUSCRIPT ADDRESS: Center for Personalized Instruction
29 Loyola Hall, Georgetown University
Washington, DC 20057

MAJOR CONTENT AREAS: Educational

ARTICLES USUALLY ACCEPTED: Research, theoretical, review, abstracts, technical notes, case studies

TOPICS PREFERRED: Those related to personalized instruction

INAPPROPRIATE MANUSCRIPTS: Those dealing with group-oriented, lock-step-instruction or totally machine mediated instructic

INDEXED/ABSTRACTED IN: Not yet indexed (new journal)

SUBSCRIPTION ADDRESS: Center for Personalized Instruction
29 Loyola Hall, Georgetown University
Washington, DC 20057

SUBSCRIPTION COST:	$15 individual, $20 institutional		
PUBLICATION LAG TIME:	2-6 months	STYLE SHEET:	Yes
EARLY PUBLICATION OPTION:	No	STYLE REQUIREMENTS:	Own style
REVIEW PERIOD:	1-6 months	CIRCULATION:	700
ACCEPTANCE RATE:	40%	REPRINT POLICY:	Purchase required

JOURNAL TITLE: Journal of Phenomenological Psychology

MANUSCRIPT ADDRESS: Psychology Department
Duquesne University
Pittsburgh, PA 15219

MAJOR CONTENT AREAS: Phenomenological psychology

ARTICLES USUALLY ACCEPTED: All types of articles with a phenomenological viewpoint

TOPICS PREFERRED: None

INAPPROPRIATE MANUSCRIPTS: Papers on humanistic psychology

INDEXED/ABSTRACTED IN: PA, CCSBS, CIJE

SUBSCRIPTION ADDRESS: Humanities Press
Atlantic Highlands, NJ 07716

SUBSCRIPTION COST:	$9		
PUBLICATION LAG TIME:	1 year	STYLE SHEET:	No
EARLY PUBLICATION OPTION:	No	STYLE REQUIREMENTS:	APA
REVIEW PERIOD:	6 months	CIRCULATION:	Not given
ACCEPTANCE RATE:	Not given	REPRINT POLICY:	25 free

JOURNAL TITLE: The Journal of Primal Therapy

MANUSCRIPT ADDRESS: 620 North Almont Drive
Los Angeles, CA 90069

MAJOR CONTENT AREAS: Psychotherapy

ARTICLES USUALLY ACCEPTED: All types of articles if related to primal therapy

TOPICS PREFERRED: Anything connected with primal therapy

INAPPROPRIATE MANUSCRIPTS: Poetry

INDEXED/ABSTRACTED IN: EBSCO

SUBSCRIPTION ADDRESS: 620 North Almont Drive
Los Angeles, CA 90069

SUBSCRIPTION COST:	$11		
PUBLICATION LAG TIME:	1 issue	STYLE SHEET:	Yes
EARLY PUBLICATION OPTION:	No	STYLE REQUIREMENTS:	Chicago
REVIEW PERIOD:	Up to 6 weeks	CIRCULATION:	2,000
ACCEPTANCE RATE:	50%	REPRINT POLICY:	1 free

JOURNAL TITLE: Journal of Psychiatric Nursing and Mental Health Services

MANUSCRIPT ADDRESS: Margaret Carnine, R.N., Managing Editor
Charles B. Slack, Inc., 6900 Grove Road
Thorofare, NJ 08086

MAJOR CONTENT AREAS: All areas related to psychiatric nursing

ARTICLES USUALLY ACCEPTED: Research, review, theoretical, book review

TOPICS PREFERRED: Psychiatric nursing and mental health services

INAPPROPRIATE MANUSCRIPTS: None

INDEXED/ABSTRACTED IN: PA, CINL, CCCP

SUBSCRIPTION ADDRESS: Charles B. Slack, Inc.
6900 Grove Road
Thorofare, NJ 08086

SUBSCRIPTION COST:	$12		
PUBLICATION LAG TIME:	Not known	STYLE SHEET:	Yes
EARLY PUBLICATION OPTION:	Yes	STYLE REQUIREMENTS:	JAMA
REVIEW PERIOD:	2-3 months	CIRCULATION:	4,000
ACCEPTANCE RATE:	Not given	REPRINT POLICY:	Optional purchase

JOURNAL TITLE: Journal of Psychiatric Research

MANUSCRIPT ADDRESS: Dr. Seynour Kety, Editor-in-Chief
Psychiatric Research Labs, R-4
Mass. General Hospital, Boston, MA 02114

MAJOR CONTENT AREAS: Psychiatric research

ARTICLES USUALLY ACCEPTED: Research reports

TOPICS PREFERRED: Clinical, biological, psychological and
sociological research on psychiatric issues

INAPPROPRIATE MANUSCRIPTS: Not given

INDEXED/ABSTRACTED IN: BA, CA, HLI, IM, PA, SCI, SSCI

SUBSCRIPTION ADDRESS: Pergamon Press
Maxwell House, Fairview Park
Elmsford, NY 10523

SUBSCRIPTION COST: $25 individual, $50 institutional

PUBLICATION LAG TIME:	Not given	STYLE SHEET:	Not given
EARLY PUBLICATION OPTION:	Not given	STYLE REQUIREMENTS:	WLSP
REVIEW PERIOD:	Not given	CIRCULATION:	Not given
ACCEPTANCE RATE:	Not given	REPRINT POLICY:	Optional purchase

JOURNAL TITLE: The Journal of Psychiatry and Law

MANUSCRIPT ADDRESS: Dianne Nashel
28 Morris Road
Tenafly, NJ 07670

MAJOR CONTENT AREAS: Behavior therapy, psychoanalysis, psychotherapy,
psychiatry and law

ARTICLES USUALLY ACCEPTED: Research, book review on all subjects dealing
with the interface between psychiatry or
psychology and the law

TOPICS PREFERRED: Commitment of mental patients, dangerousness

INAPPROPRIATE MANUSCRIPTS: None

INDEXED/ABSTRACTED IN: PA, EM, CCSBS, IPARL, SSCI

SUBSCRIPTION ADDRESS: Federal Legal Publications, Inc.
95 Morton St.
New York, NY 10014

SUBSCRIPTION COST: $20 individual, $24 institutional

PUBLICATION LAG TIME:	4-6 months	STYLE SHEET:	Yes
EARLY PUBLICATION OPTION:	No	STYLE REQUIREMENTS:	Chicago
REVIEW PERIOD:	2-3 months	CIRCULATION:	1,500
ACCEPTANCE RATE:	33%	REPRINT POLICY:	50 free

JOURNAL TITLE: The Journal of Psychohistory

MANUSCRIPT ADDRESS: 2315 Broadway
New York, NY   10024

MAJOR CONTENT AREAS: Psychoanalysis, psychohistory

ARTICLES USUALLY ACCEPTED: Research, review, theoretical, book review

TOPICS PREFERRED: Psychohistory, history of childhood

INAPPROPRIATE MANUSCRIPTS: Those that are purely literary or purely
clinical
INDEXED/ABSTRACTED IN: PA, SA, CDA, HA, AHL

SUBSCRIPTION ADDRESS: 2315 Broadway
New York, NY   10024

SUBSCRIPTION COST: $16 individual, $24 institutional
PUBLICATION LAG TIME: 9 months   STYLE SHEET: No
EARLY PUBLICATION OPTION: No   STYLE REQUIREMENTS: Chicago
REVIEW PERIOD: 1 week   CIRCULATION: 4,000
ACCEPTANCE RATE: 5%   REPRINT POLICY: 50 free

JOURNAL TITLE: Journal of Psycholinguistic Research

MANUSCRIPT ADDRESS: R. W. Rieber, Editor, John Jay College
444 West 56th Street
New York, NY   10019
MAJOR CONTENT AREAS: Developmental, experimental, learning,
perception, psycholinguistics
ARTICLES USUALLY ACCEPTED: Research, review, theoretical

TOPICS PREFERRED: Psycholinguistics, the psychology of cognition
and language
INAPPROPRIATE MANUSCRIPTS: None

INDEXED/ABSTRACTED IN: PA, AA, BA, CCSBS, DSHA, LLBA

SUBSCRIPTION ADDRESS: Plenum Press
227 West 17th Street
New York, NY   10011
SUBSCRIPTION COST: $19.75 individual, $39.50 institutional
PUBLICATION LAG TIME: 9 months   STYLE SHEET: No
EARLY PUBLICATION OPTION: No   STYLE REQUIREMENTS: APA
REVIEW PERIOD: 3-5 months   CIRCULATION: 1,000
ACCEPTANCE RATE: Not given   REPRINT POLICY: Optional
purchase

JOURNAL TITLE: The Journal of Psychology

MANUSCRIPT ADDRESS: The Managing Editor, The Journal Press
2 Commercial Street, P.O. Box 543
Provincetown, MA 02657

MAJOR CONTENT AREAS: All areas of psychology

ARTICLES USUALLY ACCEPTED: Research, review, theoretical

TOPICS PREFERRED: General field of psychology

INAPPROPRIATE MANUSCRIPTS: Essay-type manuscripts, articles not conforming
to submission requirements

INDEXED/ABSTRACTED IN: PA, ASW, BRI, CSPA, CCSBS, CIJE, DSHA, EA,
ECEA, LLBA, PRG, WSA

SUBSCRIPTION ADDRESS: The Journal Press
2 Commercial Street, P.O. Box 543
Provincetown, MA 02657

SUBSCRIPTION COST: $45

PUBLICATION LAG TIME: Immediate publication STYLE SHEET: Yes

EARLY PUBLICATION OPTION: All immediate STYLE REQUIREMENTS: Journal Press

REVIEW PERIOD: 1 month CIRCULATION: 1,760

ACCEPTANCE RATE: 40% REPRINT POLICY: 200 free

JOURNAL TITLE: Journal of Psychology and Theology

MANUSCRIPT ADDRESS: 1409 North Walnut Grove Avenue
Rosemead, CA 91770

MAJOR CONTENT AREAS: The integration of psychology and theology

ARTICLES USUALLY ACCEPTED: Research, theoretical, review

TOPICS PREFERRED: Anything dealing with the integration of
of psychology and theology

INAPPROPRIATE MANUSCRIPTS: Those not related to the integration of
psychology and theology

INDEXED/ABSTRACTED IN: PA, IRPL, PRG, RTA, RICS, SSCI

SUBSCRIPTION ADDRESS: 1409 North Walnut Grove Avenue
Rosemead, CA 91770

SUBSCRIPTION COST: $12

PUBLICATION LAG TIME: 6 months STYLE SHEET: Yes

EARLY PUBLICATION OPTION: No STYLE REQUIREMENTS: APA

REVIEW PERIOD: 2-3 months CIRCULATION: 2,000

ACCEPTANCE RATE: 50% REPRINT POLICY: 10 free

JOURNAL TITLE: Journal of Psychosomatic Research

MANUSCRIPT ADDRESS: Dr. Denis Leigh, The Maudsley Hospital
Denmark Hill
London SE5 8AZ, England

MAJOR CONTENT AREAS: Behavior therapy, clinical, psychotherapy,
personality, social

ARTICLES USUALLY ACCEPTED: Research, book review

TOPICS PREFERRED: Anxiety, stress, aggression, biofeedback
treatment, personality and disease, sleep analysis

INAPPROPRIATE MANUSCRIPTS: None

INDEXED/ABSTRACTED IN: PA, CCSBS, LLBA

SUBSCRIPTION ADDRESS: Pergamon Press
Headington Hill Hall
Oxford OX3 OBW, England

SUBSCRIPTION COST: $25 individual, $60 institutional

PUBLICATION LAG TIME: Not given   STYLE SHEET: Yes

EARLY PUBLICATION OPTION: Not given   STYLE REQUIREMENTS: Own style

REVIEW PERIOD: Not given   CIRCULATION: 1,600

ACCEPTANCE RATE: 50-60%   REPRINT POLICY: 100 free

JOURNAL TITLE: Journal of Rehabilitation

MANUSCRIPT ADDRESS: 1522 K Street, N. W.
Washington, DC 20005

MAJOR CONTENT AREAS: Community, counseling, mental retardation,
psychotherapy, social, rehabilitation

ARTICLES USUALLY ACCEPTED: Research, review, theoretical, book review

TOPICS PREFERRED: Rehabilitation in general, physiological and
psychological

INAPPROPRIATE MANUSCRIPTS: Technical medical manuscripts dealing with
a specific disability

INDEXED/ABSTRACTED IN: PA, ASW, CCSBS, CIJE, DSHA, ERA, ECEA, GPE,
ILD, JHE, LLBA

SUBSCRIPTION ADDRESS: 1522 K Street, N.W.
Washington, DC 20005

SUBSCRIPTION COST: $10 individual, $8 institutional

PUBLICATION LAG TIME: 2 months   STYLE SHEET: Yes

EARLY PUBLICATION OPTION: No   STYLE REQUIREMENTS: Own style

REVIEW PERIOD: 6 months   CIRCULATION: 37,000

ACCEPTANCE RATE: 20%   REPRINT POLICY: 5 free copies
of issue

JOURNAL TITLE: Journal of Religion and Health

MANUSCRIPT ADDRESS: Dr. Harry C. Menserve, Editor
Box 428
Southwest Harbor, ME 04679

MAJOR CONTENT AREAS: Almost all as related to religion and health

ARTICLES USUALLY ACCEPTED: Theoretical and research material directed to the major disciplines concerned with religion and health

TOPICS PREFERRED: The interrelationships among the major disciplines concerned with religion and health

INAPPROPRIATE MANUSCRIPTS: Narrowly technical topics, superficial treatment of any topic

INDEXED/ABSTRACTED IN: PA, BS, IRPL, RTA

SUBSCRIPTION ADDRESS: Institutes of Religion and Health
3 West 29th Street
New York, NY 10001

SUBSCRIPTION COST: $8

PUBLICATION LAG TIME:	6 months	STYLE SHEET:	Yes
EARLY PUBLICATION OPTION:	Yes	STYLE REQUIREMENTS:	Chicago
REVIEW PERIOD:	6 weeks	CIRCULATION:	3,500
ACCEPTANCE RATE:	50%	REPRINT POLICY:	2 free copies of issue

JOURNAL TITLE: Journal of Research in Crime and Deliquency

MANUSCRIPT ADDRESS: 1501 Neil Avenue
Columbus, OH 43201

MAJOR CONTENT AREAS: Behavior therapy, clinical, community, counseling, criminology, psychotherapy, social

ARTICLES USUALLY ACCEPTED: Research, theoretical, review

TOPICS PREFERRED: Criminology, evaluation research, white collar crime, innovations in criminal justice

INAPPROPRIATE MANUSCRIPTS: Those at the undergraduate term paper level dealing with well settled issues

INDEXED/ABSTRACTED IN: SA, BS, CDA, CCSBS, IPARL, IPAPL

SUBSCRIPTION ADDRESS: National Council on Crime and Deliquency
411 Hackensack Avenue
Hackensack, NJ 07601

SUBSCRIPTION COST: $5

PUBLICATION LAG TIME:	12-15 months	STYLE SHEET:	Yes
EARLY PUBLICATION OPTION:	No	STYLE REQUIREMENTS:	Chicago
REVIEW PERIOD:	2 months	CIRCULATION:	1,000
ACCEPTANCE RATE:	10%	REPRINT POLICY:	5 free

JOURNAL TITLE: Journal of Research and Development in Education
MANUSCRIPT ADDRESS: Room G-3
Aderhold Bldg., University of Georgia
Athens, GA   30602
MAJOR CONTENT AREAS: Educational

ARTICLES USUALLY ACCEPTED: Research; a theme is selected 24 months in advance of publication and a guest editor is appointed who solicits articles around that theme
TOPICS PREFERRED: Themes vary

INAPPROPRIATE MANUSCRIPTS: Former term papers of people who are now assistant professors
INDEXED/ABSTRACTED IN: PA, BS, CCSBS, CIJE, EI, ECEA, LLBA

SUBSCRIPTION ADDRESS: Room G-3
Aderhold Bldg., University of Georgia
Athens, GA   30602
SUBSCRIPTION COST: $10
PUBLICATION LAG TIME: 3-4 months   STYLE SHEET: Yes
EARLY PUBLICATION OPTION: No   STYLE REQUIREMENTS: APA
REVIEW PERIOD: 1 month   CIRCULATION: 1,500
ACCEPTANCE RATE: By invitation   REPRINT POLICY: Optional purchase

JOURNAL TITLE: Journal of Research in Personality

MANUSCRIPT ADDRESS: Jerry S. Wiggins, Editor, Dept. of Psychology
University of British Columbia
Vancouver, BC, Canada
MAJOR CONTENT AREAS: Personality

ARTICLES USUALLY ACCEPTED: Research, theoretical, review, notes

TOPICS PREFERRED: Any in the area of personality

INAPPROPRIATE MANUSCRIPTS: None

INDEXED/ABSTRACTED IN: PA, CCSBS, PRG

SUBSCRIPTION ADDRESS: Academic Press, Inc.
111 Fifth Avenue
New York, NY   10003
SUBSCRIPTION COST: $18.75 individual, $37.50 institutional
PUBLICATION LAG TIME: 1 year   STYLE SHEET: Yes
EARLY PUBLICATION OPTION: No   STYLE REQUIREMENTS: APA
REVIEW PERIOD: 6-8 weeks   CIRCULATION: 1,500
ACCEPTANCE RATE: 30%   REPRINT POLICY: 50 free

JOURNAL TITLE: Journal of School Psychology

MANUSCRIPT ADDRESS: Beeman N. Phillips, Editor
Dept. of Educational Psychology,
University of Texas at Austin, Austin, TX 78712

MAJOR CONTENT AREAS: School psychology; behavior therapy, counseling,
and education as related to school psychology

ARTICLES USUALLY ACCEPTED: Research, opinions, and practices in school
psychology; articles dealing with school
psychology as a scientific specialty

TOPICS PREFERRED: Interprofessional roles, training and legal
issues, assessment, early education

INAPPROPRIATE MANUSCRIPTS: None

INDEXED/ABSTRACTED IN: PA, BS, CCSBS, CIJE, EI, ECEA, IBSS, PHRA,
PRG

SUBSCRIPTION ADDRESS: Behavioral Publications, Inc.
72 Fifth Avenue
New York, NY 10011

SUBSCRIPTION COST: $25 individual, $35 institutional

PUBLICATION LAG TIME: 1 year	STYLE SHEET:	No
EARLY PUBLICATION OPTION: No	STYLE REQUIREMENTS:	APA
REVIEW PERIOD: 6-8 weeks	CIRCULATION:	2,700
ACCEPTANCE RATE: 25%	REPRINT POLICY:	1 free copy of issue

JOURNAL TITLE: Journal for the Scientific Study of Religion

MANUSCRIPT ADDRESS: Graduate School of Social Work
University of Texas at Arlington
Arlington, TX 76019

MAJOR CONTENT AREAS: Scientific study of religion

ARTICLES USUALLY ACCEPTED: Theoretical, research

TOPICS PREFERRED: Religion from a scientific point of view

INAPPROPRIATE MANUSCRIPTS: Papers concerned with religion or theology
per se

INDEXED/ABSTRACTED IN: PA, SA, AA, BS, CCSBS, IRPL, IBSS, RTA

SUBSCRIPTION ADDRESS: Society for the Scientific Study of Religion
Box U68A, University of Connecticut
Storrs, CT 06268

SUBSCRIPTION COST: $15

PUBLICATION LAG TIME: 3 months	STYLE SHEET:	Yes
EARLY PUBLICATION OPTION: No	STYLE REQUIREMENTS:	APA
REVIEW PERIOD: 3 months	CIRCULATION:	2,500
ACCEPTANCE RATE: 15-20%	REPRINT POLICY:	Optional purchase

JOURNAL TITLE: Journal of Sex and Marital Therapy

MANUSCRIPT ADDRESS: Raul C. Schiavi, Editor, Dept. of Psychiatry
Mt. Sinai School of Medicine
Madison Ave. & 100th St., New York, NY 10029

MAJOR CONTENT AREAS: Human sexuality

ARTICLES USUALLY ACCEPTED: Research, review, theoretical, book review, case studies

TOPICS PREFERRED: Research and clinical aspects of sexuality and the marital relationship

INAPPROPRIATE MANUSCRIPTS: Topics outside of human sexuality

INDEXED/ABSTRACTED IN: PA, EM, CCSBS, SLTCPP

SUBSCRIPTION ADDRESS: Human Sciences Press
72 Fifth Avenue
New York, NY 10011

SUBSCRIPTION COST:	$15 individual, $35 institutional		
PUBLICATION LAG TIME:	6-12 months	STYLE SHEET:	Yes
EARLY PUBLICATION OPTION:	Yes	STYLE REQUIREMENTS:	Own style
REVIEW PERIOD:	Not given	CIRCULATION:	2,000
ACCEPTANCE RATE:	20%	REPRINT POLICY:	Optional purchase

JOURNAL TITLE: The Journal of Sex Research

MANUSCRIPT ADDRESS: 138 East 94th Street, 6W
New York, NY 10028

MAJOR CONTENT AREAS: Any related and pertinent to sexuality

ARTICLES USUALLY ACCEPTED: Research, theoretical

TOPICS PREFERRED: Research in sexuality, animal and human

INAPPROPRIATE MANUSCRIPTS: Sexual behavior of college students, how to make sex more joyful

INDEXED/ABSTRACTED IN: PA, SA, CCSBS

SUBSCRIPTION ADDRESS: 138 East 94th Street, 6W
New York, NY 10028

SUBSCRIPTION COST:	$20		
PUBLICATION LAG TIME:	10-12 months	STYLE SHEET:	Yes
EARLY PUBLICATION OPTION:	Yes	STYLE REQUIREMENTS:	APA
REVIEW PERIOD:	4-6 weeks	CIRCULATION:	1,500
ACCEPTANCE RATE:	Not given	REPRINT POLICY:	Optional purchase

JOURNAL TITLE: Journal of Social Issues

MANUSCRIPT ADDRESS: Dr. Jacqueline D. Goodchilds, Editor
Dept of Psychology, University of California
Los Angeles, CA 90024

MAJOR CONTENT AREAS: All areas of psychology, sociology, economics, etc. as related to social issues

ARTICLES USUALLY ACCEPTED: Original data-based overview, research, and theoretical; most are solicited

TOPICS PREFERRED: Social concerns for which social psychological professionals have research-based information

INAPPROPRIATE MANUSCRIPTS: Polemical articles and impassioned arguments

INDEXED/ABSTRACTED IN: PA, ASW, AA, BS, CSPA, CCSBS, CIJE, EAA, ECEA, IPAPL, IBSS, ILD, IPSA, LLBA, PRAJ, PHRA, RHEA, SSHI, WSA

SUBSCRIPTION ADDRESS: P. O. Box 1248
Ann Arbor, MI 48106

SUBSCRIPTION COST: $14 individual, $20 institutional
PUBLICATION LAG TIME: 1 year   STYLE SHEET: No
EARLY PUBLICATION OPTION: No   STYLE REQUIREMENTS: APA
REVIEW PERIOD: Variable   CIRCULATION: 7,000
ACCEPTANCE RATE: Most are solicited REPRINT POLICY: 100 free

JOURNAL TITLE: The Journal of Social Psychology

MANUSCRIPT ADDRESS: The Managing Editor, The Journal Press
2 Commercial Street, P.O. Box 543
Provincetown, MA 02657

MAJOR CONTENT AREAS: Community, industrial/organizational, personality, social, cross-cultural

ARTICLES USUALLY ACCEPTED: Studies of persons in group settings and of culture and personality

TOPICS PREFERRED: Field research and cross-cultural research

INAPPROPRIATE MANUSCRIPTS: Essays more suitable to popular magazines, those not conforming to submission requirements

INDEXED/ABSTRACTED IN: PA, ASW, AA, BS, CSPA, CDL, CCSBS, CIJE, DSHA, ECEA, IPAPL, IBSS, IPSA, JHE, LLBA, PRG, RHEA, WSA

SUBSCRIPTION ADDRESS: The Journal Press
2 Commercial Street, P.O. Box 543
Provincetown, MA 02657

SUBSCRIPTION COST: $45
PUBLICATION LAG TIME: 15 months   STYLE SHEET: Yes
EARLY PUBLICATION OPTION: No   STYLE REQUIREMENTS: Journal Press
REVIEW PERIOD: 1 month   CIRCULATION: 2,415
ACCEPTANCE RATE: 40%   REPRINT POLICY: 100 free

JOURNAL TITLE: Journal of Special Education

MANUSCRIPT ADDRESS: 3515 Woodhaven Rd.
Philadelphia, PA 19154

MAJOR CONTENT AREAS: Behavior therapy, educational, learning, mental retardation, psychometrics, social, perception

ARTICLES USUALLY ACCEPTED: Research, theoretical, opinion, review

TOPICS PREFERRED: Definitive and carefully documented articles from all disciplines engaged in special education

INAPPROPRIATE MANUSCRIPTS: Case studies with too small or inappropriate samples (e.g., in behavior modification)

INDEXED/ABSTRACTED IN: PA, BS, CCSBS, CKJE, DSHA, EI, ECEA, LLBA

SUBSCRIPTION ADDRESS: Grune & Stratton, Inc.
111 Fifth Ave.
New York, NY 10003

SUBSCRIPTION COST:	$18.50		
PUBLICATION LAG TIME:	8-18 months	STYLE SHEET:	Yes
EARLY PUBLICATION OPTION:	No	STYLE REQUIREMENTS:	APA
REVIEW PERIOD:	1-3 months	CIRCULATION:	3,500
ACCEPTANCE RATE:	5-10%	REPRINT POLICY:	20 free

JOURNAL TITLE: Journal for Special Educators of the Mentally Retarded

MANUSCRIPT ADDRESS: Joseph Prentky, Ed.D., Editor
179 Sierra Vista Lane
Valley Cottage, NY 10989

MAJOR CONTENT AREAS: Educational, mental retardation

ARTICLES USUALLY ACCEPTED: Review, book review, practical classroom articles on a classroom level

TOPICS PREFERRED: Any article dealing with classroom activities of the mentally retarded

INAPPROPRIATE MANUSCRIPTS: Research, behavioral, those other than education of the mentally retarded

INDEXED/ABSTRACTED IN: CCSBS, EI, ECEA

SUBSCRIPTION ADDRESS: Box 171
Center Conway, NH 03813

SUBSCRIPTION COST:	$9		
PUBLICATION LAG TIME:	6-12 months	STYLE SHEET:	Yes
EARLY PUBLICATION OPTION:	No	STYLE REQUIREMENTS:	Own style
REVIEW PERIOD:	4-6 weeks	CIRCULATION:	5,000
ACCEPTANCE RATE:	80%	REPRINT POLICY:	6 free copies of issue

JOURNAL TITLE: Journal of Speech and Hearing Disorders

MANUSCRIPT ADDRESS: Ralph L. Shelton, Ph.D., Dept. of Speech and Hearing Sciences, Building 25
Univ. of Arizona, Tuscon, AZ 85721

MAJOR CONTENT AREAS: Speech and hearing disorders

ARTICLES USUALLY ACCEPTED: Applied research, review, case studies

TOPICS PREFERRED: Speech pathology

INAPPROPRIATE MANUSCRIPTS: None

INDEXED/ABSTRACTED IN: PA, BS, CCSBS, CIJE, DSHA, EI, ECA, LLBA, WLSP

SUBSCRIPTION ADDRESS: American Speech and Hearing Association
9030 Old Georgetown Road
Washington, DC 20014

SUBSCRIPTION COST: $28
PUBLICATION LAG TIME: 1-24 months   STYLE SHEET: Yes
EARLY PUBLICATION OPTION: No   STYLE REQUIREMENTS: Own style
REVIEW PERIOD: 6 months   CIRCULATION: 30,000
ACCEPTANCE RATE: Not given   REPRINT POLICY: Purchase required

JOURNAL TITLE: Journal of Speech and Hearing Research

MANUSCRIPT ADDRESS: Thomas J. Hixon, Ph.D., Dept. of Speech and Hearing Sciences, Building 25
Univ. of Arizona, Tuscon, AZ 85721

MAJOR CONTENT AREAS: Speech and hearing

ARTICLES USUALLY ACCEPTED: Research, theoretical

TOPICS PREFERRED: Communication sciences

INAPPROPRIATE MANUSCRIPTS: None

INDEXED/ABSTRACTED IN: PA, BS, CCSBS, CIJE, DSHA, EI, ECA, LLBA, WLSP

SUBSCRIPTION ADDRESS: American Speech and Hearing Association
9030 Old Georgetown Road
Washington, DC 20014

SUBSCRIPTION COST: $28
PUBLICATION LAG TIME: Variable   STYLE SHEET: Yes
EARLY PUBLICATION OPTION: No   STYLE REQUIREMENTS: Own style
REVIEW PERIOD: 4-6 months   CIRCULATION: 30,000
ACCEPTANCE RATE: Not given   REPRINT POLICY: Purchase required

JOURNAL TITLE: Journal of Structural Learning

MANUSCRIPT ADDRESS: John Williams, Luce Research Institute
Ealing Technical College, Woodlands Ave.
Acton, London W3 9DN, England

MAJOR CONTENT AREAS: Learning

ARTICLES USUALLY ACCEPTED: Research, review, theoretical

TOPICS PREFERRED: Mathematical learning, educational evolution,
artificial intelligence, learning structures

INAPPROPRIATE MANUSCRIPTS: Conventional experiments on learning without
reference to basic learning structures

INDEXED/ABSTRACTED IN: PA, CCSBS, CIJE

SUBSCRIPTION ADDRESS: Gordon & Breach, Ltd.
42 William IV St.
London WC2, England

SUBSCRIPTION COST: $14.50 individual, $35 institutional

PUBLICATION LAG TIME: 1 year   STYLE SHEET: Yes

EARLY PUBLICATION OPTION: No   STYLE REQUIREMENTS: APA

REVIEW PERIOD: 4 months   CIRCULATION: 600

ACCEPTANCE RATE: 25%   REPRINT POLICY: 20 free

JOURNAL TITLE: Journal of Studies on Alcohol

MANUSCRIPT ADDRESS: Editoral Office
Rutgers Center of Alcohol Studies
New Brunswick, NJ 08903

MAJOR CONTENT AREAS: All areas as related to alcohol problems

ARTICLES USUALLY ACCEPTED: Research, review, theoretical, book review

TOPICS PREFERRED: Alcohol and alcohol-related problems

INAPPROPRIATE MANUSCRIPTS: Dissertations, descriptions of unevaluated
treatment procedures

INDEXED/ABSTRACTED IN: PA, IM, EM, ASW, SA, ACP, BA, BS, CA, CCSBS,
HA, PpA, PAISB, WAH

SUBSCRIPTION ADDRESS: Publications Office, Rutgers Center of Alcohol
Studies, Titsworth and Stone Roads
Piscataway, NJ 08854

SUBSCRIPTION COST: $25 individual, $35 institutional

PUBLICATION LAG TIME: 2-4 months   STYLE SHEET: Yes

EARLY PUBLICATION OPTION: No   STYLE REQUIREMENTS: CBI

REVIEW PERIOD: 4-6 months   CIRCULATION: 3,200

ACCEPTANCE RATE: 35%   REPRINT POLICY: 25 free

JOURNAL TITLE: Journal for the Theory of Social Behavior

MANUSCRIPT ADDRESS: P. F. Secord, Urban Studies
Queens College
Flushing, NY 11367

MAJOR CONTENT AREAS: All areas related to models of human behavior

ARTICLES USUALLY ACCEPTED: Theoretical

TOPICS PREFERRED: Conceptual analysis, models of human behavior, philosophy of science

INAPPROPRIATE MANUSCRIPTS: None

INDEXED/ABSTRACTED IN: PA, SA, CCSBS, LLBA, PI

SUBSCRIPTION ADDRESS: Blackwell
108 Cowley Road
Oxford OX4 1JF, England

SUBSCRIPTION COST: $10.50 individual, $15 institutional

PUBLICATION LAG TIME: 6-8 months	STYLE SHEET:	Yes
EARLY PUBLICATION OPTION: No	STYLE REQUIREMENTS:	APA
REVIEW PERIOD: 6 months	CIRCULATION:	1,000
ACCEPTANCE RATE: 15%	REPRINT POLICY:	25 free

JOURNAL TITLE: Journal of Transpersonal Psychology

MANUSCRIPT ADDRESS: Box 4437
Stanford, CA 94305

MAJOR CONTENT AREAS: All areas from a transpersonal orientation

ARTICLES USUALLY ACCEPTED: Research, review, theoretical

TOPICS PREFERRED: Human psychology, experience, and behavior from a transpersonal orientation

INAPPROPRIATE MANUSCRIPTS: "The only true way is_____."

INDEXED/ABSTRACTED IN: PA, PRG

SUBSCRIPTION ADDRESS: Box 4437
Stanford, CA 94305

SUBSCRIPTION COST: $7.50

PUBLICATION LAG TIME: 3-6 months	STYLE SHEET:	No
EARLY PUBLICATION OPTION: No	STYLE REQUIREMENTS:	Modified APA
REVIEW PERIOD: 8 weeks	CIRCULATION:	2,200
ACCEPTANCE RATE: 10%	REPRINT POLICY:	50 free

JOURNAL TITLE: Journal of Verbal Learning and Verbal Behavior

MANUSCRIPT ADDRESS: Walter Kintsch, Editor
Dept. of Psychology, University of Colorado
Boulder, CO 80302

MAJOR CONTENT AREAS: Developmental, experimental, learning

ARTICLES USUALLY ACCEPTED: Research, theoretical

TOPICS PREFERRED: Memory and language

INAPPROPRIATE MANUSCRIPTS: None

INDEXED/ABSTRACTED IN: PA, CCSBS, CIJE, DSHA, LLBA

SUBSCRIPTION ADDRESS: Academic Press, Inc.
111 Fifth Avenue
New York, NY 10003

SUBSCRIPTION COST: $22.50 individual, $49 institutional
PUBLICATION LAG TIME: 6 months STYLE SHEET: Yes
EARLY PUBLICATION OPTION: No STYLE REQUIREMENTS: APA
REVIEW PERIOD: 1-2 months CIRCULATION: 2,600
ACCEPTANCE RATE: 25% REPRINT POLICY: 50 free

JOURNAL TITLE: Journal of Vocational Behavior

MANUSCRIPT ADDRESS: Lenore W. Harmon, Editor
777 Enderis Hall, Univ. of Wisconsin-Milwaukee
Milwaukee, WI 53201

MAJOR CONTENT AREAS: Applied behavior analysis, counseling,
organizational, psychometrics, methodology

ARTICLES USUALLY ACCEPTED: Research, a few theoretical

TOPICS PREFERRED: Career development and choice, job performance,
measurement of vocational behavior concepts

INAPPROPRIATE MANUSCRIPTS: Validations of measures of job performance
using a known technology in a specific setting

INDEXED/ABSTRACTED IN: PA, CSPA, CCSBS, CIJE, ERA, WSA

SUBSCRIPTION ADDRESS: Academic Press, Inc.
111 Fifth Avenue
New York, NY 10003

SUBSCRIPTION COST: $14 individual, $28 institutional
PUBLICATION LAG TIME: 8 months STYLE SHEET: Yes
EARLY PUBLICATION OPTION: No STYLE REQUIREMENTS: APA
REVIEW PERIOD: 2 months CIRCULATION: 1,000
ACCEPTANCE RATE: 45% REPRINT POLICY: 50 free

JOURNAL TITLE: Journal of Youth and Adolescence

MANUSCRIPT ADDRESS: Dr. Daniel Offer, Dept. of Psychiatry
Michael Reese Hospital, 2959 S. Ellis Ave.
Chicago, IL 60616

MAJOR CONTENT AREAS: Clinical, developmental, personality,
social

ARTICLES USUALLY ACCEPTED: Research, theoretical, review

TOPICS PREFERRED: Scholarly research

INAPPROPRIATE MANUSCRIPTS: Case reports

INDEXED/ABSTRACTED IN: PA, IM, SA, CCSBS, LLBA

SUBSCRIPTION ADDRESS: Plenum Publishing Corp.
227 West 17th Street
New York, NY 10011

SUBSCRIPTION COST: $16 individual, $24 institutional

PUBLICATION LAG TIME: 8 months

STYLE SHEET: Yes

EARLY PUBLICATION OPTION: No

STYLE REQUIREMENTS: AIBS

REVIEW PERIOD: 2-3 months

CIRCULATION: 800

ACCEPTANCE RATE: 30%

REPRINT POLICY: Purchase
required

JOURNAL TITLE:	Language Learning: A Journal of Applied Linguistics
MANUSCRIPT ADDRESS:	H. Douglas Brown, Editor 2001 North University Bldg., Univ. of Michigan Ann Arbor, MI 48109
MAJOR CONTENT AREAS:	Language learning
ARTICLES USUALLY ACCEPTED:	Research, review, theoretical, book review
TOPICS PREFERRED:	None
INAPPROPRIATE MANUSCRIPTS:	None
INDEXED/ABSTRACTED IN:	BS, CCSBS, CIJE, DSHA, EI
SUBSCRIPTION ADDRESS:	2001 North University Bldg. University of Michigan Ann Arbor, MI 48109
SUBSCRIPTION COST:	$5 individual, $8 institutional

PUBLICATION LAG TIME:	Not given	STYLE SHEET:	No
EARLY PUBLICATION OPTION:	No	STYLE REQUIREMENTS:	LSA
REVIEW PERIOD:	3 months	CIRCULATION:	3,000
ACCEPTANCE RATE:	Not given	REPRINT POLICY:	50 free

JOURNAL TITLE:	Learning and Motivation
MANUSCRIPT ADDRESS:	J. Bruce Overmier 212 Elliott Hall, Univ. of Minnesota Minneapolis, MN 55455
MAJOR CONTENT AREAS:	Learning, motivation, comparative, experimental, general, physiological
ARTICLES USUALLY ACCEPTED:	Research, review, theoretical
TOPICS PREFERRED:	Experimental analysis of theoretical problems in learning and motivation
INAPPROPRIATE MANUSCRIPTS:	Education, clinical, community
INDEXED/ABSTRACTED IN:	PA, CCSBS
SUBSCRIPTION ADDRESS:	Academic Press, Inc. 111 Fifth Avenue New York, NY 10003
SUBSCRIPTION COST:	$21 individual, $42 institutional

PUBLICATION LAG TIME:	11 months	STYLE SHEET:	Yes
EARLY PUBLICATION OPTION:	No	STYLE REQUIREMENTS:	APA
REVIEW PERIOD:	3 months	CIRCULATION:	1,000
ACCEPTANCE RATE:	30%	REPRINT POLICY:	50 free

JOURNAL TITLE: Literature and Psychology

MANUSCRIPT ADDRESS: English Department
Fairleigh Dickinson University
Teaneck, NJ 07666

MAJOR CONTENT AREAS: Psychoanalysis applied to interpretation of literature

ARTICLES USUALLY ACCEPTED: Review, book review

TOPICS PREFERRED: Psychological interpretation of literary works, primarily expressed through psychoanalysis

INAPPROPRIATE MANUSCRIPTS: Jungian psychology applied to literary works

INDEXED/ABSTRACTED IN: PA, MLA

SUBSCRIPTION ADDRESS: English Department
Fairleigh Dickinson University
Teaneck, NJ 07666

SUBSCRIPTION COST: $5 individual, $8 institutional

PUBLICATION LAG TIME: 2-5 months   STYLE SHEET: No

EARLY PUBLICATION OPTION: No   STYLE REQUIREMENTS: MLA

REVIEW PERIOD: 3-6 months   CIRCULATION: 1,000

ACCEPTANCE RATE: 5-10%   REPRINT POLICY: 2 free copies of issue

JOURNAL TITLE: MH

MANUSCRIPT ADDRESS: 1800 North Kent Street
Arlington, VA 22209

MAJOR CONTENT AREAS: Clinical, community, psychotherapy

ARTICLES USUALLY ACCEPTED: Research, review, theoretical, book review

TOPICS PREFERRED: Prevention, community mental health

INAPPROPRIATE MANUSCRIPTS: Technical papers or Ph.D. dissertations

INDEXED/ABSTRACTED IN: PA, CSPA, IPAPL, IPARL, JHE, LLBA, MMRI, PAISB, RGPL, RHEA, WSA

SUBSCRIPTION ADDRESS: 1800 North Kent Street
Arlington, VA 22209

SUBSCRIPTION COST: $10		
PUBLICATION LAG TIME: 1-2 years	STYLE SHEET:	Yes
EARLY PUBLICATION OPTION: No	STYLE REQUIREMENTS:	Own style
REVIEW PERIOD: 3 weeks	CIRCULATION:	7,000
ACCEPTANCE RATE: 5%	REPRINT POLICY:	Optional purchase

JOURNAL TITLE: The Mankind Quarterly

MANUSCRIPT ADDRESS: 1 Darnaway Street
Edinburgh EH3 6DW, Scotland

MAJOR CONTENT AREAS: Ethnology, anthropology, demography, racial history

ARTICLES USUALLY ACCEPTED: Research

TOPICS PREFERRED: Ethnology, anthropology, demography, racial history

INAPPROPRIATE MANUSCRIPTS: None

INDEXED/ABSTRACTED IN: SA, AHL, AA, AI. BS, CCSBS, HA

SUBSCRIPTION ADDRESS: 1 Darnaway Street
Edinburgh EH3 6DW, Scotland

SUBSCRIPTION COST: $12		
PUBLICATION LAG TIME: 1-2 years	STYLE SHEET:	Yes
EARLY PUBLICATION OPTION: No	STYLE REQUIREMENTS:	Own style
REVIEW PERIOD: 2-3 weeks	CIRCULATION:	1,500
ACCEPTANCE RATE: 90%	REPRINT POLICY:	12 free

167

JOURNAL TITLE: Maternal Child Nursing Journal

MANUSCRIPT ADDRESS: 3505 Fifth Avenue
Pittsburgh, PA 15213

MAJOR CONTENT AREAS: Clinical, psychotherapy, social, clinical
nursing

ARTICLES USUALLY ACCEPTED: Research, review, theoretical, clinical
case studies

TOPICS PREFERRED: Children's coping with stress, parent-child
perceptions of illness and/or hospitalization

INAPPROPRIATE MANUSCRIPTS: Functional aspects of nursing

INDEXED/ABSTRACTED IN: PA, CINL

SUBSCRIPTION ADDRESS: 3505 Fifth Avenue
Pittsburgh, PA 15213

SUBSCRIPTION COST:	$8		
PUBLICATION LAG TIME:	6-12 months	STYLE SHEET:	Yes
EARLY PUBLICATION OPTION:	No	STYLE REQUIREMENTS:	Own style
REVIEW PERIOD:	3 months	CIRCULATION:	1,200
ACCEPTANCE RATE:	75%	REPRINT POLICY:	50 free

JOURNAL TITLE: Measurement and Evaluation in Guidance

MANUSCRIPT ADDRESS: 460 Erickson Hall
Michigan State University
East Lansing, MI 48824

MAJOR CONTENT AREAS: Counseling, educational, psychometrics

ARTICLES USUALLY ACCEPTED: Research, review, theoretical, book review

TOPICS PREFERRED: Those dealing with measurement and evaluation
in guidance

INAPPROPRIATE MANUSCRIPTS: Validity studies which belong in Educational
and Psychological Measurement

INDEXED/ABSTRACTED IN: PA, CSPA, CCSBS, CIJE, EI, ERA

SUBSCRIPTION ADDRESS: 1607 New Hampshire Avenue, N.W.
Washington, DC 20009

SUBSCRIPTION COST:	$12		
PUBLICATION LAG TIME:	1 year	STYLE SHEET:	Yes
EARLY PUBLICATION OPTION:	No	STYLE REQUIREMENTS:	APA
REVIEW PERIOD:	6 weeks	CIRCULATION:	3,000
ACCEPTANCE RATE:	33%	REPRINT POLICY:	5 free

JOURNAL TITLE: Medical Aspects of Human Sexuality

MANUSCRIPT ADDRESS: 609 Fifth Avenue
New York, NY 10017

MAJOR CONTENT AREAS: Clinical, counseling

ARTICLES USUALLY ACCEPTED: Clinical, research, review related to
sexuality

TOPICS PREFERRED: Sexuality

INAPPROPRIATE MANUSCRIPTS: Those inappropriate for physicians

INDEXED/ABSTRACTED IN: WSA

SUBSCRIPTION ADDRESS: 609 Fifth Avenue
New York, NY 10017

SUBSCRIPTION COST:	$25		
PUBLICATION LAG TIME:	Variable	STYLE SHEET:	Not given
EARLY PUBLICATION OPTION:	Not given	STYLE REQUIREMENTS:	Ind. Med.
REVIEW PERIOD:	1 month	CIRCULATION:	175,000
ACCEPTANCE RATE:	Not given	REPRINT POLICY:	Optional purchase

JOURNAL TITLE: Medicine and Science in Sports

MANUSCRIPT ADDRESS: Howard G. Knuttgen, Ph.D., Editor
1440 Monroe Street
Madison, WI 53706

MAJOR CONTENT AREAS: All areas of medicine and psychology related
to sports

ARTICLES USUALLY ACCEPTED: Research, review, book review

TOPICS PREFERRED: Physiology, clinical and athletic medicine,
biomechanics, psychology of sport

INAPPROPRIATE MANUSCRIPTS: All master's theses and most doctoral theses

INDEXED/ABSTRACTED IN: IM, EM, CA, CCCP, NSA, SCI, WSA

SUBSCRIPTION ADDRESS: 1440 Monroe Street
Madison, WI 53706

SUBSCRIPTION COST:	$18		
PUBLICATION LAG TIME:	2-4 months	STYLE SHEET:	Yes
EARLY PUBLICATION OPTION:	No	STYLE REQUIREMENTS:	Own style
REVIEW PERIOD:	4 weeks	CIRCULATION:	4,500
ACCEPTANCE RATE:	40%	REPRINT POLICY:	Optional purchase

JOURNAL TITLE: Memory and Cognition

MANUSCRIPT ADDRESS: Dr. Rudolph W. Schultz
Dept. of Psychology, University of Iowa
Iowa City, IA 52240

MAJOR CONTENT AREAS: Developmental, human experimental & learning,
memory & information processing, cognition

ARTICLES USUALLY ACCEPTED: Research, review, theoretical

TOPICS PREFERRED: Memory, information processing, psycholinguistics
problem solving, thinking, conceptual behavior

INAPPROPRIATE MANUSCRIPTS: Educational psychology, correlational studies,
applied behavior analysis, methodology

INDEXED/ABSTRACTED IN: PA, CCSBS

SUBSCRIPTION ADDRESS: Psychonomic Society, Inc.
1108 West 34th Street
Austin, TX 78705

SUBSCRIPTION COST: $15 individual, $30 institutional

PUBLICATION LAG TIME: 10 months   STYLE SHEET: Yes

EARLY PUBLICATION OPTION: No   STYLE REQUIREMENTS: APA

REVIEW PERIOD: 6-8 weeks   CIRCULATION: 1,750

ACCEPTANCE RATE: 40%   REPRINT POLICY: Purchase
encouraged

JOURNAL TITLE: Mental Retardation

MANUSCRIPT ADDRESS: Sue Allen Warren, Ph.D., Editor
Dept of Special Education, Boston University
765 Commonwealth Ave., Boston, MA 02215

MAJOR CONTENT AREAS: Mental retardation, behavior therapy,
educational, learning

ARTICLES USUALLY ACCEPTED: Research, case studies, theoretical, book
review

TOPICS PREFERRED: Learning, behavior therapy, and education as
related to mental retardation

INAPPROPRIATE MANUSCRIPTS: None

INDEXED/ABSTRACTED IN: PA, ASW, BS, CCSBS, CIJE, DSHA, ECEA,
IPAPL, LLBA

SUBSCRIPTION ADDRESS: Ana Montoulieu, AAMD
5201 Connecticut Avenue, N.W.
Washington, DC 20015

SUBSCRIPTION COST: $22

PUBLICATION LAG TIME: Up to 1 year   STYLE SHEET: Yes

EARLY PUBLICATION OPTION: No   STYLE REQUIREMENTS: APA

REVIEW PERIOD: 3-6 months   CIRCULATION: 12,000

ACCEPTANCE RATE: 33%   REPRINT POLICY: Optional
purchase

JOURNAL TITLE: Merrill-Palmer Quarterly

MANUSCRIPT ADDRESS: Editor, Department of Psychology
University of Michigan
Ann Arbor, MI 48104

MAJOR CONTENT AREAS: Developmental, experimental, learning, mental
retardation, perception, personality

ARTICLES USUALLY ACCEPTED: Research, theoretical

TOPICS PREFERRED: Human development

INAPPROPRIATE MANUSCRIPTS: Point-of-view papers that lack an empirical
or theoretical basis

INDEXED/ABSTRACTED IN: PA, ASW, SA, BS, CDA, CCSBS, CIJE, DSHA, EI,
ECEA, JHE, LLBA, MRA, SEA, WSA

SUBSCRIPTION ADDRESS: 71 East Ferry
Detroit, MI 48202

SUBSCRIPTION COST:	$11		
PUBLICATION LAG TIME:	8-12 months	STYLE SHEET:	Yes
EARLY PUBLICATION OPTION:	Yes	STYLE REQUIREMENTS:	APA
REVIEW PERIOD:	3-8 weeks	CIRCULATION:	3,500
ACCEPTANCE RATE:	20-25%	REPRINT POLICY:	50 free

JOURNAL TITLE: Military Medicine

MANUSCRIPT ADDRESS: P. O. Box 104
Kensington, MD 20795

MAJOR CONTENT AREAS: Military and federal health concerns

ARTICLES USUALLY ACCEPTED: Scientific articles related to the
health field

TOPICS PREFERRED: None

INAPPROPRIATE MANUSCRIPTS: None

INDEXED/ABSTRACTED IN: PA, IM, CCCP, DSHA, WAH

SUBSCRIPTION ADDRESS: Association of Military Surgeons
P. O. Box 104
Kensington, MD 20795

SUBSCRIPTION COST:	$20		
PUBLICATION LAG TIME:	10-12 months	STYLE SHEET:	Yes
EARLY PUBLICATION OPTION:	No	STYLE REQUIREMENTS:	Ind. Med.
REVIEW PERIOD:	1 month	CIRCULATION:	10,000
ACCEPTANCE RATE:	70%	REPRINT POLICY:	3-5 free

JOURNAL TITLE: Monographs of the Society for Research
in Child Development

MANUSCRIPT ADDRESS: Dr. Frances D. Horowitz, Editor
Dept. of Human Development, Univ. of Kansas
Lawrence, KS 66045

MAJOR CONTENT AREAS: Developmental

ARTICLES USUALLY ACCEPTED: Research, review, theoretical

TOPICS PREFERRED: None

INAPPROPRIATE MANUSCRIPTS: None

INDEXED/ABSTRACTED IN: PA, CDA, CCSBS, LLBA

SUBSCRIPTION ADDRESS: The University of Chicago Press
5801 South Ellis Ave.
Chicago, IL 60637

SUBSCRIPTION COST: $15
PUBLICATION LAG TIME: 8-12 months   STYLE SHEET: Yes
EARLY PUBLICATION OPTION: No   STYLE REQUIREMENTS: APA
REVIEW PERIOD: 3 months   CIRCULATION: 5,000
ACCEPTANCE RATE: 20%   REPRINT POLICY: 10 free

JOURNAL TITLE: Multivariate Behavioral Research

MANUSCRIPT ADDRESS: Dr. Benjamin Fruchter, Editor
Dept. of Educational Psychology
University of Texas at Austin, Austin, TX 78712

MAJOR CONTENT AREAS: Most areas if multivariate procedures or
design and analysis are employed

ARTICLES USUALLY ACCEPTED: Research, theoretical

TOPICS PREFERRED: New multivariate mathematico-statistical
procedures, new conceptual multivariate models

INAPPROPRIATE MANUSCRIPTS: None

INDEXED/ABSTRACTED IN: PA, CSPA, CCSBS, LLBA

SUBSCRIPTION ADDRESS: Box 30785
TCU Station
Fort Worth, TX 76129

SUBSCRIPTION COST: $15 individual, $24 institutional
PUBLICATION LAG TIME: 6 months   STYLE SHEET: No
EARLY PUBLICATION OPTION: No   STYLE REQUIREMENTS: APA
REVIEW PERIOD: 6 months   CIRCULATION: 1,000
ACCEPTANCE RATE: 25%   REPRINT POLICY: Optional
purchase

JOURNAL TITLE: National Council on Drug Abuse Newsletter

MANUSCRIPT ADDRESS: 8 South Michigan Avenue
Chicago, IL 60603

MAJOR CONTENT AREAS: Most areas as related to drug abuse and
alcoholism

ARTICLES USUALLY ACCEPTED: Research, review, theoretical, book review,
particularly in abstract form

TOPICS PREFERRED: Chemical abuse, drug abuse, alcoholism,
therapy techniques with drug patients

INAPPROPRIATE MANUSCRIPTS: None

INDEXED/ABSTRACTED IN: IM

SUBSCRIPTION ADDRESS: 8 South Michigan Avenue
Chicago, IL 60603

SUBSCRIPTION COST: $38 individual, $48 institutional
PUBLICATION LAG TIME: 1-3 months   STYLE SHEET: Yes
EARLY PUBLICATION OPTION: No   STYLE REQUIREMENTS: Own style
REVIEW PERIOD: 1-3 months   CIRCULATION: 15,000
ACCEPTANCE RATE: 2%   REPRINT POLICY: 10 free copies
of issue

JOURNAL TITLE: Nature

MANUSCRIPT ADDRESS: 4 Little Essex Street
London WC2, England

MAJOR CONTENT AREAS: Experimental

ARTICLES USUALLY ACCEPTED: Research, review

TOPICS PREFERRED: Experimental and observational science

INAPPROPRIATE MANUSCRIPTS: None

INDEXED/ABSTRACTED IN: PA, AA, AI, AATA, BAA, BEI, BS, CB, ISA,
LISA, PRAJ, WSA, WTA

SUBSCRIPTION ADDRESS: 4 Little Essex Street
London WC2, England

SUBSCRIPTION COST: $95
PUBLICATION LAG TIME: 7 weeks   STYLE SHEET: Yes
EARLY PUBLICATION OPTION: No   STYLE REQUIREMENTS: Own style
REVIEW PERIOD: 4 weeks   CIRCULATION: 20,000
ACCEPTANCE RATE: 30%   REPRINT POLICY: Optional
purchase

JOURNAL TITLE: Neurology

MANUSCRIPT ADDRESS: Russell N. DeJong, M.D., Editor-in-Chief
University of Michigan Hospital
Ann Arbor, MI 48109

MAJOR CONTENT AREAS: Mental retardation, clinical neurology, basic neurology

ARTICLES USUALLY ACCEPTED: Research, clinical, case reports

TOPICS PREFERRED: Clinical and basic neurology

INAPPROPRIATE MANUSCRIPTS: Those with no clinical application

INDEXED/ABSTRACTED IN: PA, IM, CCCP, DSHA, IPAPL, LLBA

SUBSCRIPTION ADDRESS: 4015 West 65th Street
Minneapolis, MN 55435

SUBSCRIPTION COST: $24
PUBLICATION LAG TIME: 7-8 months
EARLY PUBLICATION OPTION: No
REVIEW PERIOD: 1 month
ACCEPTANCE RATE: 52%

STYLE SHEET: Yes
STYLE REQUIREMENTS: Ind. Med.
CIRCULATION: 9,000
REPRINT POLICY: Optional purchase

JOURNAL TITLE: Neuropsychologia

MANUSCRIPT ADDRESS: Prof. H. Hecaen
2 ter rue d'Alesia
75014 Paris, France

MAJOR CONTENT AREAS: Experimental, physiological

ARTICLES USUALLY ACCEPTED: Research

TOPICS PREFERRED: Human and animal (primate) neuropsychology

INAPPROPRIATE MANUSCRIPTS: Psychiatry

INDEXED/ABSTRACTED IN: PA, CCSBS, LLBA

SUBSCRIPTION ADDRESS: Pergamon Press
Headington Hill Hall
Oxford OX3 OBW, England

SUBSCRIPTION COST: $25 individual, $55 institutional
PUBLICATION LAG TIME: 9-12 months
EARLY PUBLICATION OPTION: Yes
REVIEW PERIOD: 15-60 days
ACCEPTANCE RATE: 30%

STYLE SHEET: Yes
STYLE REQUIREMENTS: Own style
CIRCULATION: Not given
REPRINT POLICY: 50 free

JOURNAL TITLE: New England Journal of Medicine

MANUSCRIPT ADDRESS: 10 Shattuck Street
Boston, MA 02115

MAJOR CONTENT AREAS: All clinical and experimental areas of
medicine
ARTICLES USUALLY ACCEPTED: Research, review

TOPICS PREFERRED: Clinical investigations

INAPPROPRIATE MANUSCRIPTS: Animal experiments with limited clinical
applicability
INDEXED/ABSTRACTED IN: PA, IM, ASW, AHMS, CCCP, HA, IPARL, LLBA,
PRAJ, WSA

SUBSCRIPTION ADDRESS: 10 Shattuck Street
Boston, MA 02115

SUBSCRIPTION COST:	$22		
PUBLICATION LAG TIME:	3 months	STYLE SHEET:	Yes
EARLY PUBLICATION OPTION:	No	STYLE REQUIREMENTS:	Ind. Med.
REVIEW PERIOD:	1 month	CIRCULATION:	160,000
ACCEPTANCE RATE:	15%	REPRINT POLICY:	Optional purchase

JOURNAL TITLE: New Zealand Psychologist

MANUSCRIPT ADDRESS: R. Gregson and R. J. Irwin, Editors
Dept. of Psychology, Private Bag, Victoria
University, Wellington, New Zealand
MAJOR CONTENT AREAS: Psychology

ARTICLES USUALLY ACCEPTED: Not given

TOPICS PREFERRED: Not given

INAPPROPRIATE MANUSCRIPTS: Not given

INDEXED/ABSTRACTED IN: PA

SUBSCRIPTION ADDRESS: New Zealand Psychological Society
Dept. of Psychology, Private Bag, Victoria
University, Wellington, New Zealand

SUBSCRIPTION COST:	$2New Zealand		
PUBLICATION LAG TIME:	Not given	STYLE SHEET:	Not given
EARLY PUBLICATION OPTION:	Not given	STYLE REQUIREMENTS:	Not given
REVIEW PERIOD:	Not given	CIRCULATION:	500
ACCEPTANCE RATE:	Not given	REPRINT POLICY:	Not given

JOURNAL TITLE: Nursing Research

MANUSCRIPT ADDRESS: 10 Columbus Circle
New York, NY 10019

MAJOR CONTENT AREAS: Nursing

ARTICLES USUALLY ACCEPTED: Research, abstracts, news, book reviews

TOPICS PREFERRED: Nursing research

INAPPROPRIATE MANUSCRIPTS: None

INDEXED/ABSTRACTED IN: PA, IM, EM, AHMS, CINL, CCCP, CCSBS, HA, HLI, MCR, MRA, NSA, SSCI

SUBSCRIPTION ADDRESS: 10 Columbus Circle
New York, NY 10019

SUBSCRIPTION COST: $20
PUBLICATION LAG TIME: 1 year
EARLY PUBLICATION OPTION: No
REVIEW PERIOD: 3 months
ACCEPTANCE RATE: 30%

STYLE SHEET: Yes
STYLE REQUIREMENTS: APA
CIRCULATION: 7,500
REPRINT POLICY: Purchase required

JOURNAL TITLE: Offender Rehabilitation

MANUSCRIPT ADDRESS: Sol Chaneles, Ph.D., Editor
333 West End Avenue
New York, NY 10023

MAJOR CONTENT AREAS: All areas related to offender rehabilitation

ARTICLES USUALLY ACCEPTED: Research, review, theoretical

TOPICS PREFERRED: Social restoration

INAPPROPRIATE MANUSCRIPTS: None as yet (new journal)

INDEXED/ABSTRACTED IN: Not yet available

SUBSCRIPTION ADDRESS: The Haworth Press
174 Fifth Avenue
New York, NY 10010

SUBSCRIPTION COST: $16 individual, $30 institutional
PUBLICATION LAG TIME: 3 months   STYLE SHEET: Yes
EARLY PUBLICATION OPTION: Yes   STYLE REQUIREMENTS: Chicago
REVIEW PERIOD: 5 weeks   CIRCULATION: Not yet known
ACCEPTANCE RATE: Not yet known   REPRINT POLICY: 50 free

JOURNAL TITLE: Omega-Journal of Death & Dying

MANUSCRIPT ADDRESS: Dr. Robert Kastenbaum, Psychology Dept.
Univ. of Mass., Columbia Pt. Campus
Dorchester, MA 02125

MAJOR CONTENT AREAS: Behavior therapy, counseling and psychotherapy
as related to death and dying

ARTICLES USUALLY ACCEPTED: Research, review, theoretical, book review

TOPICS PREFERRED: Dying, terminal care, bereavement, funeral
practices, suicide, death attitudes

INAPPROPRIATE MANUSCRIPTS: Those reflecting a lack of awareness of recent
progress in the field

INDEXED/ABSTRACTED IN: PA, IM, ASW, AA, CCSBS, HA, PRG

SUBSCRIPTION ADDRESS: Baywood Publishing Co.
43 Central Drive
Farmingdale, NY 11735

SUBSCRIPTION COST: $35
PUBLICATION LAG TIME: 6-9 months   STYLE SHEET: Yes
EARLY PUBLICATION OPTION: No   STYLE REQUIREMENTS: APA
REVIEW PERIOD: 2-4 months   CIRCULATION: 1,000
ACCEPTANCE RATE: 40%   REPRINT POLICY: 20 free

JOURNAL TITLE: Organizational Behavior and Human Performance

MANUSCRIPT ADDRESS: Dr. James C. Naylor, Editor
Dept. of Psychological Sciences, Purdue Universit
West Lafayette, IN 47907

MAJOR CONTENT AREAS: Industrial/organizational

ARTICLES USUALLY ACCEPTED: Research, theoretical

TOPICS PREFERRED: Job satisfaction and motivation

INAPPROPRIATE MANUSCRIPTS: None

INDEXED/ABSTRACTED IN: PA, BS, CCSBS, JHE

SUBSCRIPTION ADDRESS: Academic Press, Inc.
111 Fifth Avenue
New York, NY 10003

SUBSCRIPTION COST:	$45 individual, $90 institutional		
PUBLICATION LAG TIME:	9 months	STYLE SHEET:	Yes
EARLY PUBLICATION OPTION:	Yes	STYLE REQUIREMENTS:	APA
REVIEW PERIOD:	2-4 months	CIRCULATION:	Not given
ACCEPTANCE RATE:	38%	REPRINT POLICY:	100 free

JOURNAL TITLE: Organizational Dynamics

MANUSCRIPT ADDRESS: 135 West 50th Street
New York, NY 10020

MAJOR CONTENT AREAS: Organizational, social

ARTICLES USUALLY ACCEPTED: Research, review

TOPICS PREFERRED: Organizational behavior in an industrial
setting

INAPPROPRIATE MANUSCRIPTS: None

INDEXED/ABSTRACTED IN: CCSBS

SUBSCRIPTION ADDRESS: Box 319, Subscription Services
American Management Association
Saranac Lake, NY 12983

SUBSCRIPTION COST:	$18		
PUBLICATION LAG TIME:	3 months	STYLE SHEET:	Yes
EARLY PUBLICATION OPTION:	No	STYLE REQUIREMENTS:	Chicago
REVIEW PERIOD:	3 months	CIRCULATION:	8,000
ACCEPTANCE RATE:	20%	REPRINT POLICY:	100 free

JOURNAL TITLE: Parapsychology Review

MANUSCRIPT ADDRESS: 29 West 57th Street
New York, NY 10019

MAJOR CONTENT AREAS: Parapsychology

ARTICLES USUALLY ACCEPTED: Research

TOPICS PREFERRED: Parapsychology

INAPPROPRIATE MANUSCRIPTS: Personal experience of paranormal phenomena

INDEXED/ABSTRACTED IN: PA

SUBSCRIPTION ADDRESS: 29 West 57th Street
New York, NY 10019

SUBSCRIPTION COST: $5
PUBLICATION LAG TIME: 2 months   STYLE SHEET: No
EARLY PUBLICATION OPTION: No   STYLE REQUIREMENTS: None
REVIEW PERIOD: 2 weeks   CIRCULATION: 2,500
ACCEPTANCE RATE: 1%   REPRINT POLICY: 2 free

JOURNAL TITLE: Pastoral Psychology

MANUSCRIPT ADDRESS: Liston O. Mills, Editor
Vanderbilt Divinity School
Nashville, TN 37240
MAJOR CONTENT AREAS: All areas as related to the work of ministry

ARTICLES USUALLY ACCEPTED: Research, theoretical

TOPICS PREFERRED: Any dealing with the work of ministry

INAPPROPRIATE MANUSCRIPTS: None

INDEXED/ABSTRACTED IN: PA, ASW, GSSRPL, IRPL, RTA, WSA

SUBSCRIPTION ADDRESS: Human Sciences Press
72 Fifth Avenue
New York, NY 10011
SUBSCRIPTION COST: $12 individual, $30 institutional
PUBLICATION LAG TIME: 6-12 months   STYLE SHEET: Yes
EARLY PUBLICATION OPTION: Yes   STYLE REQUIREMENTS: Chicago
REVIEW PERIOD: 6-8 weeks   CIRCULATION: Not yet known
ACCEPTANCE RATE: 33%   REPRINT POLICY: 1 free

JOURNAL TITLE: Pavlovian Journal of Biological Science

MANUSCRIPT ADDRESS: W. Horsley Gantt, MD., Editor
P. O. Box 7
Perry Point, MD 21902

MAJOR CONTENT AREAS: Experimental, physiological, philosophical

ARTICLES USUALLY ACCEPTED: Research, review, theoretical, editoral, book review

TOPICS PREFERRED: Physiological experimental, psychiatric, experimental psychological

INAPPROPRIATE MANUSCRIPTS: None

INDEXED/ABSTRACTED IN: PA, BA, CCSBS, PRG

SUBSCRIPTION ADDRESS: J. B. Lippincott Co., Medical Journals Dept.
East Washington Square
Philadelphia, PA 19105

SUBSCRIPTION COST: $20		
PUBLICATION LAG TIME: 3-6 months	STYLE SHEET:	Yes
EARLY PUBLICATION OPTION: No	STYLE REQUIREMENTS:	APA, Ind. Med.
REVIEW PERIOD: 3 months	CIRCULATION:	750
ACCEPTANCE RATE: 70%	REPRINT POLICY:	Optional purchase

JOURNAL TITLE: Perception

MANUSCRIPT ADDRESS: The Medical School, University Walk
Brain and Perception Lab., Dept. of Anatomy
Bristol BS8 1TD, England

MAJOR CONTENT AREAS: Perception, experimental, learning comparative, physiological

ARTICLES USUALLY ACCEPTED: Research, review, theoretical, book review, apparatus, jokes, cartoons

TOPICS PREFERRED: Artificial intelligence, philosophy, experimental aesthetics

INAPPROPRIATE MANUSCRIPTS: None

INDEXED/ABSTRACTED IN: PA, EM, CEI, CCSBS, PRG

SUBSCRIPTION ADDRESS: Pion Ltd.
207 Brondesbury Park
London NW2, England

SUBSCRIPTION COST: $19.50 individual, $39 institutional		
PUBLICATION LAG TIME: 3 months	STYLE SHEET:	Yes
EARLY PUBLICATION OPTION: No	STYLE REQUIREMENTS:	Own style
REVIEW PERIOD: 3 months	CIRCULATION:	300
ACCEPTANCE RATE: 60%	REPRINT POLICY:	50 free

JOURNAL TITLE: Perception and Psychophysics

MANUSCRIPT ADDRESS: C.W. Eriksen, Principal Editor
Psychology Bldg., University of Illinois
Champaign, IL 61820

MAJOR CONTENT AREAS: Perception

ARTICLES USUALLY ACCEPTED: Research, review, theoretical

TOPICS PREFERRED: Perception and psychophysics

INAPPROPRIATE MANUSCRIPTS: None

INDEXED/ABSTRACTED IN: PA, CCSBS, DSHA, LLBA, PRG

SUBSCRIPTION ADDRESS: Psychonomic Society
1108 West 34th Street
Austin, TX 78705

SUBSCRIPTION COST: $25 individual, $50 institutional
PUBLICATION LAG TIME: 6 months   STYLE SHEET: Yes
EARLY PUBLICATION OPTION: Yes   STYLE REQUIREMENTS: APA
REVIEW PERIOD: 6 weeks   CIRCULATION: 1,400
ACCEPTANCE RATE: 40%   REPRINT POLICY: Optional
purchase

JOURNAL TITLE: Perceptual and Motor Skills

MANUSCRIPT ADDRESS: Box 1441
Missoula, MT 59801

MAJOR CONTENT AREAS: Almost all areas

ARTICLES USUALLY ACCEPTED: Research, review, theoretical

TOPICS PREFERRED: Perception, motor skills, general
methodology

INAPPROPRIATE MANUSCRIPTS: Badly conceived questions and inadequate
designs

INDEXED/ABSTRACTED IN: PA, IM, EM, BI, BA, CSPA, CCSBS, CIJE,
DSHA, ECEA, LLBA, RHEA, SCI, WSA

SUBSCRIPTION ADDRESS: Box 1441
Missoula, MT 59801

SUBSCRIPTION COST: $39.30 individual, $78.60 institutional
PUBLICATION LAG TIME: 2 months   STYLE SHEET: No
EARLY PUBLICATION OPTION: No   STYLE REQUIREMENTS: APA
REVIEW PERIOD: 3-4 weeks   CIRCULATION: 1,800
ACCEPTANCE RATE: 55%   REPRINT POLICY: Purchase
required

JOURNAL TITLE: Personal Growth

MANUSCRIPT ADDRESS: P. O. Box 1254
Berkeley, CA 94701

MAJOR CONTENT AREAS: Humanistic psychology, exisential psychology

ARTICLES USUALLY ACCEPTED: Theoretical, interview, survey

TOPICS PREFERRED: New psychotherapies, existentialism, imagery,
phenomenology, the human potential movement

INAPPROPRIATE MANUSCRIPTS: Handwriting analysis, religion, case studies

INDEXED/ABSTRACTED IN: None

SUBSCRIPTION ADDRESS: P. O. Box 1254
Berkeley, CA 94701

SUBSCRIPTION COST:	$9.75		
PUBLICATION LAG TIME:	4-8 weeks	STYLE SHEET:	Yes
EARLY PUBLICATION OPTION:	Yes	STYLE REQUIREMENTS:	None
REVIEW PERIOD:	6 weeks	CIRCULATION:	8,000
ACCEPTANCE RATE:	10%	REPRINT POLICY:	20 free

JOURNAL TITLE: Personality and Social Psychology Bulletin

MANUSCRIPT ADDRESS: Professor Clyde Hendrick
Dept. of Psychology, Kent State University
Kent, OH 44242

MAJOR CONTENT AREAS: Personality, social

ARTICLES USUALLY ACCEPTED: Brief reports on research and theory

TOPICS PREFERRED: Brief reports on personality and social
psychology

INAPPROPRIATE MANUSCRIPTS: None

INDEXED/ABSTRACTED IN: PA

SUBSCRIPTION ADDRESS: Professor Alan E. Gross
University of Missouri at St. Louis
St. Louis, MO 63121

SUBSCRIPTION COST:	$5 individual, $15 institutional		
PUBLICATION LAG TIME:	3 months	STYLE SHEET:	Yes
EARLY PUBLICATION OPTION:	No	STYLE REQUIREMENTS:	APA, Own style
REVIEW PERIOD:	1 month	CIRCULATION:	4,000
ACCEPTANCE RATE:	35%	REPRINT POLICY:	Optional purchase

JOURNAL TITLE: Personnel and Guidance Journal

MANUSCRIPT ADDRESS: APGA
1607 New Hampshire Avenue, N.W.
Washington, DC 20009

MAJOR CONTENT AREAS: Behavior therapy, clinical, counseling,
psychotherapy, methodology, community

ARTICLES USUALLY ACCEPTED: Review, theoretical, research, book review,
dialogues, poems

TOPICS PREFERRED: Counseling and guidance

INAPPROPRIATE MANUSCRIPTS: None

INDEXED/ABSTRACTED IN: PA, ASW, BRI, BS, CSPA, CCSBS, DSHA, EI,
EAA, ERA, ECEA, IBSS, ILD, MI, MHBRI, PL,
PHRA, SEA, WSA

SUBSCRIPTION ADDRESS: APGA
1607 New Hampshire Avenue, N.W.
Washington, DC 20009

SUBSCRIPTION COST:	$20		
PUBLICATION LAG TIME:	9-12 months	STYLE SHEET:	Yes
EARLY PUBLICATION OPTION:	Yes	STYLE REQUIREMENTS:	APA
REVIEW PERIOD:	2-3 months	CIRCULATION:	46,000
ACCEPTANCE RATE:	15-20%	REPRINT POLICY:	10 free

JOURNAL TITLE: The Personnel Journal

MANUSCRIPT ADDRESS: 1131 Olympic Blvd.
Santa Monica, CA 90404

MAJOR CONTENT AREAS: Behavior therapy/applied behavior analysis,
personnel management, industrial relations

ARTICLES USUALLY ACCEPTED: Research, review, theoretical, book review,
(only on recently published books)

TOPICS PREFERRED: Personnel, industrial relations

INAPPROPRIATE MANUSCRIPTS: Those that are too specific (e.g., case history
of a hotel) to have broad appeal to readers

INDEXED/ABSTRACTED IN: PA, ADPA, BRI, BS, BPI, CSPA, CCSBS, CIJE, EE,
EAA, ERA, IPAPL, IBSS, ILD, JHE, MI, PTA, PMA,
PHRA, TMA, WSA

SUBSCRIPTION ADDRESS: P. O. Box 1520
Santa Monica, CA 90406

SUBSCRIPTION COST:	$20		
PUBLICATION LAG TIME:	6-12 months	STYLE SHEET:	Yes
EARLY PUBLICATION OPTION:	Yes	STYLE REQUIREMENTS:	Own style
REVIEW PERIOD:	3-4 months	CIRCULATION:	13,000
ACCEPTANCE RATE:	50-75%	REPRINT POLICY:	100 free

JOURNAL TITLE: Personnel Psychology

MANUSCRIPT ADDRESS: Dr. Milton D. Hakel, Editor, Dept. of Psycholgy
Ohio State Univ., 404-C West 17th Avenue
Columbus, OH 43210

MAJOR CONTENT AREAS: Personnel psychology, industrial/organizational

ARTICLES USUALLY ACCEPTED: Research methods, results, or application to
the solution of personnel problems in business,
industry or government

TOPICS PREFERRED: Personnel problems in organizations

INAPPROPRIATE MANUSCRIPTS: None

INDEXED/ABSTRACTED IN: PA, BI, BS, CCSBS, CIJE, EE, EAA, ERA, IBSS,
ILD, PMA, WSA

SUBSCRIPTION ADDRESS: Box 6965 College Station
Durham, NC 27708

SUBSCRIPTION COST:	$18		
PUBLICATION LAG TIME:	4 months	STYLE SHEET:	No
EARLY PUBLICATION OPTION:	No	STYLE REQUIREMENTS:	APA
REVIEW PERIOD:	4 months	CIRCULATION:	3,000
ACCEPTANCE RATE:	20%	REPRINT POLICY:	Optional purchase

JOURNAL TITLE: Physiological Psychology

MANUSCRIPT ADDRESS: Dr. Richard F. Thompson
Dept. of Psychobiology, Univ. of California
Irvine, CA 92717

MAJOR CONTENT AREAS: Physiological, experimental

ARTICLES USUALLY ACCEPTED: Research, review, theoretical

TOPICS PREFERRED: Any in the area of physiological psychology
if relevant to behavior

INAPPROPRIATE MANUSCRIPTS: None

INDEXED/ABSTRACTED IN: PA

SUBSCRIPTION ADDRESS: Psychonomic Society
1108 West 34th Street
Austin, TX 78705

SUBSCRIPTION COST:	$10 individual, $20 institutional		
PUBLICATION LAG TIME:	6-9 months	STYLE SHEET:	Yes
EARLY PUBLICATION OPTION:	Yes	STYLE REQUIREMENTS:	APA
REVIEW PERIOD:	2-4 weeks	CIRCULATION:	1,350
ACCEPTANCE RATE:	75%	REPRINT POLICY:	Purchase required

JOURNAL TITLE: Physiology and Behavior

MANUSCRIPT ADDRESS: Matthew J. Wayner, Editor-in-Chief
Brain Research Lab, Syracuse University
601 Univ. Ave., Syracuse, NY 13210

MAJOR CONTENT AREAS: Physiology and behavior

ARTICLES USUALLY ACCEPTED: Reports of systematic studies, brief
reports of new methods, techniques, etc.
with some review and theoretical papers

TOPICS PREFERRED: Physiological studies in behavioral context

INAPPROPRIATE MANUSCRIPTS: Not given

INDEXED/ABSTRACTED IN: BA, CA, PA

SUBSCRIPTION ADDRESS: Pergamon Press
Maxwell House, Fairview Park
Elmsford, NY 10523

SUBSCRIPTION COST: $25 individual, $200 institutional

PUBLICATION LAG TIME: 6 months	STYLE SHEET:	Not given
EARLY PUBLICATION OPTION: Not given	STYLE REQUIREMENTS:	WLSP
REVIEW PERIOD: Not given	CIRCULATION:	Not given
ACCEPTANCE RATE: Not given	REPRINT POLICY:	25 free

JOURNAL TITLE: Professional Psychology

MANUSCRIPT ADDRESS: Donald K. Freedheim, Editor
Dept of Psychology, Case Western Reserve
University, Cleveland, OH 44106

MAJOR CONTENT AREAS: The practice of psychology

ARTICLES USUALLY ACCEPTED: Original articles on conceptual and practical
issues which are of interest to psychologists
and those who want to learn about psychologists

TOPICS PREFERRED: Applications of research, standards of practice,
service delivery, training innovations

INAPPROPRIATE MANUSCRIPTS: None

INDEXED/ABSTRACTED IN: PA, CCSBS, CIJE

SUBSCRIPTION ADDRESS: APA Subscription Office
1200 17th Street, N.W.
Washington, DC 20036

SUBSCRIPTION COST: $18

PUBLICATION LAG TIME: 13 months	STYLE SHEET:	No
EARLY PUBLICATION OPTION: No	STYLE REQUIREMENTS:	APA
REVIEW PERIOD: Variable	CIRCULATION:	4,000
ACCEPTANCE RATE: 39%	REPRINT POLICY:	20 free

JOURNAL TITLE: Psychiatric Annals

MANUSCRIPT ADDRESS: 501 Madison Avenue
New York, NY 10022

MAJOR CONTENT AREAS: All areas of psychiatry

ARTICLES USUALLY ACCEPTED: Research, review, theoretical, case
studies

TOPICS PREFERRED: Any up to date trends

INAPPROPRIATE MANUSCRIPTS: None

INDEXED/ABSTRACTED IN: PA, EM, CCSBS

SUBSCRIPTION ADDRESS: 501 Madison Avenue
New York, NY 10022

SUBSCRIPTION COST:	$27.50		
PUBLICATION LAG TIME:	3-6 months	STYLE SHEET:	Yes
EARLY PUBLICATION OPTION:	No	STYLE REQUIREMENTS:	Own style
REVIEW PERIOD:	2 months	CIRCULATION:	26,770
ACCEPTANCE RATE:	60%	REPRINT POLICY:	Optional purchase

JOURNAL TITLE: Psychiatric Forum

MANUSCRIPT ADDRESS: Lucius C. Pressley, Editor
P. O. Box 119
Columbia, SC 29202

MAJOR CONTENT AREAS: Psychiatry

ARTICLES USUALLY ACCEPTED: Not given

TOPICS PREFERRED: Not given

INAPPROPRIATE MANUSCRIPTS: Not given

INDEXED/ABSTRACTED IN: EM, CCCP, PA, SSCI

SUBSCRIPTION ADDRESS: PF, South Carolina Dept. of Mental Health
P. O. Box 119
Columbia, SC 29202

SUBSCRIPTION COST:	Free		
PUBLICATION LAG TIME:	Not given	STYLE SHEET:	Not given
EARLY PUBLICATION OPTION:	Not given	STYLE REQUIREMENTS:	IM
REVIEW PERIOD:	Not given	CIRCULATION:	4,000
ACCEPTANCE RATE:	Not given	REPRINT POLICY:	Not given

JOURNAL TITLE: Psychiatric Opinion

MANUSCRIPT ADDRESS: 82 Cochituate Road
Framingham, MA 01701

MAJOR CONTENT AREAS: All areas of psychiatry

ARTICLES USUALLY ACCEPTED: Opinions regarding vital issues in the
field of mental health

TOPICS PREFERRED: Opinions covering any area of psychiatry

INAPPROPRIATE MANUSCRIPTS: Highly technical, non-opinion papers

INDEXED/ABSTRACTED IN: SLTCPP

SUBSCRIPTION ADDRESS: 82 Cochituate Road
Framingham, MA 01701

SUBSCRIPTION COST:	$15		
PUBLICATION LAG TIME:	1-12 months	STYLE SHEET:	No
EARLY PUBLICATION OPTION:	Not known	STYLE REQUIREMENTS:	Ind. Med.
REVIEW PERIOD:	1-4 weeks	CIRCULATION:	20,500
ACCEPTANCE RATE:	Not computed	REPRINT POLICY:	20 free copies of issue

JOURNAL TITLE: Psychiatric Quarterly

MANUSCRIPT ADDRESS: Behavioral Publications
72 Fifth Avenue
New York, NY 10011

MAJOR CONTENT AREAS: Psychotherapy, behavior therapy, psychoanalysis,
mental retardation, psychiatry

ARTICLES USUALLY ACCEPTED: Research, review

TOPICS PREFERRED: Theoretical and applied psychiatry and
psychotherapy

INAPPROPRIATE MANUSCRIPTS: Those not based on research, such as fringe
opinion or editorials

INDEXED/ABSTRACTED IN: PA, ASW, BS, CCCP, CCSBS, DSHA, IPAPL, LLBA,
PHRA

SUBSCRIPTION ADDRESS: Behavioral Publications
72 Fifth Avenue
New York, NY 10011

SUBSCRIPTION COST:	$15 individual, $30 institutional		
PUBLICATION LAG TIME:	6 months	STYLE SHEET:	Yes
EARLY PUBLICATION OPTION:	No	STYLE REQUIREMENTS:	Own style
REVIEW PERIOD:	2 weeks	CIRCULATION:	1,800
ACCEPTANCE RATE:	25%	REPRINT POLICY:	Purchase required

JOURNAL TITLE: Psychiatry: Journal for the Study of
Interpersonal Processes

MANUSCRIPT ADDRESS: 1610 New Hampshire Avenue, N.W.
Washington, DC 20009

MAJOR CONTENT AREAS: All areas of psychiatry

ARTICLES USUALLY ACCEPTED: Research, review, theoretical, book review

TOPICS PREFERRED: Those dealing with clinical work

INAPPROPRIATE MANUSCRIPTS: Those covering material already well
represented in the scientific literature

INDEXED/ABSTRACTED IN: PA, ASW, SA, BS, CSPA, CCSBS, HA, IPAPL,
LLBA, PRAJ, WSA

SUBSCRIPTION ADDRESS: 1610 New Hampshire Avenue, N.W.
Washington, DC 20009

SUBSCRIPTION COST:	$12.50 individual, $20 institutional		
PUBLICATION LAG TIME:	9-12 months	STYLE SHEET:	Yes
EARLY PUBLICATION OPTION:	No	STYLE REQUIREMENTS:	Own style
REVIEW PERIOD:	2-4 months	CIRCULATION:	3,400
ACCEPTANCE RATE:	20%	REPRINT POLICY:	Optional purchase

JOURNAL TITLE: The Psychoanalytic Quarterly

MANUSCRIPT ADDRESS: The Editor, Room 911
57 West 57th Street
New York, NY 10019

MAJOR CONTENT AREAS: Psychoanalysis, psychotherapy

ARTICLES USUALLY ACCEPTED: Clinical, research, theoretical, or applied
articles on psychoanalysis

TOPICS PREFERRED: Applied psychoanalysis, clinical or
theoretical

INAPPROPRIATE MANUSCRIPTS: None

INDEXED/ABSTRACTED IN: PA, IM, EM, BS, CCSBS, PRG

SUBSCRIPTION ADDRESS: 57 West 57th Street
New York, NY 10019

SUBSCRIPTION COST:	$20		
PUBLICATION LAG TIME:	1 year	STYLE SHEET:	Yes
EARLY PUBLICATION OPTION:	No	STYLE REQUIREMENTS:	Own style
REVIEW PERIOD:	3 months	CIRCULATION:	4,000
ACCEPTANCE RATE:	20%	REPRINT POLICY:	Optional purchase

JOURNAL TITLE: Psychoanalytic Review

MANUSCRIPT ADDRESS: 150 West 13th Street
New York, NY 10011

MAJOR CONTENT AREAS: Clinical, personality, psychoanalysis,
psychotherapy, history & systems

ARTICLES USUALLY ACCEPTED: Research, review, theoretical, book review

TOPICS PREFERRED: Psychoanalytic topics of interdisciplinary
interest, psychoanalysis applied to history

INAPPROPRIATE MANUSCRIPTS: Poetry, psychoanalysis applied to literature,
term papers

INDEXED/ABSTRACTED IN: PA, IM, EM, ASW, AA, AES, CCSBS, DSHA, IPAPL,
WSA

SUBSCRIPTION ADDRESS: 150 West 13th Street
New York, NY 10011

SUBSCRIPTION COST: $16
PUBLICATION LAG TIME: 2 years   STYLE SHEET: Yes
EARLY PUBLICATION OPTION: Yes   STYLE REQUIREMENTS: Own style
REVIEW PERIOD: 2-6 months   CIRCULATION: 2,000
ACCEPTANCE RATE: 25-33%   REPRINT POLICY: 2 free copies
of issue

JOURNAL TITLE: Psychological Bulletin

MANUSCRIPT ADDRESS: R. J. Herrnstein, Editor, William James Hall
Harvard University, 33 Kirkland Street
Cambridge, MA 02138

MAJOR CONTENT AREAS: All areas of psychology

ARTICLES USUALLY ACCEPTED: Evaluative reviews of substantive and
methodological issues; research that illustrates
some methodological problem or issue

TOPICS PREFERRED: Those of sufficient breadth to interest a
wide readership among psychologists

INAPPROPRIATE MANUSCRIPTS: None

INDEXED/ABSTRACTED IN: PA, ASW, BI, BS, CCSBS, DSHA, EAA, JHE,
LLBA, RHEA, WSA

SUBSCRIPTION ADDRESS: APA Subscription Office
1200 17th Street, N.W.
Washington, DC 20036

SUBSCRIPTION COST: $30
PUBLICATION LAG TIME: 11 months   STYLE SHEET: No
EARLY PUBLICATION OPTION: No   STYLE REQUIREMENTS: APA
REVIEW PERIOD: Variable   CIRCULATION: 10,000
ACCEPTANCE RATE: 15%   REPRINT POLICY: 20 free

JOURNAL TITLE: Psychological Issues

MANUSCRIPT ADDRESS: Dr. Herbert J. Schlesinger, Editor
University of Colorado Medical Center
Denver, CO 80220

MAJOR CONTENT AREAS: Psychoanalysis, psychopathology, therapy

ARTICLES USUALLY ACCEPTED: Experimental studies, controlled developmental studies, genetic explorations of psychoanalysis

TOPICS PREFERRED: Submissions on invitation only

INAPPROPRIATE MANUSCRIPTS: Not given

INDEXED/ABSTRACTED IN: IM, PA, SSCI

SUBSCRIPTION ADDRESS: International Universities Press
239 Park Avenue South
New York, NY 10003

SUBSCRIPTION COST: $15

PUBLICATION LAG TIME: Not given	STYLE SHEET: Not given
EARLY PUBLICATION OPTION: Not given	STYLE REQUIREMENTS: Not given
REVIEW PERIOD: Not given	CIRCULATION: 1,000
ACCEPTANCE RATE: Not given	REPRINT POLICY: Not given

JOURNAL TITLE: Psychological Medicine

MANUSCRIPT ADDRESS: Professor M. Shepherd
Institute of Psychiatry
De Crespigny Park, London SE5 8AF, England

MAJOR CONTENT AREAS: All clinical, biological, and psychosocial aspects of psychiatry

ARTICLES USUALLY ACCEPTED: Research, review, theoretical

TOPICS PREFERRED: Clinical, biological, and/or psychosocial research

INAPPROPRIATE MANUSCRIPTS: None

INDEXED/ABSTRACTED IN: PA, CCCP

SUBSCRIPTION ADDRESS: Subscription Manager, Cambridge Univ. Press
32 East 57th Street
New York, NY 10022

SUBSCRIPTION COST: $28 individual, $48.50 institutional

PUBLICATION LAG TIME: 6 months	STYLE SHEET: Yes
EARLY PUBLICATION OPTION: Yes	STYLE REQUIREMENTS: Own style
REVIEW PERIOD: 2 months	CIRCULATION: 1,500
ACCEPTANCE RATE: 50-55%	REPRINT POLICY: 50 free

JOURNAL TITLE: Psychological Perspectives

MANUSCRIPT ADDRESS: 10349 West Pico Boulevard
Los Angeles, CA 90064

MAJOR CONTENT AREAS: Psychology for the general public from a
Jungian orientation

ARTICLES USUALLY ACCEPTED: Book and movie reviews, scholarly articles
and essays, verse, fiction

TOPICS PREFERRED: Psychological approaches to people, social
issues, history, and mythology

INAPPROPRIATE MANUSCRIPTS: Academic articles of purely scientific
interest

INDEXED/ABSTRACTED IN: PA, PRG

SUBSCRIPTION ADDRESS: 10349 West Pico Boulevard
Los Angeles, CA 90064

SUBSCRIPTION COST: $8
PUBLICATION LAG TIME: 6-10 months
EARLY PUBLICATION OPTION: No
REVIEW PERIOD: 3 months
ACCEPTANCE RATE: 10%

STYLE SHEET: No
STYLE REQUIREMENTS: Chicago
CIRCULATION: 1,500
REPRINT POLICY: 2 free copies
of issue

JOURNAL TITLE: The Psychological Record

MANUSCRIPT ADDRESS: Charles E. Rice, Editor
Kenyon College
Gambier, OH 43022

MAJOR CONTENT AREAS: Almost all areas of psychology

ARTICLES USUALLY ACCEPTED: Research, review, theoretical, book review

TOPICS PREFERRED: Those articles which clearly relate the
work to significant problems in psychology

INAPPROPRIATE MANUSCRIPTS: Highly specialized ones that are not
relevant to readers outside the specialty

INDEXED/ABSTRACTED IN: PA, IM, BI, BA, CCSBS, DSHA, LLBA, SCI

SUBSCRIPTION ADDRESS: Charles E. Rice, Editor
Kenyon College
Gambier, OH 43022

SUBSCRIPTION COST: $6 individual, $10 institutional
PUBLICATION LAG TIME: 3 months
EARLY PUBLICATION OPTION: No
REVIEW PERIOD: 3 months
ACCEPTANCE RATE: 45%

STYLE SHEET: Yes
STYLE REQUIREMENTS: APA
CIRCULATION: 2,000
REPRINT POLICY: Optional
purchase

JOURNAL TITLE: Psychological Reports

MANUSCRIPT ADDRESS: Box 1441
Missoula, MT 59801

MAJOR CONTENT AREAS: Almost all areas of psychology

ARTICLES USUALLY ACCEPTED: Research, review, theoretical

TOPICS PREFERRED: Controversial material of scientific merit

INAPPROPRIATE MANUSCRIPTS: Badly conceived questions and inadequate
designs

INDEXED/ABSTRACTED IN: PA, BI, CSPA, CCSBS, CIJE, IPAPL, IBSS,
LLBA, PRAJ, RHEA, WSA

SUBSCRIPTION ADDRESS: Box 1441
Missoula, MT 59801

SUBSCRIPTION COST:	$39.30 individual, $78.60 institutional		
PUBLICATION LAG TIME:	2 months	STYLE SHEET:	No
EARLY PUBLICATION OPTION:	No	STYLE REQUIREMENTS:	APA
REVIEW PERIOD:	3-4 weeks	CIRCULATION:	1,800
ACCEPTANCE RATE:	55%	REPRINT POLICY:	Purchase required

JOURNAL TITLE: Psychological Research

MANUSCRIPT ADDRESS: Professor C. N. Cofer, Penn State University
417 Psychology Building
University Park, PA 16802

MAJOR CONTENT AREAS: Perception, learning, communication

ARTICLES USUALLY ACCEPTED: Research, theoretical, short communications,
apparatus notes

TOPICS PREFERRED: Those emphasizing theoretical implications of
the research reported

INAPPROPRIATE MANUSCRIPTS: None

INDEXED/ABSTRACTED IN: CCSBS, LLBA

SUBSCRIPTION ADDRESS: Springer-Verlag New York, Inc.
175 Fifth Avenue
New York, NY 10010

SUBSCRIPTION COST:	$62.50		
PUBLICATION LAG TIME:	3-4 months	STYLE SHEET:	Yes
EARLY PUBLICATION OPTION:	No	STYLE REQUIREMENTS:	Springer
REVIEW PERIOD:	Not given	CIRCULATION:	Not given
ACCEPTANCE RATE:	Not given	REPRINT POLICY:	50 free

JOURNAL TITLE: Psychological Review

MANUSCRIPT ADDRESS: George Mandler, Editor, Dept. of Psychology
University of California, San Diego
La Jolla, CA 92037

MAJOR CONTENT AREAS: All areas of psychology

ARTICLES USUALLY ACCEPTED: Those making theoretical contributions to
any area of scientific psychology

TOPICS PREFERRED: Papers that advance theory rather than review
it; theoretical rather than programmatic

INAPPROPRIATE MANUSCRIPTS: None

INDEXED/ABSTRACTED IN: PA, ASW, BI, CCSBS, CIJE, DSHA, LLBA, RHEA

SUBSCRIPTION ADDRESS: APA Subscription Office
1200 17th Street, N.W.
Washington, DC 20036

SUBSCRIPTION COST:	$20		
PUBLICATION LAG TIME:	8 months	STYLE SHEET:	No
EARLY PUBLICATION OPTION:	No	STYLE REQUIREMENTS:	APA
REVIEW PERIOD:	Variable	CIRCULATION:	8,600
ACCEPTANCE RATE:	11%	REPRINT POLICY:	20 free

JOURNAL TITLE: Psychology - A Journal of Human Behavior

MANUSCRIPT ADDRESS: P. O. Box 6495
Savannah, GA 31405

MAJOR CONTENT AREAS: All areas of psychology

ARTICLES USUALLY ACCEPTED: Research, review, theoretical, book review

TOPICS PREFERRED: Any dealing with human behavior

INAPPROPRIATE MANUSCRIPTS: Animal studies

INDEXED/ABSTRACTED IN: PA, CSPA, CCSBS

SUBSCRIPTION ADDRESS: P. O. Box 6495
Savannah, GA 31405

SUBSCRIPTION COST:	$7		
PUBLICATION LAG TIME:	3 months	STYLE SHEET:	Yes
EARLY PUBLICATION OPTION:	No	STYLE REQUIREMENTS:	APA
REVIEW PERIOD:	10-14 days	CIRCULATION:	4,000
ACCEPTANCE RATE:	50%	REPRINT POLICY:	Optional purchase

JOURNAL TITLE: Psychology in the Schools

MANUSCRIPT ADDRESS: G. B. Fuller, Editor
Psychology Dept., Central Michigan University
Mt. Pleasant, MI 48859

MAJOR CONTENT AREAS: Educational

ARTICLES USUALLY ACCEPTED: Research, evaluation, practice

TOPICS PREFERRED: Any in the area of educational psychology

INAPPROPRIATE MANUSCRIPTS: None

INDEXED/ABSTRACTED IN: PA, BS, CDA, CCSBS, CIJE, EI, ECEA, LLBA, RGPL

SUBSCRIPTION ADDRESS: 4 Conant Square
Brandon, VT 05733

SUBSCRIPTION COST: $15 individual, $25 institutional
PUBLICATION LAG TIME: 6-9 months   STYLE SHEET: Yes
EARLY PUBLICATION OPTION: No   STYLE REQUIREMENTS: APA
REVIEW PERIOD: 1 month   CIRCULATION: 2,261
ACCEPTANCE RATE: 40%   REPRINT POLICY: Optional purchase

JOURNAL TITLE: Psychology of Women Quarterly

MANUSCRIPT ADDRESS: Georgia Babladelis, Ph.D., Editor
Dept. of Psychology, California State University
Hayward, CA 94542

MAJOR CONTENT AREAS: All areas as related to the psychology of women

ARTICLES USUALLY ACCEPTED: Research, review, book review (by invitation), theoretical

TOPICS PREFERRED: Anything that contributes to our understanding of the behavior of women

INAPPROPRIATE MANUSCRIPTS: Sex difference articles of no theoretical import

INDEXED/ABSTRACTED IN: PA

SUBSCRIPTION ADDRESS: Human Sciences Press
72 Fifth Avenue
New York, NY 10011

SUBSCRIPTION COST: $12 individual, $30 institutional
PUBLICATION LAG TIME: 8-9 months   STYLE SHEET: Yes
EARLY PUBLICATION OPTION: Yes   STYLE REQUIREMENTS: APA
REVIEW PERIOD: 4 months   CIRCULATION: Not yet known
ACCEPTANCE RATE: 10-15%   REPRINT POLICY: Purchase required

JOURNAL TITLE: Psychometrika

MANUSCRIPT ADDRESS: Bert F. Green, Jr., Dept of Psychology
The Johns Hopkins University
Baltimore, MD

MAJOR CONTENT AREAS: Psychometrics, statistics, methodology

ARTICLES USUALLY ACCEPTED: The development of quantitative models for
psychological phenomena

TOPICS PREFERRED: Those dealing with the development of
psychology as a quantitative rational science

INAPPROPRIATE MANUSCRIPTS: None

INDEXED/ABSTRACTED IN: PA, BI, BA, CCSBS, CIJE, RHEA

SUBSCRIPTION ADDRESS: Howard Wainer, University of Chicago
5848 University Avenue
Chicago, IL 60637

SUBSCRIPTION COST:	$15 individual, $30 institutional		
PUBLICATION LAG TIME:	6 months	STYLE SHEET:	Yes
EARLY PUBLICATION OPTION:	No	STYLE REQUIREMENTS:	APA
REVIEW PERIOD:	3 months	CIRCULATION:	2,800
ACCEPTANCE RATE:	20%	REPRINT POLICY:	100 free

JOURNAL TITLE: Psychology Today

MANUSCRIPT ADDRESS: One Park Avenue
Room 718
New York, NY 10016

MAJOR CONTENT AREAS: All areas of interest to general readership

ARTICLES USUALLY ACCEPTED: Major overviews, research that throws light
on basic trends and news

TOPICS PREFERRED: Interpersonal relations, the trials and triumphs
of every day life, substantial scientific findings

INAPPROPRIATE MANUSCRIPTS: Poetry, personal speculation without rigor or
base

INDEXED/ABSTRACTED IN: PA, AA, BRI, BS, CSPA, CCSBS, DSHA, ECEA, GSSRPL,
IPAPL, JHE, LLBA, PRA, PHRA, RGPL

SUBSCRIPTION ADDRESS: P. O. Box 2990
Boulder, CO 80302

SUBSCRIPTION COST:	$12		
PUBLICATION LAG TIME:	3 months	STYLE SHEET:	No
EARLY PUBLICATION OPTION:	Yes	STYLE REQUIREMENTS:	Chicago
REVIEW PERIOD:	1 month	CIRCULATION:	1,100,000
ACCEPTANCE RATE:	5%	REPRINT POLICY:	50 free magazines

JOURNAL TITLE: Psychopharmacology

MANUSCRIPT ADDRESS: Dr. J. O. Cole, Boston State Hospital
591 Morton Street
Boston, MA 02124

MAJOR CONTENT AREAS: All areas in which drug effects are included as a major focus

ARTICLES USUALLY ACCEPTED: Research, review (by prior negotiation with editor)

TOPICS PREFERRED: Psychopharmacology

INAPPROPRIATE MANUSCRIPTS: None

INDEXED/ABSTRACTED IN: PA, IM

SUBSCRIPTION ADDRESS: Springer-Verlag New York, Inc.
175 Fifth Avenue
New York, NY 10010

SUBSCRIPTION COST:	$339.90		
PUBLICATION LAG TIME:	6 months	STYLE SHEET:	No
EARLY PUBLICATION OPTION:	No	STYLE REQUIREMENTS:	APA
REVIEW PERIOD:	2 months	CIRCULATION:	Not given
ACCEPTANCE RATE:	50%	REPRINT POLICY:	50 free

JOURNAL TITLE: Psychophysiology

MANUSCRIPT ADDRESS: William F. Prokasy, Editor
205 Spencer Hall, University of Utah
Salt Lake City, UT 84112

MAJOR CONTENT AREAS: All areas related to psychophysiology

ARTICLES USUALLY ACCEPTED: Research, review, theoretical ,as applied to the relationships between physiological and psychological aspects of human behavior

TOPICS PREFERRED: Psychosomatic medicine, neurology, biofeedback, conditioning, sleep

INAPPROPRIATE MANUSCRIPTS: None

INDEXED/ABSTRACTED IN: PA, IM, CCSBS, LLBA

SUBSCRIPTION ADDRESS: Society for Psychophysiological Research
2380 Lisa Lane, Route #2
Madison, WI 53711

SUBSCRIPTION COST:	$22 individual, $30 institutional		
PUBLICATION LAG TIME:	4-6 months	STYLE SHEET:	Yes
EARLY PUBLICATION OPTION:	No	STYLE REQUIREMENTS:	APA
REVIEW PERIOD:	40 days	CIRCULATION:	2,000
ACCEPTANCE RATE:	40%	REPRINT POLICY:	Optional purchase

JOURNAL TITLE: Psychosomatic Medicine

MANUSCRIPT ADDRESS: 265 Nassau Road
Roosevelt, NY 11575

MAJOR CONTENT AREAS: Physiological, experimental

ARTICLES USUALLY ACCEPTED: Research, review, theoretical, case studies

TOPICS PREFERRED: Psychobiology, neuroscience, psychosomatics

INAPPROPRIATE MANUSCRIPTS: Liaison psychiatry

INDEXED/ABSTRACTED IN: PA, ASW, CCCP, CCSBS, LLBA

SUBSCRIPTION ADDRESS: Elsevier Publishing Co., Inc.
52 Vanderbilt Avenue
New York, NY 10017

SUBSCRIPTION COST:	$19 individual, $38 institutional		
PUBLICATION LAG TIME:	6 months	STYLE SHEET:	Yes
EARLY PUBLICATION OPTION:	Yes	STYLE REQUIREMENTS:	Ind. Med.
REVIEW PERIOD:	2-6 weeks	CIRCULATION:	3,400
ACCEPTANCE RATE:	20-25%	REPRINT POLICY:	Page charges

JOURNAL TITLE: Psychosomatics

MANUSCRIPT ADDRESS: Wilfred Dorfman, M. D.
1921 Newkirk Avenue
Brooklyn, NY 11226

MAJOR CONTENT AREAS: Psychosomatic medicine

ARTICLES USUALLY ACCEPTED: Clinical, research

TOPICS PREFERRED: Psychosomatic medicine

INAPPROPRIATE MANUSCRIPTS: None

INDEXED/ABSTRACTED IN: PA, EM, ASW, CCCP, CCSBS, LLBA

SUBSCRIPTION ADDRESS: 992 Springfield Avenue
Irvington, NJ 07111

SUBSCRIPTION COST:	$20		
PUBLICATION LAG TIME:	6 months	STYLE SHEET:	No
EARLY PUBLICATION OPTION:	Yes	STYLE REQUIREMENTS:	Own style
REVIEW PERIOD:	4-6 weeks	CIRCULATION:	2,500
ACCEPTANCE RATE:	35-40%	REPRINT POLICY:	Optional purchase

JOURNAL TITLE: Psychotherapy

MANUSCRIPT ADDRESS: Eugene T. Gendlin, Editor
Dept. of Psychology, Univ. of Chicago
5848 University Ave., Chicago, IL 60637

MAJOR CONTENT AREAS: Psychotherapy

ARTICLES USUALLY ACCEPTED: Not given

TOPICS PREFERRED: Not given

INAPPROPRIATE MANUSCRIPTS: Not given

INDEXED/ABSTRACTED IN: Not given

SUBSCRIPTION ADDRESS: Department of Psychology, University of Chicago
5848 University Avenue
Chicago, IL 60637

SUBSCRIPTION COST: $10 individual, $16 institutional

PUBLICATION LAG TIME: Not given	STYLE SHEET: Not given
EARLY PUBLICATION OPTION: Not given	STYLE REQUIREMENTS: Not given
REVIEW PERIOD: Not given	CIRCULATION: 3,000
ACCEPTANCE RATE: Not given	REPRINT POLICY: Not given

JOURNAL TITLE: Psychotherapy: Theory, Research, and Practice

MANUSCRIPT ADDRESS: California School of Professional Psychology
3755 Beverly Boulevard
Los Angeles, CA 90004

MAJOR CONTENT AREAS: Clinical, psychoanalysis, psychotherapy

ARTICLES USUALLY ACCEPTED: Research, theoretical, review

TOPICS PREFERRED: None

INAPPROPRIATE MANUSCRIPTS: Counseling, rehabilitation counseling

INDEXED/ABSTRACTED IN: PA, ASW, CCSBS

SUBSCRIPTION ADDRESS: California School of Professional Psychology
3755 Beverly Boulevard
Los Angeles, CA 90004

SUBSCRIPTION COST: $16

PUBLICATION LAG TIME: 6 months	STYLE SHEET: No
EARLY PUBLICATION OPTION: No	STYLE REQUIREMENTS: APA
REVIEW PERIOD: 3 months	CIRCULATION: 6,000
ACCEPTANCE RATE: 20-25%	REPRINT POLICY: 2 free copies of issue

JOURNAL TITLE: The Public Opinion Quarterly

MANUSCRIPT ADDRESS: Journalism Bldg., Columbia University
116th Street and Broadway
New York, NY 10027

MAJOR CONTENT AREAS: General, learning, social issues, social
psychology

ARTICLES USUALLY ACCEPTED: Research, theoretical

TOPICS PREFERRED: Public opinion, survey research, communications

INAPPROPRIATE MANUSCRIPTS: None

INDEXED/ABSTRACTED IN: PA, SA, BS, CSPA, CCSBS, CIJE, EE, HA, IPAPL,
IBSS, IPSA, PAISB, SSHI, TC

SUBSCRIPTION ADDRESS: Columbia University Press
136 South Broadway
Irvington-on-the-Hudson, NY 10533

SUBSCRIPTION COST:	$12		
PUBLICATION LAG TIME:	9 months	STYLE SHEET:	Yes
EARLY PUBLICATION OPTION:	No	STYLE REQUIREMENTS:	ASA
REVIEW PERIOD:	3 months	CIRCULATION:	5,200
ACCEPTANCE RATE:	10%	REPRINT POLICY:	5 free copies of issue

JOURNAL TITLE: Public Personnel Management

MANUSCRIPT ADDRESS: International Personnel Management Association
1313 East 60th Street
Chicago, IL 60637

MAJOR CONTENT AREAS: Personnel management

ARTICLES USUALLY ACCEPTED: Research, case studies

TOPICS PREFERRED: Public personnel topics written for
practitioners

INAPPROPRIATE MANUSCRIPTS: Opinion papers

INDEXED/ABSTRACTED IN: CCSBS, PL, PMA, PAISB

SUBSCRIPTION ADDRESS: International Personnel Management Association
1313 East 60th Street
Chicago, IL 60637

SUBSCRIPTION COST:	$15		
PUBLICATION LAG TIME:	1-3 months	STYLE SHEET:	Yes
EARLY PUBLICATION OPTION:	No	STYLE REQUIREMENTS:	Chicago
REVIEW PERIOD:	2-6 months	CIRCULATION:	9,600
ACCEPTANCE RATE:	25%	REPRINT POLICY:	6 free copies of issue

JOURNAL TITLE: Public Welfare

MANUSCRIPT ADDRESS: 1155 16th Street, N.W.
Suite 201
Washington, DC 20036

MAJOR CONTENT AREAS: Casework, behavior therapy, counseling

ARTICLES USUALLY ACCEPTED: Research, analysis, field reports, theoretical, book review

TOPICS PREFERRED: Legislative analysis in the areas of welfare, food stamps, social services, etc.

INAPPROPRIATE MANUSCRIPTS: Personal experiences, articles on management theory in general not specific to welfare

INDEXED/ABSTRACTED IN: ASW, CCSBS, HA, IPAPL, IBSS, JHE, PHRA, PAISB, WSA

SUBSCRIPTION ADDRESS: 1155 16th Street, N.W.
Suite 201
Washington, DC 20036

SUBSCRIPTION COST: $8

PUBLICATION LAG TIME: 1-6 months   STYLE SHEET: Yes

EARLY PUBLICATION OPTION: No   STYLE REQUIREMENTS: Chicago

REVIEW PERIOD: 1 month   CIRCULATION: 11,000

ACCEPTANCE RATE: 10%   REPRINT POLICY: 2 free copies
of issue

JOURNAL TITLE:	Quarterly Journal of Experimental Psychology
MANUSCRIPT ADDRESS:	Professor R. Davis, Dept. of Psychology The University of Reading, Earley Gate, Whiteknights Reading RG6 2AL, U.K.
MAJOR CONTENT AREAS:	Experimental, learning, perception, physiological
ARTICLES USUALLY ACCEPTED:	Experimental work in all branches of human and animal psychology, short notes on experiment- al apparatus
TOPICS PREFERRED:	Mechanisms underlying behavior
INAPPROPRIATE MANUSCRIPTS:	None
INDEXED/ABSTRACTED IN:	PA, CCSBS, PRG
SUBSCRIPTION ADDRESS:	Academic Press, Inc. 111 Fifth Avenue New York, NY 10003

SUBSCRIPTION COST:	$31		
PUBLICATION LAG TIME:	6-9 months	STYLE SHEET:	No
EARLY PUBLICATION OPTION:	No	STYLE REQUIREMENTS:	Own style
REVIEW PERIOD:	1-3 months	CIRCULATION:	1,650
ACCEPTANCE RATE:	60%	REPRINT POLICY:	25 free

JOURNAL TITLE: Reading Improvement

MANUSCRIPT ADDRESS: Box 566
Chula Vista, CA 92010

MAJOR CONTENT AREAS: Educational, reading, early childhood education

ARTICLES USUALLY ACCEPTED: Research and others in the areas of reading improvement, early childhood education

TOPICS PREFERRED: Reading improvement

INAPPROPRIATE MANUSCRIPTS: None

INDEXED/ABSTRACTED IN: PA, CIJE, EI, LLBA

SUBSCRIPTION ADDRESS: Box 566
Chula Vista, CA 92010

SUBSCRIPTION COST: $6 individual, $8 institutional
PUBLICATION LAG TIME: 8-10 months   STYLE SHEET: Yes
EARLY PUBLICATION OPTION: Yes   STYLE REQUIREMENTS: APA
REVIEW PERIOD: 1 month   CIRCULATION: 2,500
ACCEPTANCE RATE: 50%   REPRINT POLICY: Optional purchase

JOURNAL TITLE: Rehabilitation Counseling Bulletin

MANUSCRIPT ADDRESS: Dr. Marceline E. Jaques, Editor
Christopher Baldy Hall 416, SUNY
Amherst, NY 14260

MAJOR CONTENT AREAS: Community, counseling, mental retardation, severe disability

ARTICLES USUALLY ACCEPTED: Research, review, theoretical, program descriptions

TOPICS PREFERRED: Research utilization, severe disability, practitioner's reports

INAPPROPRIATE MANUSCRIPTS: None

INDEXED/ABSTRACTED IN: PA, ASW, CCSBS, CIJE

SUBSCRIPTION ADDRESS: American Personnel and Guidance Association
1607 New Hampshire Avenue, N. W.
Washington, DC 20009

SUBSCRIPTION COST: $9
PUBLICATION LAG TIME: 2-3 months   STYLE SHEET: Yes
EARLY PUBLICATION OPTION: No   STYLE REQUIREMENTS: APA
REVIEW PERIOD: 3-4 months   CIRCULATION: Not given
ACCEPTANCE RATE: Not given   REPRINT POLICY: Optional purchase

JOURNAL TITLE: Rehabilitation Psychology

MANUSCRIPT ADDRESS: Nancy Kerr, Editor, Dept. of Ed. Psych.
Arizona State University
Tempe, AZ 85281

MAJOR CONTENT AREAS: Rehabilitation

ARTICLES USUALLY ACCEPTED: Research, review, theoretical, book review

TOPICS PREFERRED: Research which helps to establish the
conditions under which rehabilitation is facilitated

INAPPROPRIATE MANUSCRIPTS: Summaries of demonstration programs lacking
data

INDEXED/ABSTRACTED IN: PA, DSHA

SUBSCRIPTION ADDRESS: P. O. Box 26034
Tempe, AZ 85282

SUBSCRIPTION COST:	$7.50 individual, $15 institutional		
PUBLICATION LAG TIME:	2 months	STYLE SHEET:	Yes
EARLY PUBLICATION OPTION:	Yes	STYLE REQUIREMENTS:	APA
REVIEW PERIOD:	3 months	CIRCULATION:	Not given
ACCEPTANCE RATE:	60%	REPRINT POLICY:	5 free

JOURNAL TITLE: Representative Research in Social Psychology

MANUSCRIPT ADDRESS: Review Coordinator, RRSP, Dept. of Psychology
Davie Hall, University of North Carolina
Chapel Hill, NC 27514

MAJOR CONTENT AREAS: Social, social methodology

ARTICLES USUALLY ACCEPTED: Research, review, theoretical, especially
negative findings; interested in MA and
Ph.D. theses

TOPICS PREFERRED: Those that can make methodological
contributions to the field

INAPPROPRIATE MANUSCRIPTS: None in terms of content

INDEXED/ABSTRACTED IN: PA, CCSBS

SUBSCRIPTION ADDRESS: Business Manager, RRSP, Dept of Psychology
Davie Hall, University of North Carolina
Chapel Hill, NC 27514

SUBSCRIPTION COST:	$4 individual, $12 institutional		
PUBLICATION LAG TIME:	4 months	STYLE SHEET:	Yes
EARLY PUBLICATION OPTION:	No	STYLE REQUIREMENTS:	APA
REVIEW PERIOD:	3 months	CIRCULATION:	360
ACCEPTANCE RATE:	20%	REPRINT POLICY:	Optional purchase

JOURNAL TITLE: Review of Existential Psychology and Psychiatry

MANUSCRIPT ADDRESS: Thomas Lynaugh, Editor
P. O. Box 1018
New York, NY 10023

MAJOR CONTENT AREAS: Psychoanalytical studies

ARTICLES USUALLY ACCEPTED: Phenomenological approaches to psychology and psychiatry

TOPICS PREFERRED: Not given

INAPPROPRIATE MANUSCRIPTS: Not given

INDEXED/ABSTRACTED IN: PA

SUBSCRIPTION ADDRESS: P. O. Box 1018
Ansonia Station
New York, NY 10023

SUBSCRIPTION COST: $9 individual, $15 institutional
PUBLICATION LAG TIME: Not given   STYLE SHEET: Not given
EARLY PUBLICATION OPTION: Not given   STYLE REQUIREMENTS: Not given
REVIEW PERIOD: Not given   CIRCULATION: 1,300
ACCEPTANCE RATE: Not given   REPRINT POLICY: Not given

JOURNAL TITLE: Research in Higher Education

MANUSCRIPT ADDRESS: Charles F. Elton, Dept. of Higher Education
111 Dickey Hall, University of Kentucky
Lexington, KY 40506

MAJOR CONTENT AREAS: Higher education

ARTICLES USUALLY ACCEPTED: Research

TOPICS PREFERRED: Research on administrators, faculty, and students in higher education; institutional comparisons

INAPPROPRIATE MANUSCRIPTS: Case studies, opinion papers

INDEXED/ABSTRACTED IN: PA, SA, CIJE

SUBSCRIPTION ADDRESS: APS Publications, Inc.
150 Fifth Avenue
New York, NY 10011

SUBSCRIPTION COST: $28 individual, $48 institutional
PUBLICATION LAG TIME: 1 year   STYLE SHEET: Yes
EARLY PUBLICATION OPTION: No   STYLE REQUIREMENTS: APA
REVIEW PERIOD: 1 month   CIRCULATION: 986
ACCEPTANCE RATE: 35%   REPRINT POLICY: Optional purchase

JOURNAL TITLE: Research Quarterly

MANUSCRIPT ADDRESS: M. Gladys Scott, Editor
University of Iowa, Halsey Gymnasium
Iowa City, IA 52242

MAJOR CONTENT AREAS: Sports psychology

ARTICLES USUALLY ACCEPTED: Research

TOPICS PREFERRED: Physiology of exercise, attributes of sports
and athletes, physical education, biomechanics

INAPPROPRIATE MANUSCRIPTS: None

INDEXED/ABSTRACTED IN: PA, CSPA, CCSBS, ECEA, WSA

SUBSCRIPTION ADDRESS: AAHPER
1201 16th Street, N.W.
Washington, DC 20036

SUBSCRIPTION COST:	$25 individual, $15 institutional		
PUBLICATION LAG TIME:	3-6 months	STYLE SHEET:	Yes
EARLY PUBLICATION OPTION:	No	STYLE REQUIREMENTS:	APA
REVIEW PERIOD:	2-3 months	CIRCULATION:	15,000
ACCEPTANCE RATE:	50%	REPRINT POLICY:	Optional purchase

JOURNAL TITLE: Review of Educational Research

MANUSCRIPT ADDRESS: Samuel Messick, Editor
Box 2604, Educational Testing Service
Princeton, NJ 08540

MAJOR CONTENT AREAS: Educational, psychometrics, methodology

ARTICLES USUALLY ACCEPTED: Critical and integrative reviews of research
bearing on education, including reviews and
interpretation of substantive issues

TOPICS PREFERRED: Reviews of research; identification, summary,
and analysis of important studies

INAPPROPRIATE MANUSCRIPTS: None

INDEXED/ABSTRACTED IN: PA, CCSBS

SUBSCRIPTION ADDRESS: AERA
1126 16th Street, N.W.
Washington, DC 20036

SUBSCRIPTION COST:	$12 individual, $14 institutional		
PUBLICATION LAG TIME:	3 months	STYLE SHEET:	No
EARLY PUBLICATION OPTION:	No	STYLE REQUIREMENTS:	APA
REVIEW PERIOD:	3-4 weeks	CIRCULATION:	16,000
ACCEPTANCE RATE:	14-20%	REPRINT POLICY:	50 free

JOURNAL TITLE: Schizophrenia Bulletin

MANUSCRIPT ADDRESS: Dr. Loren R. Mosher, Center for Studies of Schizophrenia, NIMH, Room 10 C 26, 5600 Fishers Lane, Rockville, MD 20852

MAJOR CONTENT AREAS: All aspects of schizophrenia

ARTICLES USUALLY ACCEPTED: Review, theoretical, short reports on research or clinical practice, news items

TOPICS PREFERRED: Anything related to schizophrenia

INAPPROPRIATE MANUSCRIPTS: Those unrelated to schizophrenia, single case reports, single drug trials

INDEXED/ABSTRACTED IN: PA, IM, EM

SUBSCRIPTION ADDRESS: Superintendent of Documents
U.S. Government Printing Office
Washington, DC 20402

SUBSCRIPTION COST: $12

PUBLICATION LAG TIME: 6-12 months	STYLE SHEET:	Yes
EARLY PUBLICATION OPTION: No	STYLE REQUIREMENTS:	GPO
REVIEW PERIOD: 2-3 months	CIRCULATION:	3,539
ACCEPTANCE RATE: 33%	REPRINT POLICY:	50 free

JOURNAL TITLE: The School Counselor

MANUSCRIPT ADDRESS: Dr. Marguerite R. Carroll
Fairfield University
Fairfield, CT 06430

MAJOR CONTENT AREAS: School guidance and counseling, educational, developmental

ARTICLES USUALLY ACCEPTED: Theoretical, book review, how to do it; very little technical research

TOPICS PREFERRED: Those related to school practice

INAPPROPRIATE MANUSCRIPTS: Research that is too highly defined

INDEXED/ABSTRACTED IN: PA, CCSBS, CIJE, EI

SUBSCRIPTION ADDRESS: APGA
1607 New Hampshire Avenue
Washington, DC 20009

SUBSCRIPTION COST: $10

PUBLICATION LAG TIME: 6 months	STYLE SHEET:	Yes
EARLY PUBLICATION OPTION: No	STYLE REQUIREMENTS:	APA
REVIEW PERIOD: 1-2 months	CIRCULATION:	18,000
ACCEPTANCE RATE: 25%	REPRINT POLICY:	5 free copies of issue

JOURNAL TITLE: The School Psychology Digest

MANUSCRIPT ADDRESS: 300 Education Building
Kent State University
Kent, OH   44242

MAJOR CONTENT AREAS: Behavior therapy, counseling, educational,
social, clinical, developmental, psychometrics

ARTICLES USUALLY ACCEPTED: Research, review, theoretical; by soliciation
only

TOPICS PREFERRED: School psychology's role and function and
related material from developmental psychology

INAPPROPRIATE MANUSCRIPTS: Most unsolicited materials

INDEXED/ABSTRACTED IN: ECEA

SUBSCRIPTION ADDRESS: 300 Education Building
Kent State University
Kent, OH   44242

SUBSCRIPTION COST:	$10		
PUBLICATION LAG TIME:	45 days	STYLE SHEET:	Yes
EARLY PUBLICATION OPTION:	No	STYLE REQUIREMENTS:	APA
REVIEW PERIOD:	N/A	CIRCULATION:	4,500
ACCEPTANCE RATE:	By solicitation only	REPRINT POLICY:	Optional purchase

JOURNAL TITLE: Science

MANUSCRIPT ADDRESS: 1515 Massachusetts Avenue, N.W.
Washington, DC   20005

MAJOR CONTENT AREAS: Experimental

ARTICLES USUALLY ACCEPTED: Research, review, theoretical

TOPICS PREFERRED: Those of interdisciplinary import

INAPPROPRIATE MANUSCRIPTS: None

INDEXED/ABSTRACTED IN: PA, SA, ARGPL, AA, AATA, BRD, BRI, BAA, BS,
CSPA, CB, CIJE, DSHA, GAA, IPAPL, IPARL, ISA,
ILD, JHE, LLBA, LISA, PRAJ, RGPL, WSA, WTA

SUBSCRIPTION ADDRESS: 1515 Massachusetts Avenue, N.W.
Washington, DC   20005

SUBSCRIPTION COST:	$25 individual, $50 institutional		
PUBLICATION LAG TIME:	4-10 weeks	STYLE SHEET:	Yes
EARLY PUBLICATION OPTION:	No	STYLE REQUIREMENTS:	Own style
REVIEW PERIOD:	4-8 weeks	CIRCULATION:	145,000
ACCEPTANCE RATE:	20-25%	REPRINT POLICY:	Optional purchase

JOURNAL TITLE: Scientific American

MANUSCRIPT ADDRESS: Editors, Scientific American
415 Madison Avenue
New York, NY 10017

MAJOR CONTENT AREAS: General science

ARTICLES USUALLY ACCEPTED: Research, review

TOPICS PREFERRED: Not given

INAPPROPRIATE MANUSCRIPTS: Not given

INDEXED/ABSTRACTED IN: ARGPL, BA, BRD, CA, IM, PS, SA

SUBSCRIPTION ADDRESS: Scientific American
415 Madison Avenue
New York, NY 10017

SUBSCRIPTION COST: $15
PUBLICATION LAG TIME: Not given   STYLE SHEET: Not given
EARLY PUBLICATION OPTION: Not given   STYLE REQUIREMENTS: Not given
REVIEW PERIOD: Not given   CIRCULATION: 600,000
ACCEPTANCE RATE: Not given   REPRINT POLICY: Not given

JOURNAL TITLE: Signs: Journal of Women in Culture and
Society

MANUSCRIPT ADDRESS: 307 Barnard Hall
Barnard College
New York, NY 10027

MAJOR CONTENT AREAS: All areas as applied to women

ARTICLES USUALLY ACCEPTED: Research, theoretical; interdisciplinary
articles which focus on women

TOPICS PREFERRED: Those contributing to theory; those offering
an interdisciplinary methodology

INAPPROPRIATE MANUSCRIPTS: Narrow research reports; sex differences in
college students along a narrow dimension

INDEXED/ABSTRACTED IN: Not yet established

SUBSCRIPTION ADDRESS: University of Chicago Press
11030 Langley Avenue
Chicago, IL 60628

SUBSCRIPTION COST: $12 individual, $16 institutional
PUBLICATION LAG TIME: 12-18 months   STYLE SHEET: Yes
EARLY PUBLICATION OPTION: Yes   STYLE REQUIREMENTS: Chicago
REVIEW PERIOD: 4-6 months   CIRCULATION: 8,000
ACCEPTANCE RATE: 3-5%   REPRINT POLICY: 50 free

JOURNAL TITLE: Simulation and Games

MANUSCRIPT ADDRESS: Academic Games Associates
430 East 33rd Street
Baltimore, MD 21218

MAJOR CONTENT AREAS: Educational, experimental, general, social

ARTICLES USUALLY ACCEPTED: Research, theoretical, book and simulation/
games review

TOPICS PREFERRED: Those which include the results of research
in which a simulation or game is used

INAPPROPRIATE MANUSCRIPTS: Descriptions of simulational games which do
not report the results of a research experiment

INDEXED/ABSTRACTED IN: PA, SA, CCSBS, CIJE, IBSS, IPSA, MMRI, PHRA,
SSCI

SUBSCRIPTION ADDRESS: Sage Publications, Inc.
275 South Beverly Drive
Beverly Hills, CA 90212

SUBSCRIPTION COST:	$12 individual, $20 institutional		
PUBLICATION LAG TIME:	5 months	STYLE SHEET:	Yes
EARLY PUBLICATION OPTION:	No	STYLE REQUIREMENTS:	APA
REVIEW PERIOD:	8-12 weeks	CIRCULATION:	1,000
ACCEPTANCE RATE:	30%	REPRINT POLICY:	25 free

JOURNAL TITLE: Small Group Behavior

MANUSCRIPT ADDRESS: William Fawcett Hill, Ph.D.
Dept. of Behavioral Science, Cal. St.
Polytechnic Univ., Pomona, CA 91768

MAJOR CONTENT AREAS: Counseling and psychotherapy in groups

ARTICLES USUALLY ACCEPTED: Research, theoretical, clinical

TOPICS PREFERRED: Group therapy and counseling

INAPPROPRIATE MANUSCRIPTS: Sociology and education involving small
groups

INDEXED/ABSTRACTED IN: PA, SA, CCSBS

SUBSCRIPTION ADDRESS: Sage Publications, Inc.
275 South Beverly Drive
Beverly Hills, CA 90212

SUBSCRIPTION COST:	$10 individual, $15 institutional		
PUBLICATION LAG TIME:	18 months	STYLE SHEET:	Yes
EARLY PUBLICATION OPTION:	No	STYLE REQUIREMENTS:	Modified APA
REVIEW PERIOD:	3 months	CIRCULATION:	2,000
ACCEPTANCE RATE:	20%	REPRINT POLICY:	15 free

JOURNAL TITLE: Smith College Studies in Social Work

MANUSCRIPT ADDRESS: Lilly Hall
Northampton, MA 01060

MAJOR CONTENT AREAS: Psychoanalysis, psychotherapy, clinical
social work
ARTICLES USUALLY ACCEPTED: Clinical, research

TOPICS PREFERRED: Ego psychological perspectives on clinical
practice
INAPPROPRIATE MANUSCRIPTS: None

INDEXED/ABSTRACTED IN: PA, ASW, SA, BS, CCSBS, HA, IPARL, PAISB

SUBSCRIPTION ADDRESS: Lilly Hall
Northampton, MA 01060

SUBSCRIPTION COST: $4.50
PUBLICATION LAG TIME: 3 months   STYLE SHEET: Yes
EARLY PUBLICATION OPTION: No   STYLE REQUIREMENTS: Chicago
REVIEW PERIOD: 6 weeks   CIRCULATION: 2,000
ACCEPTANCE RATE: Not given   REPRINT POLICY: Optional
purchase

JOURNAL TITLE: Social Behavior and Personality: An
International Journal
MANUSCRIPT ADDRESS: Dr. R.A.C. Stewart
Massey University
Palmerston North, New Zealand
MAJOR CONTENT AREAS: Almost all areas of psychology

ARTICLES USUALLY ACCEPTED: Research, theoretical

TOPICS PREFERRED: Social, personality

INAPPROPRIATE MANUSCRIPTS: None

INDEXED/ABSTRACTED IN: PA, CCSBS

SUBSCRIPTION ADDRESS: Editoral Services, Ltd.
P. O. Box 6443
Wellington, New Zealand
SUBSCRIPTION COST: $NZ 8 individual, $NZ 12 institutional
PUBLICATION LAG TIME: 3-4 months   STYLE SHEET: Yes
EARLY PUBLICATION OPTION: No   STYLE REQUIREMENTS: APA
REVIEW PERIOD: 2 months   CIRCULATION: 1,000
ACCEPTANCE RATE: Not given   REPRINT POLICY: 300 free

JOURNAL TITLE: Social Biology

MANUSCRIPT ADDRESS: Room 5450, Social Science Building
1180 Observatory Drive
Madison, WI 53706

MAJOR CONTENT AREAS: Population, anthropology, medical genetics

ARTICLES USUALLY ACCEPTED: Manuscript

TOPICS PREFERRED: Population

INAPPROPRIATE MANUSCRIPTS: None

INDEXED/ABSTRACTED IN: PA, AA, CCSBS, DSHA, IBSS, WSA

SUBSCRIPTION ADDRESS: Room 5450, Social Science Building
1180 Observatory Drive
Madison, WI 53706

SUBSCRIPTION COST: $20

PUBLICATION LAG TIME: 4-6 months	STYLE SHEET:	Yes
EARLY PUBLICATION OPTION: No	STYLE REQUIREMENTS:	Chicago
REVIEW PERIOD: 4-6 months	CIRCULATION:	1,800
ACCEPTANCE RATE: 40%	REPRINT POLICY:	Purchase required

JOURNAL TITLE: Social Casework

MANUSCRIPT ADDRESS: 44 East 23rd Street
New York, NY 10010

MAJOR CONTENT AREAS: All areas of social casework

ARTICLES USUALLY ACCEPTED: Research, theoretical, practice

TOPICS PREFERRED: Social work practice, social welfare, ethnic
and minority issues

INAPPROPRIATE MANUSCRIPTS: Amateurish research reports, reviews of
literature, student papers

INDEXED/ABSTRACTED IN: PA, ASW, BRI, BS, CCSBS, HA, IPAPL, IBSS,
JHE, PHRA, SSHI, WSA

SUBSCRIPTION ADDRESS: 44 East 23rd Street
New York, NY 10010

SUBSCRIPTION COST: $12 individual, $18 institutional

PUBLICATION LAG TIME: 3-6 months	STYLE SHEET:	Yes
EARLY PUBLICATION OPTION: No	STYLE REQUIREMENTS:	Chicago
REVIEW PERIOD: 3 months	CIRCULATION:	17,000
ACCEPTANCE RATE: 20-25%	REPRINT POLICY:	5 free copies of issue

JOURNAL TITLE: Social Forces

MANUSCRIPT ADDRESS: Hamilton Hall
University of North Carolina
Chapel Hill, NC 27514

MAJOR CONTENT AREAS: Community, industrial/organizational, sociology

ARTICLES USUALLY ACCEPTED: Research, theoretical

TOPICS PREFERRED: Sociological manuscripts

INAPPROPRIATE MANUSCRIPTS: None

INDEXED/ABSTRACTED IN: PA, ASW, ABCPS, AA, BRI, BS, CSPA, CCSBS, CIJE, EAA, HA, IPAPL, PPARL, IBSS, IPSA, JHE, PRAJ, PAISB, RHEA, WSA

SUBSCRIPTION ADDRESS: Box 2288
The University of North Carolina Press
Chapel Hill, NC 27514

SUBSCRIPTION COST: $10 individual, $12 institutional

PUBLICATION LAG TIME: 1 year

EARLY PUBLICATION OPTION: No

REVIEW PERIOD: 1 month

ACCEPTANCE RATE: 15%

STYLE SHEET: Yes

STYLE REQUIREMENTS: Chicago

CIRCULATION: 4,900

REPRINT POLICY: 1 free copy of issue

JOURNAL TITLE: Social Policy

MANUSCRIPT ADDRESS: 184 Fifth Avenue
New York, NY 10010

MAJOR CONTENT AREAS: All issues of social policy

ARTICLES USUALLY ACCEPTED: Research, review, book review, criticism

TOPICS PREFERRED: Education, economics, sociology, urban development, women, health, race issues

INAPPROPRIATE MANUSCRIPTS: None

INDEXED/ABSTRACTED IN: CSPA, CCSBS, CIJE, MSRS, PHRA, SSCI, WSA

SUBSCRIPTION ADDRESS: 184 Fifth Avenue
New York, NY 10010

SUBSCRIPTION COST: $10 individual, $15 institutional

PUBLICATION LAG TIME: 1-12 months

EARLY PUBLICATION OPTION: No

REVIEW PERIOD: 2-4 weeks

ACCEPTANCE RATE: 30%

STYLE SHEET: No

STYLE REQUIREMENTS: Chicago

CIRCULATION: 4,000

REPRINT POLICY: 4 free

JOURNAL TITLE: Social Problems

MANUSCRIPT ADDRESS: Arlene Kaplan Daniels, Editor
Dept. of Sociology, Northwestern University
Evanston, IL 60201

MAJOR CONTENT AREAS: Social problems

ARTICLES USUALLY ACCEPTED: Research, theoretical, social policy,
critical

TOPICS PREFERRED: Any area of social problems

INAPPROPRIATE MANUSCRIPTS: None

INDEXED/ABSTRACTED IN: PA, ASW, SA, BS, CSPA, CCSBS, CIJE, ERA,
IPAPL, IPARL, IBSS, ILD, IPSA, JHE, PRAJ,
PHRA, PAISB, WSA

SUBSCRIPTION ADDRESS: SSSP, 114 Rockwell Hall
State Univ. College, 1300 Elmwood Avenue
Buffalo, NY 14222

SUBSCRIPTION COST: $15 individual, $25 institutional

PUBLICATION LAG TIME: 3-6 months   STYLE SHEET: No

EARLY PUBLICATION OPTION: No   STYLE REQUIREMENTS: ASA

REVIEW PERIOD: 6-10 weeks   CIRCULATION: 5,000

ACCEPTANCE RATE: 10%   REPRINT POLICY: 5 free copies
of issue

JOURNAL TITLE: Social Psychiatry

MANUSCRIPT ADDRESS: Dr. N. Kreitman, Dept. of Psychiatry
Royal Edinburgh Hosp., Morningside Park
Edinburgh EH10 5HF, Scotland, U.K.

MAJOR CONTENT AREAS: Community, social

ARTICLES USUALLY ACCEPTED: Research, invited reviews

TOPICS PREFERRED: Social psychiatry

INAPPROPRIATE MANUSCRIPTS: Purely clinical studies, descriptive
accounts of services

INDEXED/ABSTRACTED IN: PA, IM, CCSBS, SCI, WSA

SUBSCRIPTION ADDRESS: Springer-Verlag New York, Inc.
175 Fifth Avenue
New York, NY 10010

SUBSCRIPTION COST: $47.60

PUBLICATION LAG TIME: 5 months   STYLE SHEET: No

EARLY PUBLICATION OPTION: No   STYLE REQUIREMENTS: Ind. Med.

REVIEW PERIOD: 1 month   CIRCULATION: Not given

ACCEPTANCE RATE: 50%   REPRINT POLICY: 50 free

JOURNAL TITLE: Social Research

MANUSCRIPT ADDRESS: New School for Social Research
65 Fifth Avenue, Room 341
New York, NY 10003

MAJOR CONTENT AREAS: Social sciences

ARTICLES USUALLY ACCEPTED: Theoretical

TOPICS PREFERRED: Interdisciplinary treatment of social science issues by integrating philosophy and history

INAPPROPRIATE MANUSCRIPTS: None

INDEXED/ABSTRACTED IN: SA, ABCPS, AA, BRI, BS, CCSBS, ERA, IPAPL, IBSS, ILD, IPSA, JHE, PRAJ, PAISB, RHEA, WSA, WAH

SUBSCRIPTION ADDRESS: New School for Social Research
65 Fifth Avenue, Room 341
New York, NY 10003

SUBSCRIPTION COST: $10 individual, $12 institutional
PUBLICATION LAG TIME: 3-10 months   STYLE SHEET: Yes
EARLY PUBLICATION OPTION: No   STYLE REQUIREMENTS: Own style
REVIEW PERIOD: 6 weeks   CIRCULATION: 6,000
ACCEPTANCE RATE: 5%   REPRINT POLICY: 50 free

JOURNAL TITLE: Social Science Information

MANUSCRIPT ADDRESS: International Social Science Council
UNESCO, 1 rue Miollis
75015 Paris, France

MAJOR CONTENT AREAS: Ethnology, organizations, sociology of science

ARTICLES USUALLY ACCEPTED: Theoretical, research

TOPICS PREFERRED: Computers and the social sciences, human societies and ecosystems, man and his environment

INAPPROPRIATE MANUSCRIPTS: None

INDEXED/ABSTRACTED IN: PA, ABCPS, BI, CCSBS, IBSS, ILD, IPSA

SUBSCRIPTION ADDRESS: Mouton & Co.
Post Office Box 482
The Hague, Netherlands

SUBSCRIPTION COST: 98 FF individual, 140 FF institutional
PUBLICATION LAG TIME: Variable   STYLE SHEET: Yes
EARLY PUBLICATION OPTION: No   STYLE REQUIREMENTS: Own style
REVIEW PERIOD: 1-6 months   CIRCULATION: 1,500
ACCEPTANCE RATE: Varies with subject   REPRINT POLICY: 30 free

214

JOURNAL TITLE: Social Science Research

MANUSCRIPT ADDRESS: Peter H. Rossi, Editor
Dept. of Sociology, Univ. of Massachusetts
Amherst, MA 01002

MAJOR CONTENT AREAS: Interdisciplinary social science

ARTICLES USUALLY ACCEPTED: Research

TOPICS PREFERRED: Methodology and quantitative research

INAPPROPRIATE MANUSCRIPTS: Not given

INDEXED/ABSTRACTED IN: PA

SUBSCRIPTION ADDRESS: Academic Press
111 Fifth Avenue
New York, NY 10003

SUBSCRIPTION COST: $32.50		
PUBLICATION LAG TIME: Not given	STYLE SHEET: Not given	
EARLY PUBLICATION OPTION: Not given	STYLE REQUIREMENTS: ASA	
REVIEW PERIOD: Not given	CIRCULATION: Not given	
ACCEPTANCE RATE: Not given	REPRINT POLICY: 25 free	

JOURNAL TITLE: Social Service Review

MANUSCRIPT ADDRESS: 969 East 60th Street
Chicago, IL 60637

MAJOR CONTENT AREAS: Social welfare

ARTICLES USUALLY ACCEPTED: Research, review

TOPICS PREFERRED: Social welfare topics

INAPPROPRIATE MANUSCRIPTS: None

INDEXED/ABSTRACTED IN: ASW, CCSBS, HA, IPAPL, IBSS, JHE, PHRA,
PAISB, WSA, WAH

SUBSCRIPTION ADDRESS: University of Chicago Press
5801 South Ellis
Chicago, IL 60637

SUBSCRIPTION COST: $12 individual, $16 institutional		
PUBLICATION LAG TIME: 6 months	STYLE SHEET: Yes	
EARLY PUBLICATION OPTION: No	STYLE REQUIREMENTS: Chicago	
REVIEW PERIOD: 3 months	CIRCULATION: 7,000	
ACCEPTANCE RATE: 25%	REPRINT POLICY: 25 free	

JOURNAL TITLE: Social Thought

MANUSCRIPT ADDRESS: Dorothy Bird Daly, Editor, Suite 307
1346 Connecticut Avenue, N. W.
Washington, DC 20036

MAJOR CONTENT AREAS: Clinical social work, social problems

ARTICLES USUALLY ACCEPTED: Research, theoretical, book review,
experimental practice reports

TOPICS PREFERRED: Analysis of social problems and policy

INAPPROPRIATE MANUSCRIPTS: None

INDEXED/ABSTRACTED IN: ASW

SUBSCRIPTION ADDRESS: Suite 307
1346 Connecticut Avenue, N. W.
Washington, DC 20036

SUBSCRIPTION COST: $12
PUBLICATION LAG TIME: Variable
EARLY PUBLICATION OPTION: No
REVIEW PERIOD: 2 months
ACCEPTANCE RATE: 33%

STYLE SHEET: Yes
STYLE REQUIREMENTS: Chicago
CIRCULATION: 2,000
REPRINT POLICY: 25 free

JOURNAL TITLE: Social Work

MANUSCRIPT ADDRESS: 2 Park Avenue
New York, NY 10016

MAJOR CONTENT AREAS: All areas of social work

ARTICLES USUALLY ACCEPTED: Research, theoretical, review, book review
(solicited), notes for practice, viewpoints

TOPICS PREFERRED: New insights into established practices,
controversial articles, critical analyses

INAPPROPRIATE MANUSCRIPTS: None

INDEXED/ABSTRACTED IN: PA, ASW, CCSBS, CIJE, ECEA, HA, IBSS,
ILD, JHE, PAISB, WSA

SUBSCRIPTION ADDRESS: 49 Sheridan Avenue
Albany, NY 12210

SUBSCRIPTION COST: $20
PUBLICATION LAG TIME: 2-3 months
EARLY PUBLICATION OPTION: No
REVIEW PERIOD: 2-3 months
ACCEPTANCE RATE: 10%

STYLE SHEET: Yes
STYLE REQUIREMENTS: Own style
CIRCULATION: 75,000
REPRINT POLICY: 5 free

JOURNAL TITLE: Social Work in Health Care

MANUSCRIPT ADDRESS: Sylvia S. Clarke, MSW, ACSW, Director
Social Services Dept., The Roosevelt Hospital
428 W. 59th St., New York, NY 10019

MAJOR CONTENT AREAS: All areas of social work in health care settings

ARTICLES USUALLY ACCEPTED: Book review, theoretical, review, research

TOPICS PREFERRED: Practice, education, administration, and delivery in health care

INAPPROPRIATE MANUSCRIPTS: None

INDEXED/ABSTRACTED IN: PA, EM, ASW, CLA, HA, HLI, MCR

SUBSCRIPTION ADDRESS: The Haworth Press
174 Fifth Avenue
New York, NY 10010

SUBSCRIPTION COST:	$15 individual, $30 institutional		
PUBLICATION LAG TIME:	4 months	STYLE SHEET:	Yes
EARLY PUBLICATION OPTION:	Yes	STYLE REQUIREMENTS:	Own style
REVIEW PERIOD:	2-12 weeks	CIRCULATION:	2,700
ACCEPTANCE RATE:	35%	REPRINT POLICY:	50 free

JOURNAL TITLE: Social Work Today

MANUSCRIPT ADDRESS: 16 Kent Street
Birmingham B5 6RD, England

MAJOR CONTENT AREAS: Clinical social work, community mental health, medical social work, social work practice

ARTICLES USUALLY ACCEPTED: Research, case studies

TOPICS PREFERRED: Social work practice

INAPPROPRIATE MANUSCRIPTS: Academic, theoretical, rambling articles vaguely connected with social work

INDEXED/ABSTRACTED IN: ASW, AHMS

SUBSCRIPTION ADDRESS: 16 Kent Street
Birmingham B5 6RD, England

SUBSCRIPTION COST:	$20		
PUBLICATION LAG TIME:	1-6 months	STYLE SHEET:	Yes
EARLY PUBLICATION OPTION:	Yes	STYLE REQUIREMENTS:	Own style
REVIEW PERIOD:	1 month	CIRCULATION:	18,000
ACCEPTANCE RATE:	40%	REPRINT POLICY:	25 free

JOURNAL TITLE: Society

MANUSCRIPT ADDRESS: Rutgers University
New Brunswick, NJ 08903

MAJOR CONTENT AREAS: Educational, industrial/organizational,
personality, social
ARTICLES USUALLY ACCEPTED: Those that show how social science can help
right long-standing wrongs

TOPICS PREFERRED: Education, political psychology

INAPPROPRIATE MANUSCRIPTS: Solutions to the problems of the world in
20 pages or less
INDEXED/ABSTRACTED IN: CSPA, CCSBS, CIJE, PHRA, RGPL

SUBSCRIPTION ADDRESS: Rutgers University
New Brunswick, NJ 08903

SUBSCRIPTION COST: $9.75 individual, $12.50 institutional
PUBLICATION LAG TIME: 6-12 months   STYLE SHEET: Yes
EARLY PUBLICATION OPTION: Yes   STYLE REQUIREMENTS: Own style
REVIEW PERIOD: 4 months   CIRCULATION: 75,000
ACCEPTANCE RATE: 10%   REPRINT POLICY: Optional
purchase

JOURNAL TITLE: Sociology and Social Research: An
International Journal
MANUSCRIPT ADDRESS: Managing Editor
University of Southern California
Los Angeles, CA 90007
MAJOR CONTENT AREAS: All areas of sociology

ARTICLES USUALLY ACCEPTED: Research, book review

TOPICS PREFERRED: Those contributing to the practical
application of sociological research methods
INAPPROPRIATE MANUSCRIPTS: Personal experiences

INDEXED/ABSTRACTED IN: PA, ASW, SA, BS, CSPA, CCSBS, EE, ERA, HA,
IPAPL, IBSS, IPSA, JHE, PAISB, RHEA, WAH

SUBSCRIPTION ADDRESS: Managing Editor
University of Southern California
Los Angeles, CA 90007
SUBSCRIPTION COST: $7.50 individual, $15 institutional (may change)
PUBLICATION LAG TIME: 8 weeks   STYLE SHEET: Yes
EARLY PUBLICATION OPTION: Yes   STYLE REQUIREMENTS: ASA
REVIEW PERIOD: 8 weeks   CIRCULATION: 3,000
ACCEPTANCE RATE: 47%   REPRINT POLICY: 25 free

JOURNAL TITLE: Sociology of Work and Occupations: An International Journal

MANUSCRIPT ADDRESS: P. O. Box 4348
Chicago, IL 60680

MAJOR CONTENT AREAS: Work, labor force

ARTICLES USUALLY ACCEPTED: Research, review, theoretical, book review

TOPICS PREFERRED: Inter-relations between occupations and organizations, comparative studies of occupations

INAPPROPRIATE MANUSCRIPTS: Nonscholarly papers, management research

INDEXED/ABSTRACTED IN: CCSBS

SUBSCRIPTION ADDRESS: Sage Publications
275 S. Beverly Drive
Beverly Hills, CA 90212

SUBSCRIPTION COST:	$12 individual, $20 institutional		
PUBLICATION LAG TIME:	9-12 months	STYLE SHEET:	Yes
EARLY PUBLICATION OPTION:	No	STYLE REQUIREMENTS:	Own style
REVIEW PERIOD:	3-6 months	CIRCULATION:	Not given
ACCEPTANCE RATE:	15%	REPRINT POLICY:	25 free

JOURNAL TITLE: Sociometry

MANUSCRIPT ADDRESS: Dept. of Sociology
University of Oregon
Eugene, OR 97403

MAJOR CONTENT AREAS: Social

ARTICLES USUALLY ACCEPTED: Research, theoretical

TOPICS PREFERRED: Attitudes, small groups, personal space, exchange theory, balance theory

INAPPROPRIATE MANUSCRIPTS: Clinical psychology, psychotherapy, counseling, educational psychology

INDEXED/ABSTRACTED IN: PA, ASW, SA, BS, CSPA, CCSBS, EAA, ECEA, IPAPL, IBSS, IPSA, JHE, PRAJ, RHEA, WSA

SUBSCRIPTION ADDRESS: American Sociological Association
1722 N Street, N.W.
Washington, DC 20036

SUBSCRIPTION COST:	$12 individual, $16 institutional		
PUBLICATION LAG TIME:	6 months	STYLE SHEET:	No
EARLY PUBLICATION OPTION:	No	STYLE REQUIREMENTS:	ASA
REVIEW PERIOD:	4 months	CIRCULATION:	4,000
ACCEPTANCE RATE:	10%	REPRINT POLICY:	Optional purchase

JOURNAL TITLE: Special Children

MANUSCRIPT ADDRESS: AASE
107-20   125 Street
Richmond Hill, NY   11419

MAJOR CONTENT AREAS: Special children, mental retardation, educational

ARTICLES USUALLY ACCEPTED: Tips for teachers and parents of exceptionals, social and rehabilitation activities, legislation

TOPICS PREFERRED: Nature and needs of the handicapped, service-oriented stories in a narrative format

INAPPROPRIATE MANUSCRIPTS: Clinical and research findings, job opportunities, physical education

INDEXED/ABSTRACTED IN: None

SUBSCRIPTION ADDRESS: AASE
Box 168
Fryeburg, ME   04037

SUBSCRIPTION COST: $10

PUBLICATION LAG TIME: 6 months

EARLY PUBLICATION OPTION: No

REVIEW PERIOD: 1 month

ACCEPTANCE RATE: Not given

STYLE SHEET: Yes

STYLE REQUIREMENTS: Own style

CIRCULATION: 5,000

REPRINT POLICY: 2 fee copies of issue

JOURNAL TITLE: Spring, An Annual of Archetypal Psychology and Jungian Thought

MANUSCRIPT ADDRESS: Patricia Berry, Manuscript Editor
Postfach 190
8024 - Zurich, Switzerland

MAJOR CONTENT AREAS: Jungian psychology, psychoanalysis, psychotherapy

ARTICLES USUALLY ACCEPTED: Those that inter-relate with other fields (e.g., science, literature, law, etc.); philosophical and religious articles

TOPICS PREFERRED: Depth psychology, particularly Jungian

INAPPROPRIATE MANUSCRIPTS: None

INDEXED/ABSTRACTED IN: Not given

SUBSCRIPTION ADDRESS: Postfach 190
8024 - Zurich, Switzerland

SUBSCRIPTION COST: $7.50

PUBLICATION LAG TIME: 6 months

EARLY PUBLICATION OPTION: No

REVIEW PERIOD: 9 weeks

ACCEPTANCE RATE: Not given

STYLE SHEET: No

STYLE REQUIREMENTS: Chicago

CIRCULATION: 4,000

REPRINT POLICY: 20 free

JOURNAL TITLE: Suicide and Life-Threatening Behavior

MANUSCRIPT ADDRESS: Edwin S. Schneidman, Ph.D., UCLA NPI
760 Westwood Plaza
Los Angeles, CA 90024

MAJOR CONTENT AREAS: All aspects of suicide and life-threatening behavior

ARTICLES USUALLY ACCEPTED: Research, review, clinical, theoretical

TOPICS PREFERRED: Suicide, death, life-threatening behaviors

INAPPROPRIATE MANUSCRIPTS: Anecdotes about suicide, suicide prevention, suicide prevention centers

INDEXED/ABSTRACTED IN: PA, CCSBS

SUBSCRIPTION ADDRESS: Betsy S. Comstock, M.D., Dept. of Psychiatry
Baylor College of Medicine, 1200 Moursund Ave.
Houston, TX 72025

SUBSCRIPTION COST:	$7 individual, $20 institutional		
PUBLICATION LAG TIME:	6-9 months	STYLE SHEET:	Yes
EARLY PUBLICATION OPTION:	No	STYLE REQUIREMENTS:	APA
REVIEW PERIOD:	1 month	CIRCULATION:	1,000
ACCEPTANCE RATE:	50%	REPRINT POLICY:	Optional purchase

JOURNAL TITLE: Synthesis, the Realization of the Self

MANUSCRIPT ADDRESS: 830 Woodside Road
STE 5
Redwood City, CA 94061

MAJOR CONTENT AREAS: Behavior therapy, developmental, personality, psychotherapy, social

ARTICLES USUALLY ACCEPTED: Research, theoretical, case studies

TOPICS PREFERRED: Case histories

INAPPROPRIATE MANUSCRIPTS: None

INDEXED/ABSTRACTED IN: Not given

SUBSCRIPTION ADDRESS: 830 Woodside Road
STE 5
Redwood City, CA 94061

SUBSCRIPTION COST:	$8		
PUBLICATION LAG TIME:	9 months	STYLE SHEET:	No
EARLY PUBLICATION OPTION:	No	STYLE REQUIREMENTS:	None as yet
REVIEW PERIOD:	3-6 months	CIRCULATION:	28,000
ACCEPTANCE RATE:	1%	REPRINT POLICY:	100 free

JOURNAL TITLE: Teachers College Record

MANUSCRIPT ADDRESS: 525 West 120th Street
New York, NY 10027

MAJOR CONTENT AREAS: All areas related to education

ARTICLES USUALLY ACCEPTED: Research, theoretical, issue-oriented, book review, analyses; emphasis on national or international levels

TOPICS PREFERRED: Scholarly work on issues of education and related disciplines

INAPPROPRIATE MANUSCRIPTS: None

INDEXED/ABSTRACTED IN: PA, SA, BRD, BRI, CSPA, CCSBS, CIJE, EI, EAA, ECEA, HA, IPAPL, LLBA, LISA, PHRA, RHEA, SSCI, WSA, WAH

SUBSCRIPTION ADDRESS: 525 West 120th Street
New York, NY 10027

SUBSCRIPTION COST: $12
PUBLICATION LAG TIME: 9 months
EARLY PUBLICATION OPTION: No
REVIEW PERIOD: 6 weeks
ACCEPTANCE RATE: 4%

STYLE SHEET: No
STYLE REQUIREMENTS: Chicago
CIRCULATION: 7,000
REPRINT POLICY: 50 free

JOURNAL TITLE: Teaching Exceptional Children

MANUSCRIPT ADDRESS: B. Aiello, Editor
1920 Association Drive
Reston, VA 22091

MAJOR CONTENT AREAS: Behavior therapy, educational, mental retardation, exceptionality

ARTICLES USUALLY ACCEPTED: Practitioner oriented articles, practical suggestions teachers can use when working with exceptional children

TOPICS PREFERRED: How-to-do-it articles for working with multiply handicapped/gifted programs

INAPPROPRIATE MANUSCRIPTS: Those written in a research format

INDEXED/ABSTRACTED IN: CIJE, DSHA, EI, ECEA, LLBA

SUBSCRIPTION ADDRESS: S. Jackson
1920 Association Drive
Reston, VA 22091

SUBSCRIPTION COST: $6.50
PUBLICATION LAG TIME: 3-6 months
EARLY PUBLICATION OPTION: No
REVIEW PERIOD: 3 months
ACCEPTANCE RATE: 30%

STYLE SHEET: Yes
STYLE REQUIREMENTS: APA
CIRCULATION: 75,000
REPRINT POLICY: 5 free

JOURNAL TITLE: Teaching of Psychology

MANUSCRIPT ADDRESS: Dr. R. Daniel
McAlester Hall, University of Missouri
Columbia, MO 65201

MAJOR CONTENT AREAS: Teaching of any area of psychology

ARTICLES USUALLY ACCEPTED: Research, review, essay, commentary, innovative
course descriptions

TOPICS PREFERRED: Professional problems of teachers, curriculum
designs, demonstration and laboratory projects

INAPPROPRIATE MANUSCRIPTS: Theoretical articles on substantive
topics

INDEXED/ABSTRACTED IN: PA

SUBSCRIPTION ADDRESS: Dr. R. Daniel
McAlester Hall, University of Missouri
Columbia, MO 65201

SUBSCRIPTION COST: $4 individual, $10 institutional

PUBLICATION LAG TIME: 6-8 months

EARLY PUBLICATION OPTION: No

REVIEW PERIOD: 2 months

ACCEPTANCE RATE: 60%

STYLE SHEET: No

STYLE REQUIREMENTS: APA

CIRCULATION: 3,400

REPRINT POLICY: 3 free copies
of issue

JOURNAL TITLE: Theory and History in Psychology

MANUSCRIPT ADDRESS: Dr. W. Van Hoorn
Rijkeuniversitat Leiden, Ryinsburgerweg 169
Leiden, The Netherlands

MAJOR CONTENT AREAS: History and systems

ARTICLES USUALLY ACCEPTED: Theoretical, review

TOPICS PREFERRED: None

INAPPROPRIATE MANUSCRIPTS: None

INDEXED/ABSTRACTED IN: PA

SUBSCRIPTION ADDRESS: Interdisciplinary Communications Media, Inc.
15 Canal Road
Pelham Manor, NY 10803

SUBSCRIPTION COST: $15 individual, $40 institutional

PUBLICATION LAG TIME: 9 months

EARLY PUBLICATION OPTION: No

REVIEW PERIOD: 3-4 months

ACCEPTANCE RATE: Not yet known

STYLE SHEET: Yes

STYLE REQUIREMENTS: APA

CIRCULATION: New journal

REPRINT POLICY: Purchase
required

JOURNAL TITLE: Theory Into Practice

MANUSCRIPT ADDRESS: 116 Ramseyer Hall, Ohio State University
29 West Woodruff Avenue
Columbus, OH 43210

MAJOR CONTENT AREAS: Educational

ARTICLES USUALLY ACCEPTED: Theoretical and review around a central theme; most are solicited

TOPICS PREFERRED: Those relating educational theory and practice

INAPPROPRIATE MANUSCRIPTS: Research reports

INDEXED/ABSTRACTED IN: CIJE, EI, EAA, ECEA, IPAPL

SUBSCRIPTION ADDRESS: 149 Arps Hall, Ohio State University
1945 North High Street
Columbus, OH 43210

SUBSCRIPTION COST: $5
PUBLICATION LAG TIME: Variable
EARLY PUBLICATION OPTION: No
REVIEW PERIOD: 2-3 months
ACCEPTANCE RATE: Not given

STYLE SHEET: Yes
STYLE REQUIREMENTS: Chicago
CIRCULATION: 5,000
REPRINT POLICY: 11 free

JOURNAL TITLE: Tower International Journal of Life Sciences

MANUSCRIPT ADDRESS: P. O. Box 4594
Philadelphia, PA 19131

MAJOR CONTENT AREAS: Behavior therapy, perception, physiological

ARTICLES USUALLY ACCEPTED: Research

TOPICS PREFERRED: Behavior science

INAPPROPRIATE MANUSCRIPTS: None

INDEXED/ABSTRACTED IN: PA, IM

SUBSCRIPTION ADDRESS: P. O. Box 4594
Philadelphia, PA 19131

SUBSCRIPTION COST: $21
PUBLICATION LAG TIME: 1 year
EARLY PUBLICATION OPTION: Yes
REVIEW PERIOD: 6 months
ACCEPTANCE RATE: 60%

STYLE SHEET: Yes
STYLE REQUIREMENTS: Ind. Med.
CIRCULATION: 500
REPRINT POLICY: 50 free

JOURNAL TITLE:	Transactional Analysis Journal
MANUSCRIPT ADDRESS:	1772 Vallejo Street San Francisco, CA 94123
MAJOR CONTENT AREAS:	Transactional analysis
ARTICLES USUALLY ACCEPTED:	Any type of article on transactional analysis
TOPICS PREFERRED:	Any using transactional analysis
INAPPROPRIATE MANUSCRIPTS:	Those using professional jargon rather than everyday language
INDEXED/ABSTRACTED IN:	PA, SSCI, SLTCPP
SUBSCRIPTION ADDRESS:	1772 Vallejo Street San Francisco, CA 94123

SUBSCRIPTION COST:	$15		
PUBLICATION LAG TIME:	1-12 months	STYLE SHEET:	Yes
EARLY PUBLICATION OPTION:	Yes	STYLE REQUIREMENTS:	APA
REVIEW PERIOD:	2-8 weeks	CIRCULATION:	12,000
ACCEPTANCE RATE:	33%	REPRINT POLICY:	10 free

JOURNAL TITLE: Urban and Social Change Review

MANUSCRIPT ADDRESS: Karen Feinstein, Editor
McGuinn Hall, Boston College
Chestnut Hill, MA 02167

MAJOR CONTENT AREAS: Social problems, social service

ARTICLES USUALLY ACCEPTED: Research, review, theoretical, book review
program evaluations

TOPICS PREFERRED: Interdisciplinary solutions to urban & social
problems, integration of research with practice

INAPPROPRIATE MANUSCRIPTS: Purely historical themes

INDEXED/ABSTRACTED IN: ASW, ABCPS, CECD, CCSBS, HA, IBSS, LLBA, PMA

SUBSCRIPTION ADDRESS: Karen Feinstein, Editor
McGuinn Hall, Boston College
Chestnut Hill, MA 02167

SUBSCRIPTION COST: $5 individual, $8 institutional

PUBLICATION LAG TIME: 3 months

EARLY PUBLICATION OPTION: Yes

REVIEW PERIOD: 3 months

ACCEPTANCE RATE: 8%

STYLE SHEET: Yes

STYLE REQUIREMENTS: Chicago

CIRCULATION: 2,500

REPRINT POLICY: 5 free

JOURNAL TITLE: Vision Research

MANUSCRIPT ADDRESS: Thorne Shipley, Bascom Palmer Eye Inst.
P. O. Box 520875
Miami, FL 33152

MAJOR CONTENT AREAS: Experimental, perception, physiological

ARTICLES USUALLY ACCEPTED: Research

TOPICS PREFERRED: Vision and perception

INAPPROPRIATE MANUSCRIPTS: Far out theories of perceptual function

INDEXED/ABSTRACTED IN: PA, IM, EM, OL, VI

SUBSCRIPTION ADDRESS: Pergamon Press
Headington Hill Hall
Oxford OX3 OBW, England

SUBSCRIPTION COST: $25 individual, $130 institutional		
PUBLICATION LAG TIME: 6-8 months	STYLE SHEET: Yes	
EARLY PUBLICATION OPTION: No	STYLE REQUIREMENTS: Own style	
REVIEW PERIOD: 6-8 weeks	CIRCULATION: 2,500	
ACCEPTANCE RATE: 60%	REPRINT POLICY: 50 free	

JOURNAL TITLE: Vocational Guidance Quarterly

MANUSCRIPT ADDRESS: 6401 Linda Vista Road
San Diego, CA 92111

MAJOR CONTENT AREAS: Counseling

ARTICLES USUALLY ACCEPTED: Research, review, theoretical

TOPICS PREFERRED: Anything related to the role of work/
leisure in people's lives

INAPPROPRIATE MANUSCRIPTS: None

INDEXED/ABSTRACTED IN: PA, ASW, BS, CSPA, CCSBS, CIJE, EI, ILD,
MMRI, SEI

SUBSCRIPTION ADDRESS: 1607 New Hampshire Avenue, N.W.
Washington, DC 20009

SUBSCRIPTION COST: $10		
PUBLICATION LAG TIME: 4-6 months	STYLE SHEET: Yes	
EARLY PUBLICATION OPTION: No	STYLE REQUIREMENTS: APA	
REVIEW PERIOD: 2-3 months	CIRCULATION: 15,000	
ACCEPTANCE RATE: 25%	REPRINT POLICY: 5 free copies of issue	

JOURNAL TITLE: Voices: Journal of the American Academy of Psychotherapists

MANUSCRIPT ADDRESS: 815 Indian Road
Glenview, IL 60025

MAJOR CONTENT AREAS: Psychotherapy

ARTICLES USUALLY ACCEPTED: First person articles

TOPICS PREFERRED: Psychotherapy from the view of the experiencing therapist

INAPPROPRIATE MANUSCRIPTS: None, although very few research reports or "scientific" third person articles are published

INDEXED/ABSTRACTED IN: PA

SUBSCRIPTION ADDRESS: AAP
1040 Woodcock Road
Orlando, FL 32803

SUBSCRIPTION COST: $15 individual, $17 institutional

PUBLICATION LAG TIME: Variable

EARLY PUBLICATION OPTION: No

REVIEW PERIOD: Variable

ACCEPTANCE RATE: 40%

STYLE SHEET: Yes

STYLE REQUIREMENTS: Own style

CIRCULATION: 2,000

REPRINT POLICY: Optional purchase

JOURNAL TITLE: World Journal of Psychosynthesis

MANUSCRIPT ADDRESS: 820 North Capitol
Lansing, MI   48906

MAJOR CONTENT AREAS: All areas

ARTICLES USUALLY ACCEPTED: Research, review, theoretical, book review,
case studies

TOPICS PREFERRED: Family, technical, clinical, and scientific
aspects of world community mental health

INAPPROPRIATE MANUSCRIPTS: None

INDEXED/ABSTRACTED IN: Not given

SUBSCRIPTION ADDRESS: Psychodiagnostic Test Company
Box 859
East Lansing, MI   48823

SUBSCRIPTION COST: $12 individual, $20 institutional

PUBLICATION LAG TIME: 1-4 months   STYLE SHEET: Yes

EARLY PUBLICATION OPTION: No   STYLE REQUIREMENTS: Own style

REVIEW PERIOD: 1-3 months   CIRCULATION: Not given

ACCEPTANCE RATE: Not given   REPRINT POLICY: Optional
purchase

JOURNAL TITLE: Zygon: Journal of Religion and Science

MANUSCRIPT ADDRESS: 1100 East 55th Street
Chicago, IL 60615

MAJOR CONTENT AREAS: Any area of the psychosocial sciences that
say something significant about religion

ARTICLES USUALLY ACCEPTED: Research, review, theoretical, book review

TOPICS PREFERRED: Scientific understanding of human values
and religion and theology

INAPPROPRIATE MANUSCRIPTS: Those that are too elementary or superficial
in their cognizance of religion or science

INDEXED/ABSTRACTED IN: AHL, BI, BS, GSSRPL, HA, IRPL, PI, RTA

SUBSCRIPTION ADDRESS: University of Chicago Press
11030 Langley Avenue
Chicago, IL 60628

SUBSCRIPTION COST: $12 individual, $16 institutional

PUBLICATION LAG TIME: 5-24 months   STYLE SHEET: Yes

EARLY PUBLICATION OPTION: No   STYLE REQUIREMENTS: Chicago

REVIEW PERIOD: 1-24 months   CIRCULATION: 2,300

ACCEPTANCE RATE: 20%   REPRINT POLICY: Optional
purchase

JOURNAL TITLE: Child and Youth Services

MANUSCRIPT ADDRESS: Jerome Beker, Ed.D., Senior Editorial Consultant
c/o The Haworth Press, 174 Fifth Avenue
New York, NY 10010

MAJOR CONTENT AREAS: All clinical, developmental, community, and
organizational aspects of child and youth services

ARTICLES USUALLY ACCEPTED: Review articles only

TOPICS PREFERRED: Only review articles that relate to child
and youth services

INAPPROPRIATE MANUSCRIPTS: None

INDEXED/ABSTRACTED IN: Not yet known (new journal)

SUBSCRIPTION ADDRESS: The Haworth Press
174 Fifth Avenue
New York, NY 10010

SUBSCRIPTION COST: $14 individual, $24 institutional

PUBLICATION LAG TIME: 4-8 months	STYLE SHEET:	Yes
EARLY PUBLICATION OPTION: No	STYLE REQUIREMENTS:	Chicago
REVIEW PERIOD: 2-3 months	CIRCULATION:	Not yet known
ACCEPTANCE RATE: Not yet known	REPRINT POLICY:	50 free

JOURNAL TITLE: Educational Gerontology

MANUSCRIPT ADDRESS: Dr. D. Barry Lumsden, Adult Education Program
School of Education, Virginia Commonwealth Univ.
Richmond, VA 23284

MAJOR CONTENT AREAS: Gerontological services, counseling, social work
practice

ARTICLES USUALLY ACCEPTED: Research, theoretical

TOPICS PREFERRED: Education and aging

INAPPROPRIATE MANUSCRIPTS: Impressionistic reports lacking in
generalizability

INDEXED/ABSTRACTED IN: PA, EM, ASW, AEI, BI, BEI, CEI, CCSBS, CIJE,
EI, IEA, RGPL, RHEA, SSCI

SUBSCRIPTION ADDRESS: Hemisphere Publishing Corp.
1025 Vermont Avenue, N.W.
Washington, DC 20005

SUBSCRIPTION COST: $19.50 individual, $39.60 institutional

PUBLICATION LAG TIME: 4 months	STYLE SHEET:	Yes
EARLY PUBLICATION OPTION: Yes	STYLE REQUIREMENTS:	APA
REVIEW PERIOD: 4 weeks	CIRCULATION:	600
ACCEPTANCE RATE: 45%	REPRINT POLICY:	Optional purchase

JOURNAL TITLE: Essence

MANUSCRIPT ADDRESS: Dr. S. Fleming, Dept. of Psychology
Atkinson College, York Univ., 4700 Keele St.
Downsview, Ontario, Canada

MAJOR CONTENT AREAS: Clinical, gerontology, health care,
psychotherapy

ARTICLES USUALLY ACCEPTED: Research, review, theoretical, case studies

TOPICS PREFERRED: Aging, dying, death

INAPPROPRIATE MANUSCRIPTS: None yet

INDEXED/ABSTRACTED IN: IM (under review), SSCI

SUBSCRIPTION ADDRESS: Dr. S. Fleming, Dept. of Psychology
Atkinson College, York Univ., 4700 Keele St.
Downsview, Ontario, Canada

SUBSCRIPTION COST:	$12		
PUBLICATION LAG TIME:	3-6 months	STYLE SHEET:	Yes
EARLY PUBLICATION OPTION:	No	STYLE REQUIREMENTS:	APA
REVIEW PERIOD:	4-6 weeks	CIRCULATION:	470
ACCEPTANCE RATE:	35%	REPRINT POLICY:	10 free

JOURNAL TITLE: Experimental Aging Research

MANUSCRIPT ADDRESS: P. O. Box 85
Bar Harbor, ME   04609

MAJOR CONTENT AREAS: Developmental, community, gerontological
services

ARTICLES USUALLY ACCEPTED: Research, review, theoretical, book review,
brief communications, methodological notes

TOPICS PREFERRED: Developmental or aging research

INAPPROPRIATE MANUSCRIPTS: None

INDEXED/ABSTRACTED IN: PA, IM, BA, CA, CCSBS

SUBSCRIPTION ADDRESS: P. O. Box 85
Bar Harbor, ME   04609

SUBSCRIPTION COST:	$28 individual, $65 institutional		
PUBLICATION LAG TIME:	2 months	STYLE SHEET:	Yes
EARLY PUBLICATION OPTION:	Yes	STYLE REQUIREMENTS:	APA
REVIEW PERIOD:	2 months	CIRCULATION:	Not given
ACCEPTANCE RATE:	65%	REPRINT POLICY:	20 free

JOURNAL TITLE: Intelligence

MANUSCRIPT ADDRESS: Douglas K. Detterman, Editor
Dept. of Psychology, Case Western Reserve University
Cleveland, OH 44106

MAJOR CONTENT AREAS: Mental retardation, intelligence

ARTICLES USUALLY ACCEPTED: Research, review, theoretical

TOPICS PREFERRED: Intelligence and mental retardation

INAPPROPRIATE MANUSCRIPTS: None

INDEXED/ABSTRACTED IN: Not yet known

SUBSCRIPTION ADDRESS: Ablex Publishing Corp.
355 Chestnut Street
Norwood, NJ 07648

SUBSCRIPTION COST: Not yet available
PUBLICATION LAG TIME: Not yet available   STYLE SHEET: Yes
EARLY PUBLICATION OPTION: No   STYLE REQUIREMENTS: APA
REVIEW PERIOD: 8 weeks   CIRCULATION: Not yet known
ACCEPTANCE RATE: 45%   REPRINT POLICY: Optional purchase

JOURNAL TITLE: International Journal of Psychology

MANUSCRIPT ADDRESS: J. Leroux, Editor, Dept. of Psychology
University of Leuven, 104, Tiensestraat
3000 Leuven, Belgium

MAJOR CONTENT AREAS: Cross-cultural psychology, experimental,
developmental, personality

ARTICLES USUALLY ACCEPTED: Research, review, theoretical

TOPICS PREFERRED: Cross-cultural comparisons of psychological
phenomena, international issues in psychology

INAPPROPRIATE MANUSCRIPTS: None

INDEXED/ABSTRACTED IN: PA, CCSBS, LLBA, PRG, SSI

SUBSCRIPTION ADDRESS: Centrale des Revues Dunod-Gasether-Villars
70 rue de Saint Mande B.P. 119
93104 Montreuil, France

SUBSCRIPTION COST: 95 FF
PUBLICATION LAG TIME: 6-9 months   STYLE SHEET: Yes
EARLY PUBLICATION OPTION: No   STYLE REQUIREMENTS: APA
REVIEW PERIOD: 2-4 months   CIRCULATION: 1,500
ACCEPTANCE RATE: 30%   REPRINT POLICY: 50 free

233

JOURNAL TITLE: International Social Work

MANUSCRIPT ADDRESS: International Council on Social Welfare
P.O. Box 1496
Bombay 400 001, India

MAJOR CONTENT AREAS: All social work areas

ARTICLES USUALLY ACCEPTED: Research, review, theoretical, case studies

TOPICS PREFERRED: Social welfare, social development

INAPPROPRIATE MANUSCRIPTS: None

INDEXED/ABSTRACTED IN: ASW, IBSS, ILD, WSA

SUBSCRIPTION ADDRESS: International Council on Social Welfare
P. O. Box 1496
Bombay 400 001, India

SUBSCRIPTION COST:	$7		
PUBLICATION LAG TIME:	6 months	STYLE SHEET:	Yes
EARLY PUBLICATION OPTION:	No	STYLE REQUIREMENTS:	None
REVIEW PERIOD:	6 months	CIRCULATION:	Not given
ACCEPTANCE RATE:	Not given	REPRINT POLICY:	2 free copies of issue

JOURNAL TITLE: Journal of the American Academy of Psychiatry and Neurology

MANUSCRIPT ADDRESS: 17 Kingston Road
Scarsdale, New York 10583

MAJOR CONTENT AREAS: Behavior therapy, community psychiatry and mental health, social psychiatry, psychoanalysis, etc.

ARTICLES USUALLY ACCEPTED: Research, review, and theoretical articles, case studies, book reviews

TOPICS PREFERRED: Clinical aspects of psychiatry, neurology, and psychoanalysis

INAPPROPRIATE MANUSCRIPTS: Quickly written, nonsubstantive articles

INDEXED/ABSTRACTED IN: CCSBS, SSCI, EM, IM

SUBSCRIPTION ADDRESS: 17 Kingston Road
Scarsdale, New York 10583

SUBSCRIPTION COST:	$25.00 individual; $30.00 institutional		
PUBLICATION LAG TIME:	2-3 months	STYLE SHEET:	Yes
EARLY PUBLICATION OPTION:	Yes	STYLE REQUIREMENTS:	Chicago
REVIEW PERIOD:	2-3 weeks	CIRCULATION:	10,000
ACCEPTANCE RATE:	75%, AAPN members only	REPRINT POLICY:	Purchase required

JOURNAL TITLE: Journal of Comparative Family Studies

MANUSCRIPT ADDRESS: Dr. George Kurian, Editor, Dept. of Sociology
University of Calgary, 2920 24th Ave., NW
Calgary, Alberta, Canada

MAJOR CONTENT AREAS: Family planning, social issues, social
psychology, health care, human sexuality

ARTICLES USUALLY ACCEPTED: Research, review

TOPICS PREFERRED: Cross-cultural studies

INAPPROPRIATE MANUSCRIPTS: None

INDEXED/ABSTRACTED IN: PA, ASW, AA

SUBSCRIPTION ADDRESS: Dr. George Kurian, Editor, Dept. of Sociology
University of Calgary, 2920 24th Ave., NW
Calgary, Alberta, Canada

SUBSCRIPTION COST: $16 individual, $32 institutional
PUBLICATION LAG TIME: Not given   STYLE SHEET: Yes
EARLY PUBLICATION OPTION: No   STYLE REQUIREMENTS: ASA
REVIEW PERIOD: 2 months   CIRCULATION: 500
ACCEPTANCE RATE: 75%   REPRINT POLICY: Optional
                                                           purchase

JOURNAL TITLE: Journal of Divorce

MANUSCRIPT ADDRESS: Esther Oshiver Fisher, LL.B., Ed.D.
1050 Park Avenue
New York, NY 10028

MAJOR CONTENT AREAS: Clinical, psychotherapy, human sexuality,
and legal issues as related to divorce

ARTICLES USUALLY ACCEPTED: Research, theoretical, case studies

TOPICS PREFERRED: All topics concerned with the divorce process

INAPPROPRIATE MANUSCRIPTS: None

INDEXED/ABSTRACTED IN: Not yet known (new journal)

SUBSCRIPTION ADDRESS: The Haworth Press
174 Fifth Avenue
New York, NY 10010

SUBSCRIPTION COST: $18 individual, $35 institutional
PUBLICATION LAG TIME: 6 months   STYLE SHEET: Yes
EARLY PUBLICATION OPTION: No   STYLE REQUIREMENTS: Chicago
REVIEW PERIOD: 2 months   CIRCULATION: Not yet known
ACCEPTANCE RATE: Not yet known   REPRINT POLICY: 50 free

JOURNAL TITLE: Motivation and Emotion

MANUSCRIPT ADDRESS: M. H. Appley, Editor, c/o The President's Office
Clark University
Worcester, MA 01610

MAJOR CONTENT AREAS: Experimental, physiological, social

ARTICLES USUALLY ACCEPTED: Research, review, theoretical

TOPICS PREFERRED: Motivation, emotion, psychological stress,
environmental psychology

INAPPROPRIATE MANUSCRIPTS: None

INDEXED/ABSTRACTED IN: None as yet (new journal)

SUBSCRIPTION ADDRESS: Plenum Publishing Corp.
227 West 17th Street
New York, NY 10011

SUBSCRIPTION COST: $16 individual; $32 institutional

PUBLICATION LAG TIME:	6 months	STYLE SHEET:	Yes
EARLY PUBLICATION OPTION:	No	STYLE REQUIREMENTS:	APA
REVIEW PERIOD:	2 months	CIRCULATION:	150
ACCEPTANCE RATE:	25%	REPRINT POLICY:	Purchase optional

JOURNAL TITLE: The Paraclete, The Journal of the National
Association of Christians in Social Work

MANUSCRIPT ADDRESS: Box 84
Wheaton, IL 60187

MAJOR CONTENT AREAS: All clinical and social areas as related
to Christianity and social work

ARTICLES USUALLY ACCEPTED: Research, review, theoretical, case studies,
book reviews

TOPICS PREFERRED: Christianity applied to social work
practice

INAPPROPRIATE MANUSCRIPTS: Those whose contents are irrelevant to
social work and Christianity

INDEXED/ABSTRACTED IN: Not given

SUBSCRIPTION ADDRESS: Box 84
Wheaton, IL 60187

SUBSCRIPTION COST: $6

PUBLICATION LAG TIME:	3 months	STYLE SHEET:	Yes
EARLY PUBLICATION OPTION:	No	STYLE REQUIREMENTS:	Chicago
REVIEW PERIOD:	2-6 months	CIRCULATION:	2,000
ACCEPTANCE RATE:	Not given	REPRINT POLICY:	One free

JOURNAL TITLE: Psychological Issues Monograph Series

MANUSCRIPT ADDRESS: Herbert J. Schlesinger, Ph.D., Editor
4200 E. Ninth Ave., Box C-270
U. of Col. Medical Ctr., Denver, CO 80262

MAJOR CONTENT AREAS: All experimental areas, general, history &
systems, social, psychotherapy, personality

ARTICLES USUALLY ACCEPTED: Monographs (100-200 + printed pages) that confront
fundamental psychological issues; manuscripts are
typically by invitation

TOPICS PREFERRED: Basic psychological issues that might contribute
to a general psychoanalytic theory of behavior

INAPPROPRIATE MANUSCRIPTS: None

INDEXED/ABSTRACTED IN: PA, IM, CCSBS, PRG, SSCI

SUBSCRIPTION ADDRESS: International Universities Press
315 Fifth Avenue
New York, NY 10016

SUBSCRIPTION COST: $27.50 individual, $37.50 institutional

PUBLICATION LAG TIME:	7-18 months	STYLE SHEET:	Yes
EARLY PUBLICATION OPTION:	No	STYLE REQUIREMENTS:	Own style
REVIEW PERIOD:	2-4 months	CIRCULATION:	1,300
ACCEPTANCE RATE:	75%	REPRINT POLICY:	5 free

JOURNAL TITLE: Religious Education

MANUSCRIPT ADDRESS: 409 Prospect Street
New Haven, CT 06510

MAJOR CONTENT AREAS: Developmental, educational, religious education,
education and social issues

ARTICLES USUALLY ACCEPTED: Research, theoretical

TOPICS PREFERRED: All aspects of religious education

INAPPROPRIATE MANUSCRIPTS: None

INDEXED/ABSTRACTED IN: PA, BS, CCSBS, EI, GSSRPL, IPAPL, IRPL, RTA,
WSA

SUBSCRIPTION ADDRESS: 409 Prospect Street
New Haven, CT 06510

SUBSCRIPTION COST: $20

PUBLICATION LAG TIME:	9-12 months	STYLE SHEET:	Yes
EARLY PUBLICATION OPTION:	No	STYLE REQUIREMENTS:	Chicago
REVIEW PERIOD:	3 months	CIRCULATION:	5,000
ACCEPTANCE RATE:	10-20%	REPRINT POLICY:	Optional purchase

237

JOURNAL TITLE:	Teaching of Organizational Behavior
MANUSCRIPT ADDRESS:	Graduate School of Business Stanford University Stanford, CA 94305
MAJOR CONTENT AREAS:	Teaching theory and techniques of administration and organizational psychology
ARTICLES USUALLY ACCEPTED:	Research, theoretical, case studies
TOPICS PREFERRED:	Different ways in which people have taught organizational behavior
INAPPROPRIATE MANUSCRIPTS:	None
INDEXED/ABSTRACTED IN:	None yet
SUBSCRIPTION ADDRESS:	Graduate School of Business Stanford University Stanford, CA 94305
SUBSCRIPTION COST:	$7.50

PUBLICATION LAG TIME:	6 months	STYLE SHEET:	Yes
EARLY PUBLICATION OPTION:	No	STYLE REQUIREMENTS:	APA
REVIEW PERIOD:	2 months	CIRCULATION:	1,000
ACCEPTANCE RATE:	40%	REPRINT POLICY:	Optional purchase

JOURNAL TITLE:	Work Performance
MANUSCRIPT ADDRESS:	500 NW 34th Street Suite 112 Pompano Beach, FL 33064
MAJOR CONTENT AREAS:	Applied behavior analysis, industrial/ organizational
ARTICLES USUALLY ACCEPTED:	Case studies
TOPICS PREFERRED:	Increasing the productivity of workers using behavioral science
INAPPROPRIATE MANUSCRIPTS:	None
INDEXED/ABSTRACTED IN:	Not given
SUBSCRIPTION ADDRESS:	500 NW 34th Street Suite 112 Pompano Beach, FL 33064
SUBSCRIPTION COST:	$24

PUBLICATION LAG TIME:	1-2 months	STYLE SHEET:	Yes
EARLY PUBLICATION OPTION:	No	STYLE REQUIREMENTS:	Not given
REVIEW PERIOD:	Immediate	CIRCULATION:	Not given
ACCEPTANCE RATE:	50%	REPRINT POLICY:	5 free

SUBJECT, TITLE AND KEYWORD INDEX

This Index will refer the reader to the page numbers on which journals are listed. Journals are listed by title, subject, and key words within their title.

In addition, if a journal's editor indicated a clear preference for certain types of manuscripts, these "manuscript preference subject areas" are also included as indexing terms. The reader will therefore be able to search for appropriate journals for article submission according to the general subject areas in which his or her article falls.

K, L